"Rewilding Children's Imaginations does a magical job of combining cross-curricular skills with creative activities inspired by the natural world and multi-cultural folktales. The detailed yet easy-to-follow plans offer a range of playful and stimulating ideas for children to develop their confidence in oracy and storytelling. Learning should always look like this: child-centred and discussion-led with rich and diverse material to ignite the imagination." – **Marina Lewis-King**, Programme Manager, A New Direction

"Rewilding Children's Imaginations is a must-read for all practitioners of primary-aged children. This easy-to-follow guide connects the magic of the outside world with the children they teach. Rich with stories from around the globe, it offers an escape from the digital world and 'bottom in seats' educating, into the depths of exploration and creativity that all children deserve. It promotes exciting storytelling, brimming with language, oracy and drama which can be used to support in all established curriculums. Connecting with nature can help the children to see that they are part of something much bigger, freeing children's imaginations." – **Zoe Bagheri**, Assistant Headteacher and Senior Mental Health Lead

"One of the greatest tragedies of modern civilization has to be the divide we created in our imagination between nature and humans. This book provides a brilliantly written and researched account of just why that divide is a fantasy. It is an inspirational and practical guide for those who want to show our children the pathway back."
– **Dr Eugene Hughes**, Psychotherapist, Co-Founder of *Lead Like a River*: The Times Top 20 Life Changing Experiences

REWILDING CHILDREN'S IMAGINATIONS

Rewilding Children's Imaginations is a practical and creative resource designed to engage children in the natural world through folktales, storytelling, and artmaking.

The guide introduces 21 folklore stories from across the world alongside 99 creative activities, spanning nature and the four seasons of the year. Using the lens of folktales and myths of the land, children are encouraged to explore a variety of activities and exercises across different arts media, from visual art making to storytelling, drama, and movement.

This resource:

- Helps teachers and group facilitators to build confidence in offering a range of creative learning experiences, inspired by nature.

- Provides a collection of easy-to-use, cross-curricular, and storytelling activities.

- Allows children to connect with nature, their imagination, and folktales from around the world.

- Builds new skills in oracy, artmaking, collaboration, wellbeing, care of the environment, diversity, respect, tolerance, and more.

- Inspires children to tell stories and make art both individually and collaboratively, helping them build confidence as active creators in their community.

- Shares creative tools and positive learning experiences to inspire children, teachers, and parents across the school year.

Rewilding Children's Imaginations brings together nature, art, and oral storytelling in easy and accessible ways to help children connect with the world around them, as well as with their own creative and emotional landscapes. It is essential and enjoyable reading for primary teachers and early years professionals, outdoors practitioners, therapists, art educators, community and youth workers, home schoolers, parents, carers, and families.

Pia Jones is an author, creative workshop facilitator and integrative arts psychotherapist, having trained at The Institute for Arts in Therapy and Education. Pia has worked with children and adults in a variety of school, health, and community settings. A love for myth, art, and nature underpins her practice.

Sarah Pimenta is an artist, educator, creative workshop facilitator, illustrator, and lecturer in creativity. She has delivered art and print-making workshops in over 250 schools, diverse communities, and public venues internationally. Nature and social change are huge inspirations in her art and creative workshops.

Tamsin Cooke is an internationally published and award-winning children's author, workshop facilitator, and former primary school teacher. She designs and runs innovative creative writing and drama workshops in schools across the UK and globally online.

REWILDING CHILDREN'S IMAGINATIONS

99 CREATIVE ACTIVITIES
INSPIRED BY NATURE AND FOLKTALES
FROM AROUND THE WORLD

Pia Jones, Sarah Pimenta & Tamsin Cooke

Routledge
Taylor & Francis Group

LONDON AND NEW YORK

Designed cover image: Sarah Pimenta

First published 2023
by Routledge
4 Park Square, Milton Park, Abingdon, Oxon OX14 4RN

and by Routledge
605 Third Avenue, New York, NY 10158

Routledge is an imprint of the Taylor & Francis Group, an informa business

British Library Cataloguing-in-Publication Data
A catalogue record for this book is available from the British Library

Library of Congress Cataloging-in-Publication Data
A catalog record has been requested for this book

ISBN: 978-1-032-01456-2 (hbk)
ISBN: 978-1-032-01451-7 (pbk)
ISBN: 978-1-003-17868-2 (ebk)

DOI: 10.4324/9781003178682

Typeset in DIN Schriften
by Deanta Global Publishing Services, Chennai, India

Access the Support Material: https://resourcecentre.routledge.com/speechmark

CONTENTS

Contents

Contents

Contents

ACKNOWLEDGEMENTS

Rewilding Children's Imaginations has been a creative journey that has taken us all over the world (metaphorically) in search of folktales that connect with the seasons. The development of practical, creative activities needed a three-visioned lens of teaching, art education, and art therapy. It couldn't have happened without collaboration at its core. The authors truly needed each other to bring this book to life.

A special thanks must also go to Clare Ashworth, our editor at Speechmark, for seeing this book's potential straightaway, and guiding us steadily along the away. Many thanks to Molly Kavanagh for all her attention and care alongside Speechmark's production team who turned *Rewilding Children's Imaginations* into such a practical and beautiful resource.

A special thanks also to Katy Potts Skelsey for helping plant the initial seed. Thanks also to Antonella Mancini for her continued support along the way. Thanks must also go to our families and friends for supporting our absences and distraction, as we disappeared to go foraging for stories across the seasons.

Finally, thanks must go to all the storytellers who so generously share folktales from their own culture and others, to keep these stories alive for this generation and those to come.

Pia, Sarah & Tamsin

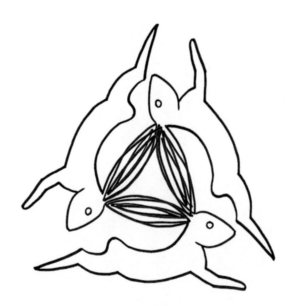

FOREWORD BY L ROYLES

In my 15+ years working as an outdoors educator, my work has centred on art and nature to help diverse groups connect and discover new aspects about themselves and their surroundings. Frameworks such as forest school, forest bathing, and horticultural therapy underpin my practice. A decision to work outside has given me many titles – gardener, forest school practitioner, Scout leader, community activist, learning support assistant, and cob builder. It is wearing these hats that I find myself reading *Rewilding Children's Imaginations*.

What makes this resource unique is how it weaves together folktales, creativity, learning, play, and nature. Like a series of handy road maps with tips for traversing and diving into the imagination, its range of art and drama activities invites us to travel the world. This practical resource pulls all these gems neatly into the four seasons, accompanied by 90+ creative activities and ready-prepared lesson plans to support busy teachers, youth leaders, and outdoor practitioners. The authors evidently know the challenges and they deliver. I can really see how this resource would help teachers grow confidence in nature-inspired learning.

Sadly, not all schools come with access to woods or outdoor spaces. It's crushing to see how many schools are removing trees and replacing grass with Astroturf. As our entire world faces the challenges of climate change, children and young people will have to step into an active relationship with the natural world to protect the planet that sustains us.

We know how creativity, play, and being in the natural world shifts our attention, affects our mood, helps us focus and restores us. What's so useful about *Rewilding Children's Imaginations*, is that it doesn't rely on having a woodland close by. Deep rooted in its approach is that it helps groups of all ages and abilities build bridges and connect with nature, from close and afar. In offering activities across the seasons, we are invited to connect to the natural changes around us, across the year. As we move towards rewilding green spaces, this timely book offers much by way to guide and remind us to rewild our imaginations too.

As I reflect upon my work with marginalised groups, often displaced, this book makes me question why I don't work with folktales and traditions. *Rewilding Children's Imaginations* is a call to build more bridges with those belonging or connected to another country of origin. I can see its application as much in my intergenerational work as well as work with cub Scouts. The book offers creative activities that can be used with a wide variety of groups and settings.

My hope is that this resource will facilitate new dialogues in and out of the classroom and spark new ideas. May it validate what many of us know instinctively about the role of nature, art, and storytelling to support creativity, growth, and wellbeing for all ages. Let it guide and remind us where to focus our attention and imagination, in all stages of our lives.

L. Royles
Founder and Director of Urban Forest School Collective and Cob in the Community CIC

INTRODUCTION

Welcome to *Rewilding Children's Imaginations*, a practical and creative guide designed to engage children in the natural world through folktales, storytelling, and artmaking. It is aimed primarily at children aged seven to eleven (Key Stage 2), although many exercises can be adapted to suit other age groups. In our guide, we introduce a total of 21 folktales from across the world, and 99 creative activities spanning nature and the four seasons of the year.

The aims of the guide are two-fold. Firstly, to help teachers and group facilitators to:

- Build confidence in offering creative learning experiences connected to nature
- Use a range of easy-to-use creative and storytelling activities (cross-curricular)
- Offer new learning experiences around oracy and artmaking

Secondly, creative activities are designed to help children and participants to:

- Learn to connect with nature, their imaginations, and stories across the world
- Be inspired to tell stories and make art individually and collaboratively
- Feel alive, grounded, and well in their community

In our modern world, it's easy to forget that once, all humans lived close to nature. With the rapid rise of cities and modern living, many of us no longer do. It's also easy to forget once stories weren't read or written – they were spoken aloud. This guide attempts to bring together nature, art, and oral storytelling in easy, accessible ways so children can find their own voice by connecting with the natural world around them.

Although *Rewilding Children's Imaginations* has been designed mainly for helping Key Stage 2 primary school teachers develop creative sessions inspired by the seasons in nature, we hope that other groups and communities are inspired to explore the natural world through creativity. Audiences might include the following.

- Teachers, teaching assistants, learning support, youth workers, home schoolers
- Art educators, storytellers, creative group facilitators, community artists
- Guides, Scouts, Forest School, outdoors practitioners, youth groups
- Community groups, parents, carers, families, and individuals

DOI: 10.4324/9781003178682-1

Whereas creative activities from this guide can be organised outside, we recognise that for many schools, groups, and organisations, this is not always possible. We believe participants can equally benefit from indoor learning inspired by nature and the outside.

After an introduction to the benefits of nature in education and wellbeing, and a section on folktales and the arts, we briefly look at some of the challenges when working outdoors, offering some practical tips for class/group management.

To introduce the theme of oral storytelling, we draw upon a first folktale, along with six activities to introduce working with nature and different creative arts media. The guide is then structured around the four seasons, starting with autumn in tune with the cycle of UK school year. Each season starts off with a tailored sensory walk outside, followed by five folktales from across the world, each with four creative activities. We've aimed to tell folktales in short and captivating ways to help the storyteller/teacher/group facilitator. Creative activities have been placed one to a page, where possible, for ease of use. Each season finishes off with a group activity, and a creative idea to try at home. This guide can be either be used chronologically, or dipped into as and when, across the seasons. At the end of the book, there are links to interesting organisations supporting a love of folktales, natural play, storytelling, and rewilding of children's creativity and learning.

Finally, *Rewilding Children's Imaginations* was born out of the UK lockdown during the coronavirus pandemic, where nature and creativity supported all three authors' wellbeing, as well as their families. It reflects the lifelong care and passion for nature, story, art, and multicultural diversity held by its authors. This book comes from a creative collaboration between:

> *Pia Jones:* Integrative arts psychotherapist, creative workshop facilitator, and author of the *Therapeutic Fairy Tales* series, focusing on using nature as a support for children and families' wellbeing. A love of myth, storytelling, art, and nature is at the centre of her work.
> *Sarah Pimenta:* Artist, arts educator, and workshop facilitator. Sarah integrates nature into her work inside classrooms and outside. She is the illustrator of the existing and upcoming *Therapeutic Fairy Tales* series published by Routledge, where nature inspires her illustrations.
> *Tamsin Cooke:* Award-winning international author, creative workshop facilitator, and former primary school teacher. Her love of myths, folktales, and nature can be seen in her books: *Cat Burglar, Mission Gone Wild, Stunt Double* and *Jungle Curse*.

We hope that *Rewilding Children's Imaginations* offers a range of stories and creative ideas to inspire a love of working with nature and creativity. In helping connect children with nature and their own imaginations, we hope they build confidence in becoming active participants, storytellers, and creators in the world.

Chapter 1

BENEFITS OF CREATIVE NATURE-INSPIRED LEARNING FOR CHILDREN

'I go to nature to be soothed, healed and have my senses put in order.'

– John Burroughs (naturalist and author)

As humans, we all live in the natural world. Even if we live in cities and towns, nature is ever present – in the trees, plants, and creatures we encounter in parks and gardens; the changing skies and weather; the orbits of sun and moon; the food we eat; and pets we bring into our homes. Given the busy pace of modern living in developed countries and the ever-increasing reliance on technology and being indoors, sometimes it can be easy to forget our own place in the natural world, our own physical bodies. Nature forms part of our habitat, and humans are equally creatures of nature. Nature is inside us all. And being in nature is one of the simplest ways to restore balance and wellbeing in times of pressure and difficulty.

The role of nature in educational settings

Outdoors learning has played a vital role in pre-schools and reception class in the UK for years, as children are encouraged to play outside to aid social, emotional, physical, sensory, and motor development. City parks and farms, and garden areas in schools, introduce nature in safe ways to children, providing essential opportunities to explore and learn about the world we live in (Stuart-Smith, 2020). By contrast, outdoors learning for older children, was seen mainly as an alternative to the norm, led by Steiner and the Forest School movements. However, in recent years, Forest Schools in the UK have seen a rise in popularity (Forest Research, 2022) Originally created for early years and nursery settings, Forest Schools have started to enter the primary school education system, as well as reach older year groups. The child-centric, immersive teaching has been proven to create high levels of engagement as children connect with themselves and others, their creativity, and nature in an outdoors environment. A growing body of research is proving the specific

DOI: 10.4324/9781003178682-2

benefits a connection with nature brings to children's learning and well-being (Sheldrake et al., 2019) Nature's unpredictability can help children improve practical and physical skills, risk-taking, creativity, as well as scientific and social skills (Waites et al., 2016)

The essential role of nature in actively promoting mental, emotional, and physical wellbeing

However, children's relationship with nature is under threat. A report from The National Trust, *Natural Childhood* (Moss, 2012) highlighted that many of us, especially children, aren't getting enough time in nature, and are showing symptoms of Nature Deficit Disorder. This term, first coined by Louv (2005), includes a 'diminished use of the senses, attention difficulties, and higher rates of physical and emotional illnesses.' Humans innately suffer from a lack of being outdoors, and children are roaming outside much less (Moss, 2012).

Most of us instinctively know the benefits nature brings to mental, emotional, and physical wellbeing. A walk or a view of the sky can bring stillness, soothing, and grounding after a stressful, busy day. Trips to nature destinations such as parks, beaches, rivers, mountains, and countryside places help us relax, roam, and play. Writers, poets, artists, and philosophers across history have proclaimed the benefits of maintaining an active relationship with nature, often as an antidote to the ever increasingly fast pace of modern life (Stuart-Smith, 2020). Examples of benefits described are a sense of calmness, stillness, slowness, a greater capacity to reflect, an increased ability to notice and pay attention, and a way to sit more easily and digest feelings. Nature is a powerful tool to teach mindfulness (Allen, 2021). In creating a calm, open, and receptive mind, the benefits of being in nature can contribute to building children's receptivity in both educational and family settings. The very act of slowing down can help give us space to listen and see what's going on, both inside and outside of us.

Being outside in nature also enables us to get in touch with our physical bodies. Sometimes we forget that emotions are experienced and sensed first through the body. It is by being in contact with our bodies that we can learn to ground feelings. In this way, nature can support emotional regulation by helping activate the parasympathetic nerve function, known as 'rest and digest' in contrast to the 'fight, freeze, flight' stress responses of the sympathetic nerve function (Allen, 2021). New research is showing how being outdoors in safe spaces can support children and adults' wellbeing and capacity to relax (Stuart-Smith, 2020). Being out in nature can help us slow down, take deeper breaths, be in the present, and become more mindful. Older teenagers' cognition and mental health can also benefit from experiences in woodland and natural environments (Maes et al., 2021).

Further scientific study of the Japanese practice of *shinrin-yoku* – translated as forest-bathing – which means being in the presence of trees using the five senses, is proven to lower heart rate and blood pressure, reduce stress hormone production, boost the immune system, and improve overall feelings of wellbeing (Li, 2010). The invisible chemicals released by trees, known as phytoncides, have the potential to reduce stress hormones like cortisol, lower blood pressure, and improve immunity. The increased oxygen in woodland areas has been shown to help improve concentrations levels. Scientific research is now proving what some people have always been known: that being in nature has the potential to contribute to our psychological, emotional, and physical wellbeing (Hansen et al, July 2017).

Biophilia, a phrase first coined by psychoanalyst Erich Fromm (1964) was further expanded by biologist and naturalist Edward Wilson (1984) to highlight that human beings have an innate need for a relationship and connection with nature. Psychoanalyst and psychiatrist Carl Jung also proposed that many ailments arose from a human disconnection from nature (Sabini, 2002).

The role of nature in providing a mirror for our internal and emotional states

What may be less known, however, is how nature can also serve to help us make sense of our lives by playing the role of a mirror (Siddons Heginworth and Nash, 2019). A broken branch, an upside-down beetle struggling to right itself, a sunny day, dark clouds, high winds, a squashed fly, green shoots; all can serve as metaphors that may mirror inner states of growth and upset. What we are drawn to outside may resonate with what is going on inside. It's what poets naturally do (Oliver, 2016). In similar ways, engaging with the seasons of the year or different climates, can help teach us about changing inner states, be they calm or stormy. The weather can be a useful tool to explore changing feelings and 'inner weather', showing how nothing stays the same and all passes eventually (Allen, 2021). The cycles of nature can help teach children about their own cycles of rest and activity. The varying scales found in nature, both small as with insects, and huge with the sky, can help explore different perspectives. Dangers and fears of nature, such as getting lost in the woods, being stung by a bee, or struck by lightning, can also help children externalise and talk about their fears and anxieties. There is so much focus on resilience in the current narrative that many children don't feel it's acceptable to share other more vulnerable or fearful parts of themselves. In contrast, for children who might be more shy or quiet, nature can support them in finding ways to express their own 'song' or 'roar.' By providing a mirror and enabling children to project their own inner world onto the outside world, nature can help open up conversations around feelings and experiences in less direct and more non-threatening ways. This process is at the root of the ever-growing field of nature therapy and environmental arts therapy (Siddons Heginworth and Nash, 2019). In engaging with metaphors in nature and building a relationship with the natural world, children can be encouraged to understand and tell their own stories while creating new ones. This innate capacity in nature to encourage storytelling and children's creativity will be explored in greater depth in the next chapter on folktales.

Why wellbeing matters for children in educational settings

If there has ever been a time that children need support with their mental and physical wellbeing, it is now. Research shows the rising levels of anxiety, feelings of isolation, depression, and self-harm in children and young people (NHS national survey, 2017). This upward trend has increased during the recent coronavirus pandemic (Shum et al., 2021).

The pressures of modern life risk taking a generation of children and adults away from experiencing the simple yet restorative benefits of the natural world. Children are increasingly monitored and assessed in their school settings. As important as academic targets are for enabling children to reach their potential, they also bring pressures. For children who find reading and writing or maths difficult, they can often feel lost and unworthy in the school system. Experiences in nature can offer these students a chance to develop different skills.

The dramatic growth of digital technology and 'screen-time' has become an integral facet of children's lives (Moss, 2012). Study, work, entertainment, and human connection increasingly take place across digital and social media platforms leading to many children and adults spending more time indoors. With the recent coronavirus pandemic, digital technology became essential as children across the world were engaged in home-schooling on online platforms. Yet, even when we are outdoors, nature is sometimes only viewed through the lens of a phone or device. Beautiful shots are captured and shared online to gain likes and followers on social media, as opposed to being savoured and experienced for their own benefit. Nature becomes a product or commodity to consume instead of being a restorative time-out that we relate to through our senses. (Baker, 2009). Some researchers are worried that we risk 'an extinction of experience' (Pyle, 2003).

Helping children learn to take care of the natural world

Connecting to nature isn't only important on a personal and social level. It's also about our wider community and the needs of the planet. If we can give children positive experiences in relating to the natural world, children can feel part of nature rather than separate to it. Learning to take care of plants and animals teaches compassion, respect, and responsibility for the natural world (Sheldrake, Amos and Reiss, 2019). Empathy increases for the plants and creatures around them (Sobel 1996). Research shows how children's experiences of nature in early years determine then how they relate to the natural world as they grow older. Educators can inspire children's relationships to nature and provide an experience of wonder that they can take onwards in life (Wilson, 1993).

Nature's role in teaching children about biodiversity of lands, community, and people

Additionally, we propose that teaching children how to engage with their environment helps them learn about the stories of the land where they live, which may be different from parents' or carers' birthplaces. Across the world, cultures have their own relationship with nature depending on the unique features of each habitat. Children from other cultures who have travelled abroad to their families may have experienced very different landscapes to the one at home. The exploration of one specific location can show children the innate diversity of plants, trees, insects, birds, animals; that there is not one part that outweighs the other in importance; that there is an interdependency between all flora and fauna. Engaging with nature can help teach children about diversity and difference in empowering and non-judgmental ways.

A need for creative vehicles to help children engage with nature and the natural world

As we hope to have shown in this chapter, there are numerous benefits to be gained for children through engaging with nature-inspired learning in an educational setting, both for learning goals, and for mental and emotional wellbeing. That said, it's not always easy for all children to engage with the natural world. In an age that is defined by a fast pace, with a focus on achieving goals and high levels of stimulation, nature can often feel too still or boring for children and adults. Or in instances of intense weather fluctuations – storms, floods, fires, droughts – the opposite becomes true. Too much happens, and nature becomes frightening and overwhelming, associated with destruction and loss.

To help children start to build their own relationship with nature in an educational setting, one of the most powerful tools in cultures all over the world is the creative arts. In the following chapter, we shall show how much of oral storytelling and folktales is rooted in nature and is therefore a natural fit for outside learning or bringing nature inside the classroom. Storytelling and the arts can serve as a bridge to connect children with nature outdoors by using their own senses and creativity.

Summary of benefits of outdoor learning and nature-based experience

Educational:

- Develop greater physical, sensory, and motor skills

- Improve observational skills, recording, and note-taking skills

- Gain hands-on learning about the local land, lifecycles, ecosystems, and natural world

- Engage with ideas around risk in an outdoors environment

- Learn collaboration, social, creative, teambuilding, and presentation skills

- Develop care and consideration for the natural world and our place in it

- Encourage respect for diversity and multi-cultural differences

- Recognise our interdependence and interconnection with the rest of the world

Mental health and general wellbeing:

- Help children feel mentally and physically grounded

- Help children to slow down and process feelings

- Connect with nature to promote mindfulness and emotional self-regulation

- Access emotional landscapes, building a relationship between inside & outside

- Connect children to self and others in a natural environment

- Help children bring different parts of themselves and see different parts in others

- To explore and accept different habitats and cultures

- Use nature as a tool to connect with stories, and develop new stories

- To combat some of the symptoms of Nature Deficit Disorder

Chapter 2

HOW FOLKLORE AND ORAL STORYTELLING CAN SUPPORT CHILDREN

"The protagonist of folktale is always, and intensely, a young person moving through ordeals into adult life...."

© Jill Paton Walsh (author)

An introduction to folklore & oral storytelling

Storytelling is part of an ancient human tradition, a way for us to make sense of the world and give structure to our lives (Campbell, 1993). Stories show us characters and heroes' journeys and relationships, to others, to the land, and to our own selves. One of the earliest and oldest forms of story are folktales.

Folklore and folktales are described in the dictionary (Oxford English, 2012) as stories born from a community and passed on to generations by word of mouth. All cultures across the world have told them. It's interesting how many folktales have survived through time and made it into print in a modern era. Something in these old stories resonates and sticks. Yet in their essence, folk stories were originally created to be told aloud and shared in groups (Jones, 1996).

Oral storytellers often held important roles in communities showing how their contribution was valued (Levine, 1992). In some cultures, such as First Nation and Aboriginal, storytellers are still actively valued, and their stories seen as sacred and vital communication. The traditions of storytelling and folktales are currently enjoying a resurgence in the UK. We might say that teachers also perform important storytelling roles with children and adults, standing up in classrooms and giving live lessons. Parents and caregivers continue the tradition of oral storytelling when they make up bedtime stories for children and leave the storybook behind. You can see children's eyes sometimes light up in anticipation when they say, "tell me a story." The practice of live theatre continues this trend of oral storytelling. You could also argue that some aspects of social media draw upon oral storytelling.

DOI: 10.4324/9781003178682-3

By engaging children with oracy, folktales can provide a different kind of storytelling experience away from the more individual and technical experience of reading. Folktales can help some less confident children find their own voice and speak up.

For children who may find some aspects of literacy difficult, oral storytelling in groups can open up new possibilities of understanding and communicating story. In providing bite-size dramatic stories, children can develop confidence in new storytelling and presentation skills. Folklore stories introduce a whole range of characters, often animals. In introducing mice who are heroes, or lions who are cowards, folktales offer an opportunity to experiment with different parts of ourselves, be that quieter or louder.

Folktales – multi-cultural stories showing people's relationship to land, nature, and ancestors

Due to their ancient roots, folktales inevitably reflect the time and place from which they arose. Our ancestors lived much closer to the land, both in terms of living from it and the proximity to the wilderness surrounding them. As a result, folktales often refer to local landscapes and nature, making them an invaluable tool to engage people with aspects of nature and histories (Hunter, 2020). Many tales live in the outdoors. Folklore stories introduce a range of animals, birds, trees, plants, mountains, deserts, rivers, and seas. Folktales present stories across different seasons or weather systems. They don't reflect an idealised, gentle face of nature but show us its unpredictable and uncontrollable forces too. These tales often bring in more destructive, dangerous elements of nature such as droughts, floods, fires, and storms. By locating themselves in a range of habitats, folktales can introduce the listener to new wild places, introducing themes of diversity and multi-cultural difference. In doing so, folklore stories can play a unique role in helping children engage and connect with different habitats across the world. Folktales can also connect us to our ancestors' stories, our own roots, and histories (Campa, 1965).

Folktales – a set of unruly and wild stories

It's not only its setting that makes the average folktale a little bit wild. Characters are larger than life and their relationships are full of extremes (Warner, 1994). The natural world is personified and reflects how the principle of animism – a living soul in all natural phenomena – is part of culture (Bird-David, 1999). Elemental forces such as fire, water, earth, and air/winds become fickle gods and goddesses. Rocks and trees take on life as magical and sometimes monstrous entities. It's hard to know whose side anybody is on. Talking animals, giants, and monsters abound (Bettelheim, 1976). Animal wisdom and magical objects save the day. Ghosts and wild spirits roam the countryside. Wild weathers and habitats provide the backdrops to characters' story arcs. Yet before we write these elements off as old-fashioned or babyish, these folkloric traditions have inspired writers and made their way into some our most popular and memorable novels, both child and adult, such as *The Lord of the Rings*. Folktales by nature are not sanitised. Threats loom large in polar opposite themes of life and death, freedom and oppression, monsters and helpers, and cruelty and trickery. Folktales tend to present an old and sometimes gory justice system based on revenge, one that can sit uneasily with adults and modern-day thinking, However, these raw and unsophisticated elements can often resonate directly and deeply with children (Bettelheim, 1976). Folktales and folklore characters can be invaluable tools to help children engage with the natural world outside, and human nature inside them, including our darker aspects. So, what is it in a folktale that can fascinate and capture the imagination of a child so fully? And what relevance can these stories play in supporting children's mental wellbeing?

History of storytelling traditions as tools of growth, both individually and in a community

In times past, story wasn't seen as something solely for entertainment and distraction. A range of psychologists and thinkers proposed that folktales, like fairy tales, legends, and myths, served as tools for psychological understanding and growth; that story also played a role in maintaining and supporting the wellbeing of individuals and communities (Jung, 1964; Bettelheim, 1976; Campbell, 1993; Warner, 2014). They proposed that these kinds of stories drew upon a well of universal and archetypal symbols and images to tap into our individual and collective psyches.

Folktales communicate through the medium of metaphor, with which children often feel at ease (Mills & Crowley, 1986). Trees and animals talk; magic abounds. Giants, elves, and fairies abiding in wild settings interact with humans. By capturing our imaginations through magic and metaphor, these stories create an exaggerated as-if world, one different from our own. Yet in doing so, a character's extraordinary journey could mirror psychological processes in a child and adult's own development. Different characters become imaginary vessels upon which we project our own experiences. Some psychologists believe we are not only attaching to one character in a story but all of them; that could be the baddie, the goodie, the tyrant king, the younger brother/sister or a magical beast (Jung, 1964). The characters in a folktale or story could represent and speak to our own inner cast of characters.

As a result, folktales can resonate with personal life journeys, both individually and collectively. Through the means of metaphor, stories can help us face the fears and challenges of being human and get in touch with our deeper nature.

Story as medicine for the community

In nearly all ancient traditions, the shaman was seen as the healer for the community. Storytelling, music, and art were deemed part of the remedy to help people (Winkelman, 2002). If a person became ill, it was believed they had become soul-sick, separate from their own nature. To heal a person, shamans would take them on a guided journey in their imagination, using stories and the beating of a drum as support to get them there, as well as bring them back. Like shamans, many writers, artists, and therapists believe that stories can still serve as a medicine for modern day people, enabling people to get closer to their true feelings by providing a bit of distance through metaphor (Levine, 1992).

Folktales' ability to help children link nature with creativity and the imagination

These short, archetypal stories can serve to wake up children's imaginations in an outdoors setting. If you are imagining little people, or faery lore, who live in the flowers, or tree spirits that hide underground, the outside world can be transformed into a playground of possibility. Wild worlds exist out there. If children are struggling to engage with the stillness of nature, folktales can engage the imagination to bring back some of the innate drama, and the sense of secret, magical worlds that hide and unfold behind the appearance of not much going on. The award winning BeWILDerwood theme park which originally opened in Norfolk, UK, complete with fairy doors and a sprinkling of imagination, has now opened another park in Cheshire, showing folklore stories can still hold appeal across a range of ages, both child and adult.

The need for rewilding; children's imaginations, play, and stories

Have our children, like the land, become a bit over harvested, and domesticated? There is a growing movement across the world surrounding the urgent need in the natural world for rewilding, for reclaiming some of the lands of agriculture to give them back to nature, to bring back a richness of life and biodiversity in our eco-systems. (Foreman, 1993; Soule & Noss, 1998). Perhaps we can also apply a need for 'rewilding' to child's play and their imaginations. With the growth of cities and populations, we've already seen how many children don't roam outside in the ways that their parents and grandparents did. The zone of play and independent mobility of children has shrunk dramatically in recent times (Moss, 2012).

We propose that we can apply the same thinking to the imagination. Perhaps we also need to roam and play more freely here too. Technical ability can sometimes seem more important than the exploration of our own ideas and creative expression. We have all become part of a complex system of monitoring and assessments. And whereas these systems enable institutions to track and meet the needs of many, there are inevitable pressures that come with it. The pace of study and work have become increasingly fast. Even our entertainment comes at high speed, with a constant stream of games and TV programmes on demand. Mobile devices keep us busy and connected. Silence, solitude, and space have become outdated and undervalued, despite the fact they are proven to contribute to our psychological and emotional wellbeing. Making time for silence and mental space forms part of the mindfulness movement, providing a useful counterbalance to highly stimulated living and learning environments. Invaluable reflection and processing can take place in the silence if we remember to leave gaps. Having resting places can support our capacity for learning and wellbeing. Slowing down can help with digestion, concentration, and absorption of both facts and feelings.

There are ongoing pressures on children (and adults) to meet various targets. Reading, literacy, and maths are key measures. If as a child you struggle to engage fully with these mental activities, it can leave you feeling like a failure as a student.

Yet as we have seen, stories weren't always about technical reading/writing skills; they belonged to the wild, to the outside, to our senses, and to oral storytellers who brought folktales to life in a group setting. If we can bring more focus on inspiring the imagination in an outdoors setting, perhaps folktales can help children engage in creative ways with their own nature for their own well-being. By bringing folktales into an outdoors setting, perhaps children can benefit from this rehoming of stories and their own imaginative selves back in the wild.

Summary of what folklore can bring to children's nature-inspired learning

Educational benefits:

- Teach children confidence and ability in oracy, presentation, and storytelling skills

- Connect and engage children creatively with the natural world

- Help children from diverse backgrounds identify histories in nature

- Build confidence in groupwork and collaboration

- Support a curriculum that embraces diversity and inclusion

- Encourage the use of the imagination in an outdoors environment

- Develop self-directed story making, individually and in a group

- Encourage and hone self-directed creativity

- A rewilding and reawakening of children's imaginations and play

Mental health and general wellbeing:

- Help children build a connection with their imagination as an inner resource

- Connect children with their own internal cast of characters

- Help build a relationship between the inner world and outside environment

- Introduce ideas of conflict and integration in interesting, safe, and creative ways

- To help children bring different parts of themselves and see different parts in others

- Help children find symbols for suffering, difficulty, and growth

- Encourage self-expression through safe vehicles of metaphor and story

- Explore personal and collective myths as metaphors for struggles and growth

- Help build a positive relationship with nature as a mental wellbeing resource

Chapter 3

HOW ARTMAKING CREATES
A BRIDGE WITH NATURE

'Guided by the place itself, you usher yourself into new territory, where you become creators, adventurers, takers of risk, generous givers and bestowers of beauty.'

Trebbe Johnson (author, founder of Radical Joy for Hard Times)

Arts as a sensory vehicle to experience the natural world

Like folktales, the visual and performing arts are another valuable vehicle to help connect children to nature, both the natural world and their own nature too. As we have already seen, there is growing evidence that many modern children suffer from diminished access to their senses (Louv, 2005). The arts can allow a safe experience of nature by giving them a sensory channel through which to engage with the natural world.

Humans have used nature as inspiration for image-making from the beginnings of cave art dated around 50,000 years ago (Stonard, 2021). Everyday artists paint *plein air* (painting outside). Poets are inspired by the natural world (Stuart-Smith, 2020) and stories are written about the creatures with which we share the world. The creative arts can connect us to the outside world, and you don't have to be an artist to participate or benefit. Maslow (1971) wrote that arts education was a useful tool, not for turning out artists but more whole human beings, able to feel more fully, and think creatively.

Multi-disciplinary approach to the arts

Engaging with the natural world activates all our different senses, seeing colour and form, listening to sounds, picking up smells in the air, and feeling surfaces/textures and different temperatures. For children unfamiliar with being in nature, the sensory nature of art making in all its forms can help build a connection to nature in calm and grounding ways. Not only is our body how we literally make sense of our environment, but this is also the instrument through which art can be made. People transform sight, sound, and touch into visual, verbal,

DOI: 10.4324/9781003178682-4

musical and sculptural creations through paint, voice, their body. The arts are close to our psychological *and* biological identity (Maslow, 1971).

Given the multi-sensory aspect of nature, in this guide we have proposed a multi-disciplinary approach to artmaking. Throughout the seasons, we offer a range of activities including visual arts, music, drama, and storytelling that enable participants to use all their senses to connect with the different themes of nature.

Helping children find focus and build confidence as makers and performers

Art activities focus the experience by engaging and evoking the senses and the naturally playful, inquisitive nature of children. When bringing something to life through painting, drawing, sculpture, music, or drama, children naturally develop their imaginations as well as their making, focussing, and concentration skills. As creativity abounds in nature's patterns and designs, it can instigate children's innate abilities as designers and inventors. From our experience, working creatively can help people build confidence in their own way of seeing the world.

Rewilding children's imaginations, be it outside or inside

Whilst we offer a wide range of creative activities in our guide, the objective is not about developing technical artistic skills, but rather engaging children's vivid imaginations with the world around them through the landscapes contained in the selection of seasonal folklore stories that inspired our activities. Activities have been designed to give children opportunities to articulate their own individual experiences of meeting with nature and being inspired by it, be that inside or outside. As Cezanne was often quoted, 'Painting from nature is not copying the object; it is realising one's sensations.'

Creating the right conditions for creativity to thrive

Art making in all its different forms asks us to step into the role of creator and share our ideas with the outside world. Building a sense of safety and permission to experiment with different art forms is vital if children are going to take creative risks and put themselves out there. To help children 'rewild the imagination,' and build confidence in their own creative visions, we have listed a few guiding principles below.

- Try to place the focus on the creative process and not the technical outcome

- Encourage all ideas, however apparently silly, as they can all lead to something else

- Encourage a sense of permission by avoiding statements of right/wrong, good/bad

- Model a welcoming and positive response to all ideas whatever shape or size

- Allow children to offer contributions in their own way... be it quiet or loud

We hope that our approach can help children build a rich and playful relationship with their creativity. In this way, we can help silence the inner critic and unhelpful doubts which so often stop people from trying new interests and expressing themselves, in whatever form.

By building confidence in their abilities as verbal and visual storytellers, children can feel less afraid to bring their own unique ideas into the world. In our experience, children can often surprise themselves with their own stories and creations!

Finally, it's not always possible to be outdoors, and we know how children are less free to roam wild these days in comparison to 100 years ago. Weather and location do not always permit it and safety can also be a factor. However, imagination has no boundaries, and creative activities are a key that can unlock it. Some of our activities invite the participant to imagine being outside instead or to bring the outside into the classroom. In this way, children can still benefit from building connections with the natural world.

Summary of what the arts can bring to children's nature-inspired learning

Educational benefits:

- Teach children confidence in their own creative and imaginative abilities

- Show children that they each have their own creative source

- Connect and engage children through senses with the natural world

- Discover the richness in nature where different animals/plants live side by side

- Learn how to appreciate the beauty of the natural world and respect nature

- Foster a relationship with being outside

- Engage in play-based learning

- Encourage experimentation

- Build confidence in groupwork and collaboration

- Offer fun and engaging ways to engage with nature-inspired work

- Develop self-directed art making, individually and in a group

- Encourage and hone self-directed creativity

- A rewilding and awakening of children's visual imaginations and sensory play

Mental health and general wellbeing:

- Help children build a connection with their imagination and senses as inner resource

- Learn that just like leaves are unique and sometimes imperfect, we can be too

- Help build a relationship between the inner world and outside environment

- Introduce ideas of conflict and integration in interesting, safe, creative ways

- To help children bring different parts of themselves and see different parts in others

- Help children find visual symbols for suffering, difficulty, and growth

- Encourage self-expression through safe vehicles of visual and performing arts

- Explore personal and collective images as metaphors for growth

- Help build a positive relationship with nature as a mental wellbeing resource

Tips on working outside in nature and sit-spots

Our activities, inspired by nature, are designed to be carried out either inside or outside depending on the needs of the group/organisation. However, being outside does allow children to have direct and personal experiences of the benefits being in nature.

> 'Inside you know what it's like and everything stays the same, but the outdoors is always changing.'
>
> *Y6 student, THE MAKE SPACE: Sunshine Painting Project at Watts Gallery, Guildford in 2021.*

Working outside with children can be incredibly rewarding but at the same time is not without its challenges. Students can become over-excited or distracted, particularly if it's a whole class; it may take some time for children to get used to outdoors learning and some students may forget the rules of the classroom as they associate being outside with break time.

Small groups

Often, it will be beneficial to take the children out in small groups to help acclimatise to being outside (depending on the availability of teaching assistants and parent helpers) and to make the sessions more focused and manageable. Outdoors learning provides a useful alternative to the classroom space for more than sports activities.

> 'Working in the fresh air is more peaceful and I feel more focused.'
>
> *Y6 student, Watts Gallery 2021.*

Clear Boundaries

Educators will know that it will be important to highlight the boundary of any outdoors area as an introduction and to be clear on thresholds, such as defining when the outdoors experiences will begin and end. If you are in a public outdoor space then children will need to be always supervised by adults.

Sit-spots in nature

Throughout history, humans have found favoured places to sit in nature and meditate on the views around them. Poets and artists show us theirs in their work. Outdoors practitioners, forest therapy, and wilderness awareness programmes often call such places sit-spots. These resting places can be a useful tool to help children connect to nature in a grounded way. Weather dependent, a sit-spot is a safe place to sit down and *be* in nature. The idea is that we feel supported by the earth, be it the grass, a tree, a rock. Or if inside, looking at a view from a comfortable chair or cushion might be our sit-spot. It's also a place to return to, becoming a favourite place or home-base that can help us connect to our senses, and equally the nature around us. If there is a big enough area on site, children can be invited to find their own sit-spot on school grounds or on a trip to a nature area, which they can come back to. Sit-spots can help encourage mindfulness in nature, as children can observe and use their senses to make sense of what is going on both around and inside them.

Code of conduct

At the start of term, it can be beneficial to create a code of conduct as a group to illustrate how children need to behave outside. This works even better if the students come up with the rules themselves, as it empowers them to take responsibility of their own behaviour. It can be a fun starter activity where together you decide what is important.

For example, we all will:

- Respect the boundaries and keep within the nature area
- Listen to whoever is in charge
- Respect each other
- Actively respect the outside world
  - No trampling or picking flowers or plants; leave any animals alone
- Be involved in working actively with the elements – keep an eye on the wind and rain!
- Carry any art/natural materials to and from a nature area
- Look after each other's creative work – rescue anything that blows away!
- Get permission before collecting any natural materials
- Clear up any materials – leaving no trace

Perhaps even have the children sign it so it becomes a contract between you all. With clear boundaries, everyone gets to take advantage of the wonders that nature offers. And when outside, often children forget they're 'working' as they are motivated, inspired, and having fun. The outside is such a rich, multi-sensory environment.

> Outside things are so vibrant – there are so many more creative ideas.
>
> *Y6 student Watts Gallery, 2021.*

Wet weather resources

Elements such as wind and rain can inspire children but might not seem like the ideal working environment. However, on some occasions, with waterproofs, tarpaulins, and by wrapping up warm, children can still enjoy working outside. It adds to the adventure and gives a different perspective to the activity. A collection of second-hand wellies might also prove valuable!

Being aware of the risks of working outside

As with any activities, teachers and group leaders are well versed in risk assessment. It can be useful also to remind children that being out in nature brings its own risks. We can all be stung by wasps, nettles, and/or caught up in brambles. It's worth finding out beforehand about any allergies, including hay fever, so that children can be forewarned, and prevention taken where possible. Avoiding being out under trees after high winds is important, to avoid any falling branches. A conversation around risk in nature can be useful so that children can learn how to stay safe in any outdoor environment.

Building up a box of recycled creative resources and natural materials

To avoid unnecessary waste of creative materials, it can be a great idea to encourage groups to build up their own creative resource-box, and to fill this with found natural objects such as leaves or stones, and equally recycled materials from home. Groups can then be introduced to the joys of recycling and upcycling, working with whatever materials you have found.

Transportation of resources

Involve children in the transportation of any creative or natural materials to and from the outside space, so that they feel ownership around the setting and clearing up.

Story dens

If possible, it can be incredibly rewarding to have a storytelling area set up with logs to sit on. This is the children's space – their 'story den' – where they can connect with nature and folklore, while wind is rustling through the trees. Perhaps in the colder seasons, it can be turned into a cosy space with tarpaulins, protecting children from the rain as they drink hot chocolate. Creating a safe environment and a home-base can be a real treat and add to the magic and power of storytelling. Students who find the technicalities of reading and writing difficult, but have vibrant imaginations and wonderful oracy skills, will have a chance to shine. Other students who fear speaking aloud may grow in confidence, realising that this is a safe space to practice.

In urban environments, or when rural areas are compounded by the weather, schools can find a location indoors for their story den. Filled with blankets and beanbags, it can create an inviting space for the children to share their stories. Perhaps the students can design the environment themselves, taking inspiration from nature.

Whether schools are bringing nature indoors or taking art materials outside, creativity can flourish. We are a great believer in the principle minimum resources, maximum imagination.

Chapter 4

INTRODUCTION TO FOLKTALES, STORYTELLING, AND CREATIVE ACTIVITIES

'Three apples fell from the heavens – one apple for the teller, one apple for the listener, and one apple for the person who takes the story to heart.'

(Armenian proverb)

Guiding principles behind our choice of folktales

Folktales are by nature ever-changing. Oral traditions pass on stories that migrate across borders to be retold again and again. In the retelling, story offshoots take new forms in different places. Although collections of folktales have been printed in books, the real tradition is not reading/writing them, but the speaking of them aloud. So, in the great tradition of folktales, and spirit of storytelling, we have adapted the stories in our guide too, while trying to keep true to their essence.

The whole world is rich and alive with folklore traditions and oral storytelling. Our *Rewilding Children's Imaginations* guide offers a collection, but unfortunately not every culture can be represented. There are far too many, and we had to be selective. Coming from a temperate habitat, we have chosen folktales to explore the four seasons. Most of our stories come from the Northern Hemisphere, and we are curious to learn more about those being told in the Southern Hemisphere. Due to different weather systems and habitats, some parts of the world don't divide their year in four, but into two – the dry and wet season. Some folktales aren't rooted in nature, others aren't child friendly, and some are just a little too long to place here. With some folktales, we didn't want to risk offending religious or cultural sensibilities. Other folktales, we simply won't have found! We chose folktales or folklore characters ultimately to inspire children and adults to engage with nature, seasons, storytelling, and artmaking.

Whereas most of our stories in our guide are from older times, we are mindful that for some cultures, oral storytelling remains an integral part of their ongoing lives. These stories

DOI: 10.4324/9781003178682-5

and traditions are very much alive. By including folktales and art practices from First Nation, and Aboriginal/Torres Strait Island peoples, we would like to introduce readers to a different and rich way of engaging with nature. We offer these stories in the spirit of cultural appreciation, and an acknowledgement that we have much to learn about how to connect with the land in respectful ways from indigenous cultures.

We have endeavoured to offer story sources where possible, yet this is not always possible. So many we have been told through the course of life. There are inevitable disputes by folklorists on authenticity and place of origin. Also, oral stories are often translated, written down, and perhaps edited by scholars who don't come from the origin culture. Perhaps in the end, just like nature itself, folklore is a little wild, and not easily contained within the neatness of modern life and clearly defined garden borders. We like to think of folktales like brambles; they grow around the edges yet offer such great fruit if you notice them, so often out of sight.

In our retelling of folktales, we hope that like any good story, they inspire the imagination and encourage a further interest in folktales from across the world. We have kept them 'short and sweet' to help the storyteller and so that you may be inspired to retell them in your own words. We hope that these stories can open our senses to the wild and natural world outside and inside us, the parts that so need our care and attention.

In this chapter, we start with a folktale from West Africa and accompanying six creative activities to introduce the dual themes of oral storytelling and nature. Following onto Chapter Five, we move through the four seasons, with a variety of folktales from across the world, and creative activities that draw upon storytelling, drama, creative writing, and artmaking.

A retelling of *Anansi Brings Stories into the World*

- Making an Animal-Guide Postcard
- Finding Our Roar or Squeak
- Enacting an Animal Scene from the Anansi Folktale
- Creating a Trickster Scene for a Folktale
- Creating an Animal Story in the Round
- Mythical Animal 'Nonsense & Consequences' Game

Folktale from the Akan peoples in Ghana, West Africa

A retelling of *Anansi Brings Stories into the World*

The Anansi character originates from West Africa. Often taking the form of a spider, Anansi is seen as a god of wisdom, knowledge, and speech. His story travelled during the transatlantic slave trade to become part of storytelling traditions in Jamaica, the West Indies, and the Caribbean. Anansi is a symbol of resistance against oppressive power.

Once, there was a time when there were no stories in the world. Nyame, the Sky-God, kept them all for himself. Anansi, the spider-man, thought humans would benefit from being given stories to tell, so he climbed the tallest tree and called out to Nyame: "Please give me your stories. I can pay you for them, whatever you ask."

Nyame, the Sky-God, laughed when he heard Anansi's request, and named his price. "I'll give you the stories, but only if you bring me Onini the python, Osebo the leopard, and the Mmoboro hornets." Then Nyame smiled. These creatures were too fierce for Anansi!

"You have a deal," said Anansi, scuttling down the tree. Firstly, Anansi spoke to his wife, Aso, and they came up with a plan together. Anansi visited the tree where the python lived.

"I think Nyame is wrong," said Anansi in a loud voice, waving a branch. "You are definitely shorter than this stick."

Onini appeared instantly and frowned at the stick. "I am far longer," said the python, stretching out his body proudly to its full length.

"Prove it," said Anansi. "I'll tie you to this branch to make sure we can measure you."

Onini nodded. After allowing himself to be tied to the branch, he was caught! Secondly, Anansi spoke to his wife, Aso, again and formed another plan. He watched the route the leopard took every night to get from his home to the watering hole. One day, while Osebo was sleeping, Anansi dug a deep pit along the route, and the leopard fell inside.

"Would you like some help getting out?" called Anansi peering over the edge, and Osebo, the leopard nodded, desperately. Anansi threw a thick thread of web down and shouted, "Wind my web around your tail." Then he heaved the leopard out, winding his thread around the wild cat's body as he pulled. By the time the leopard was at the top, he was trapped in a cocoon of webbing.

Thirdly, after speaking with his wife, Aso, Anansi scuttled to where the hornets lived. He emptied a gourd of water onto the leaves and said, 'It's pouring with rain. Dear hornets, get in here, and the calabash will keep you dry."

The hornets flew into the calabash and Anansi screwed on the lid as tightly as he could. Then using his webbing, he lugged all the creatures up the tree and to the Sky-God.

Nyame was astonished. "You have proven yourself to be the smartest creature, Anansi. Here are all the stories." And he gave Anansi all the stories and tales known as AnansiStories today.

ACTIVITY: MAKING AN ANIMAL-GUIDE POSTCARD		
Subject: Creative arts **Curriculum Links**: Art, PSHE	**Key Skills:** Artmaking, design	**Duration:** 1 hour plus
Resources & Creative Materials: Blank postcards, or postcard-sized white card Pens, pencils, felt tips	**Location:** Inside	

Learning Objectives:

- To learn about comfort zones, for animals and humans
- To discuss some of the challenges of being creative and putting ourselves 'out there'
- To normalise nerves and fears in creative activities – drama, oracy, artmaking

Introduction & Warm-Up: *20 minutes*
Like humans, there are times when animals feel shy and need reassurance. Let's think about how animals behave, wild or domesticated, when faced with a new situation.

- Ask anyone if they have a pet, or come across a wild creature, a bird, mouse, fox?
- What kind of behaviours do these animals show? What noises, actions?
- How do we make animals feel safe enough to approach and trust us?

Introduce the idea of a comfort zone. Humans, like animals, have a personal comfort zone, and need help to feel safe, especially when they step out of it. Comfort zones can be very different. One person feels confident doing one thing, but not another.

Key Activity:
Activity 1 – Discussion on creativity and personal comfort zones – whole class/group activity

- How do we feel when asked to present something out loud, make art, or write?
- We all have our preferences... for one person something is easy, for someone else the same thing is hard.
- Discuss what we each find easy or hard, with the teacher/facilitator joining in too.
- Brainstorm what we need to hear/see from others when we risk something new.
- E.g. A friend stands next to us, smiles, nods, offers reassurance
  o E.g. You can do it, I've got your back, don't worry about the final product, this is about the journey, have fun experimenting, allow yourself to let go.

Activity 2 – Animal-Guide or Animal-Friend postcard
In folktales, animals are often used to support people as symbols of wisdom or guides. We are each going to make an Animal-Friend postcard, an imaginary animal who will offer us support for when we are trying out new activities, like creative writing, drama or artmaking.

- Individually, choose an animal to be your friend, any animal you like.
- Draw this animal on the front.
- On the back of the postcard write down the words and behaviours that you would imagine the animal would say to you as support. Such as: "You can do it." "You've got this." "I'm here with you."
- Really think about what you need to hear/see to grow in confidence.

Sharing/Reflecting:
Share Animal-Guide postcards and examples of the phrases that animals said as comfort and support. Make sure you keep your Animal-Friend postcard in a safe place.

Key Vocabulary/ Questions Comfort-zone, animals as guides, folklore What do animals give us humans in our lives?	**Extension Activities** Create a class box to keep the animal postcards safe.

ACTIVITY: FINDING OUR 'ROAR' OR 'SQUEAK'		
Subject: Performing arts **Curriculum Links**: English, PSHE	**Key Skills:** Oracy, drama	**Duration:** 1 hour
Resources & Creative Materials: Anansi folktale		**Location:** Inside or outside

Learning Objectives:

- To rethink ideas and assumptions around 'performance'
- To develop more confidence in devising and self-expression in performing arts
- To help children find their voice, however quiet or loud

Introduction & Warm-Up: *10 minutes*
What do we all hear when someone says we're going to do drama or performing arts?

- Brainstorm responses – dread, excitement, nervous, a bit of both?
- Fears that someone might call us a show off or laugh at us

It's a bit like the Sky-God in the Anansi tale who doesn't believe he is capable. Explain how it can be daunting to act or read aloud and some of us might need support. Lots of animals in the world are naturally shy too in some situations, yet brave and bold in others. Discuss examples of animals being both brave and shy... a squirrel can seem of shy of humans but enjoys chasing its friends around a tree. Together, let's think of other examples, like a bird singing loudly in the morning, then flying away from a cat!

Key Activity: *30 minutes*
Activity 1: *10 minutes*
In the large group, invite all participant to imagine they are a shy lion/lioness

- Can you all mew very quietly, almost a whisper?
- Can you feel a little bit braver and growl a bit louder?
- Can you be even braver and growl even louder?
- Can you feel very brave and roar?
- Can you roar as loud as you possibly can?

As leader, move arms up and down to signal volume, and ask children to follow your lead.

Activity 2: *20 minutes (10 minutes each)*
In pairs, each child chooses a favourite animal – can be a pet or any animal they like.

- Together each pair is going to work together to design a short drama sketch – 1 minute – where both animals interact, and take turns being shy and bold.
- If you are stuck for ideas, you can also enact Anansi tricking one of the animals too, who pretends to be shy and quiet so he can get the animals to do what he wants!
- Encourage children to help each other in bringing their animal to life.

Sharing/Reflecting: *15 minutes*
Explain how an audience is just as important as the performers. Giving attention to a story and a performer, really makes it come alive. In any performing activities, everyone needs to feel safe and respected. Invite pairs to show their short performance, stating that there is no pressure. End the session with a few more rounds of a timid lioness finding their roar (same activity as the warm-up).

Key Vocabulary/ Questions Roar, dialling up/down volume, respect What role does the audience play in drama?	**Extension Activities** Create a short play on how a shy lion/lioness finds their roar.

ACTIVITY: ENACTING AN ANIMAL SCENE FROM THE ANANSI FOLKTALE		
Subject: Performing arts **Curriculum Links**: English, Drama	**Key Skills:** Drama, improvisation, mime, confidence, oracy, listening	**Duration:** 1 hour
Resources & Creative Materials: *Anansi Brings Stories into the World* folktale		**Location:** Inside or outside

Learning Objectives:

- To build confidence in improvisation and performing arts
- To work collaboratively to create a scene and new characters
- To learn how to be a great audience

Introduction & Warm-Up: *10 minutes*

In groups of four or five, invite children to become 'moving sculpts' of animals. This is where we use our bodies to create shapes and movements. The idea is not to have much time to prepare, but to work together collaboratively and spontaneously, and to have fun...

- Groups have one minute to create 'moving sculpts' and try to move as one.
- The facilitator calls out different creatures, e.g. spider, horse, turtle, slug, eagle, etc.
- Invite each group to think of an animal as a challenge to the other groups.
- How do they embody the qualities of an animal through mime and movement?

Have a brief brainstorm about what we need from an audience when we are performing and the important of attention and listening, to help serves as *witnesses* for the story.

Key Activity: *40 minutes*

Activity 1: *Enacting Anansi Animal Stories – 30 minutes*

In groups of four or five, participants are going to bring to life one of the Anansi animal trickster scenes in a short drama piece, with each play lasting only about one minute. Choose from:

1. When Anansi tricks the python.
2. When Anansi tricks the leopard.
3. When Anansi tricks the hornets.

- Invite children to work together to perform the scene. The challenge is everyone must be in it. Perhaps there is another animal watching or someone pretends to be the rope or calabash/gourd.
- Invite children to improvise their own lines – what do they imagine the characters would say? How will they embody the animals?

Activity 2: *Sharing Anansi Scenes with another group – approx. 10 minutes*

- Invite children to perform their animal scenes to another group, reminding the class about the importance of the audience as witness.
- Try to perform to as many groups as possible in the given time to build confidence.

Sharing/Reflecting: *10 minutes*

Ask if any groups are feeling brave enough to show their animal scene to the entire class. Invite participants to give feedback on the creative process. How was it to work collaboratively? How was it to perform in front of others? What was it like to be an audience member?

Key Vocabulary/ Questions	**Extension Activities**
Improvisation, AnansiStories, collaboratively, mime, movement, witness, sculpts, calabash/gourd Why is the audience so important in performance?	Invite the children to enact a different trickster scene from the folktale.

ACTIVITY: CREATING A TRICKSTER SCENE FOR A FOLKTALE		
Subject: Creative Writing **Curriculum Links**: English	**Key Skills:** Imagination, creative writing, collaboration, oracy	**Duration:** 1 hour
Resources & Creative Materials: *Anansi Brings Stories into the World* folktale Paper, pens/pencils	**Location:** Inside	

Learning Objectives:

- To use our imaginations to write a new scene for a folktale
- To devise our own trickster scene with animals
- To learn how to collaborate and bounce ideas off each other
- To practise reading and performing folktales to an audience

Introduction & Warm-Up: *15 minutes*

Reread the folktale, *Anansi Brings Stories into the World.* In folktales, the 'trickster' is a character that often appears, who tricks animals or opponents that are much bigger.

- Discuss each trickster scene – how does Anansi trick each of the animals? He doesn't use strength of the body but strength of the mind. He is cunning and clever.
- As a group, brainstorm other animals Nyame, the Sky-God, might have asked Anansi to bring to him as his price.
- Brainstorm together how Anansi might devise new tricks for these creatures. For example, does Anansi spin a web between two trees and have a honey pot on the other side to catch a bear? Does Anansi say a lion can't fit into a large calabash/gourd? Then once the lion jumps inside, he finds a way to seal the gourd shut.
- Don't worry how silly or far-fetched your ideas might sound... see how far you can push Anansi's abilities!

Key Activity: *30 minutes*

In pairs, choose an animal that the Sky-God wants as payment for his stories.

- To make the story more exciting, you might want to choose a fierce creature that won't be easy to catch, or a rare creature hard to find.
- Together, plan a scene where Anansi uses his cunning to trick the animal.
- Either in pairs or individually, ask the children to write the scene.

Sharing/Reflecting: *15 minutes*

Invite the children to read out their scenes, and gain responses to the creative process. How was is it to work together to create a new scene? Any challenges or surprises?

Gain responses from the audience – any similar or different scenes or themes? What are your favourite and funniest tricks played?

Key Vocabulary/ Questions: A trickster story, cunning, ingenious, collaboration, calabash/gourd Why is cunning and cleverness so important for Anansi?	**Extension Activities:** Act out the trickster scenes. Make an AnansiStories class book with illustrations or cartoons.

ACTIVITY: CREATING AN ANIMAL STORY-IN-THE-ROUND		
Subject: Performing arts **Curriculum Links**: English	**Key Skills:** Storytelling, listening, recall	**Duration:** 1 hour
Resources & Creative Materials: One minute timer	**Location:** Inside or outside	

Learning Objectives:

- To build confidence in storytelling, and telling stories of our own
- To practice our listening skills, taking note of details
- To see how stories told by word of mouth often evolve with each retelling
- To lose a bit of fear around getting something 100% right!

Introduction & Warm-Up: *15 minutes*
Explain how folktales were told and retold aloud rather than read. In the retellings, often these stories would evolve and change. Things might be omitted, other things included.

- Discuss how it feels to hear a story told to us, rather than reading it ourselves.
- Brainstorm together what makes a good listener, and a good audience.
- How do we *feel* when someone really listens to us?
- How do we know when someone is listening to us closely? Signs and behaviours?

Explain how we are going to tell a short animal story – either fictional or real – to another person, lasting no longer than one minute.

Key Activity: *30 minutes*
Invite participants to close their eyes and think of an animal story that will last no longer than one minute. It could be an experience they've had themselves, or maybe a story a family member or friend told them, e.g. being chased by an animal, or seeing a wild animal up close, or they may prefer to make up a story.

- Invite children to get into pairs, calling the participants 'Storyteller' and 'Listener.'
- The 'Storyteller' in each pair tells their animal story to the 'Listener.' (The teacher/facilitator uses the timer to ensure stories last no longer than one minute.)
- The 'Listener' then retells the story to the 'Storyteller' who cannot interrupt.
- Afterwards they discuss how close the retelling is to the original. Were there any changes?
- Then each pair swap roles (the 'Storyteller' becomes the 'Listener' and visa versa) and the process is repeated.
- The children find another pair and try telling their partner's story to three of them.
- When all four stories have been told, discuss how close they are to the original. Did anyone include new details to fill in the gaps? Did they become longer or shorter?

Sharing/Reflecting: *15 minutes*
Invite participants to share any short stories they heard to the entire class. Remind participants that folktales often change and evolve with each retelling, especially if stories have been handed down from generation to generation – there can be embellishments or omissions. Storytellers might also want to make the tales current for each generation.

Key Vocabulary/Questions: Oral storytelling, evolve, omissions, embellishment Generations; why do we think folktales change? What do folktales appeal? What makes them different?	**Extension Activities:** Repeat the activity with a two-minute story. Ask older family members if they know any folktales and bring stories back to the class.

ACTIVITY: MYTHICAL ANIMAL 'NONSENSE & CONSEQUENCES' GAME		
Subject: Visual arts **Curriculum Links**: Art	**Key Skills:** Creativity, drawing, play, improvisation, collaboration	**Duration:** 1 hour
Resources & Creative Materials: White A4 paper, pencils, pens, coloured pencils	**Location:** Inside or outside	

Learning Objectives:

- To flex the imagination in a playful, fun way
- To develop more confidence in spontaneous artmaking and improvisation
- To enjoy the creative process and not worry about outcomes

Introduction & Warm-Up: *10 minutes*

Today we are going to play a fun warm-up game, making up our own magical folktale characters! Many characters found in myths and our most loved stories are a hybrid between one or more creatures – fauns, centaurs, hippogriffs. Ask the group what different animals make up these creatures, and if they can think of any examples from books or films.

Key Activity: *30 minutes*

- Today we are going to work together to create our own mythical, magical folktale creatures.
- Divide the class into groups of four children (so they are sitting next to each other).
- Give each child an A4 piece of paper, and ask to fold into 4 equal sections.
- We're going to create our mish-mash animals – keeping them secret while making.
- Don't worry about technical results – see if you can make yourself laugh!

Step 1:

1. Draw an animal head and neck ONLY, any creature you like, on the 1st quarter of paper, making sure no-one else in your group can see what you are drawing.
2. Once finished, fold the paper over to hide your creation and draw 2 small lines into the next connected blank section beneath to show where the head/neck will attach to the next body part.
3. When everyone has finished drawing, pass the paper onto the next person in the group.

Step 2:

Repeat in this order:

1. Draw the head.
2. Draw the torso i.e., arms/wings/fins.
3. Draw legs.
4. Draw feet i.e. paws/hooves, fish tail – when you draw your next creature-part, do not draw the same animal/bird/fish as before... go for variety!

Step 3:
Once all four sections are completed pass the paper. This person gets to open the paper to *reveal* the new character. The hard part is not to share it yet! Very quickly, without thinking too much... invent a name for your new animal. Play with words, adjectives, alliteration. Don't worry if it doesn't make sense... it's just like the animals! If you're stuck, you can start it off with Dr, Lord, Lady, Professor, Queen/King, Sir/Madam, and use adjectives, like the most lazy, fluffy, mysterious... etc.Step 4: The Big Reveal – introduce your magical hybrid creatures by name to your group.Step 5. Colour in the hybrid creatures to bring them to life a bit more!

Sharing/Reflecting: *15 minutes*
Ask for volunteers to share with the whole group and gain responses. Explore the creative process – any challenges, surprises, insights?

Key Vocabulary/Questions: Improvisation, alliteration, hybrid, mythological	**Extension Activities:** Write a story about your creature.

FOLKTALES

Chapter 5 – Folktales: Introduction to the Seasons

If we picture our ancestors living in small hunter-gatherer communities – with no electricity, no central heating, no screens, no technology, no clocks, no photos, no science, no cars, no supermarkets, no schools – we can quickly imagine how their lives were unrecognisable from ours today. Unlike the many of us living in cities, once everyone lived directly off the land. To eat, you grew your own food, reared animals, and traded goods. To survive, you had to observe the passage of the seasons. Finding ways to grow, harvest, and store food were essential so that you could eat in WINTER when plants did not grow.

When so much of life was out of people's control, it must have brought security and relief to observe these regular cycles in nature. Today, satellites and science tell us much of our natural world. Yet, ancient people didn't know where the sun went at night, why the moon appeared, or why it became colder/warmer through the seasons. They had no idea we lived on a planet, in a solar system, in a galaxy.

Folktales were most likely an attempt in part to understand nature's mysteries and patterns. Many stories centre around changes in the natural world. These older belief systems pre-date the monotheistic religions – Christianity, Islam, Judaism – and tend to focus on the land, weather, and seasons. If we see lightning, large waves, or a hurricane, there is something awe-inspiring and humbling in these forces of nature. Suddenly human beings can feel very small and vulnerable indeed. Equally, a tiny seed growing into food we can eat, must have appeared magical. It's not surprising then that forces of nature were given identities in the form of nature gods and magical spirits.

In Northern/Southern hemispheres, peoples' lives and stories often focused on seasonal changes; the shortest and longest days of the year, the seasonal midpoints, the SUMMER, and WINTER Solstice (Matthews and Matthews, 1998); and the Equinoxes in SPRING and AUTUMN, when day and night hours are equal. Even the monotheistic religions that arrived much later, often placed important rituals and festivals on seasonal change-points. The calendar we follow was invented by the Romans to try and structure nature's orbits – the solar and lunar patterns – into time that could be measured. The first clocks were sundials (Koscielniak, 2014), using the sun's movements across the sky to measure time. If we look at the language roots behind the days of the week, it shows the mix of influences coming from different places and times– the names of days in English are a mix of Norse (Viking) gods and planets, which the Greeks/Romans saw as gods associated with nature.

One idea about the changes in seasons comes from the Ancient Celts, a tribe of people who migrated and lived in the British Isles. They believed the sun was a wheel that turned the seasons (Siddons-Heginworth, 2008). And it's not that far from the truth. The Earth's orbits around the sun do determine the seasons.

AUTUMN

'AUTUMN glows upon us like a splendid evening;
it is the very sunset of the year...'

Mary Russell Mitford (British poet)

September, October, November in

Northern Hemisphere

March, April, May in

Southern Hemisphere

AUTUMN SEASON, FOLKTALES, AND CREATIVE ACTIVITIES

- Introduction to AUTUMN

- Opening Activity – AUTUMN Stroll and Word Collection

A retelling of *Autumn Colour* from Oneida tribe, First Nation, Upstate New York, USA

- Bringing the Bear Folktale to Life through Drama

- Creating a Folklore Legend to Explain Why Leaves Fall in AUTUMN

- Creating Leaf Lacing Patterns and Symbols

- Creating a Dot-to-Dot Animal Star Constellation

A retelling of *Dagda's Magic Harp – The Oak of Two Blossoms* from Ireland

- Bringing *Dagda's Magic Harp* to Life through Drama and Music

- Making Musical Instruments from Natural Resources

- Bringing the AUTUMN Season to Life through Music and Art

- Creating an Acorn Poem

A retelling of *Two Brothers, a Swallow, and a Pumpkin* from Korea

- A Little Bird told Me – Retelling the Story from the Swallow's Point of View

- Creating a Picture Book about a Magic Seed

- Creating Pumpkin List Poems – either Joyful or Scary

- Designing AUTUMNAL Artwork for a Pumpkin or Squash Carving

A retelling of *The Magic Herb and the Hedgehog* from Baltic and Slavic regions

- Creating a Folklore Legend based on *The Magic Herb and the Hedgehog*

- Creating Story Whispers

- Creating an AUTUMN Treasure Map

- Hedgehog Book Art around Themes of Hibernation

DOI: 10.4324/9781003178682-7

A Retelling of *The Spirit-Wind Horse of AUTUMN* folktale from the southwest of England

• 'Winds' Mindfulness Image-Making

• Creating Our Own AUTUMN Spirit-Wind Horse

• Creating Actions And Mimes to Embody Aspects of Nature

• Creating A Rhyming Poem – A Summoning Spell

Closing exercise

• Personal/collective Associations with AUTUMN and Giant Group Mandala

Try this at home

• AUTUMN Bingo on a Nature Walk (plus resources)

Introduction to AUTUMN

As we enter AUTUMN, it's a time of striking changes. Leaves turn orange, red, yellow before falling and leaving a carpet of colour on the ground. We see a new palette of warm, deep red colours, alongside blues and greys. For agricultural communities across the world, AUTUMN marks the crucial time of the harvest, when ripe crops are collected and stored. In ancient times, when there were no supermarkets or freezers, any food grown would have had to last until the next year.

For those of us in cities and towns, harvesting activity can be seen in local parks, such as squirrels storing nuts. AUTUMN is a time for late berries and the nutting season. Depending on where you live, AUTUMN may still feel hot. However, for many people, AUTUMN marks the end of summer (and school holidays). Eventually, the weather will turn cooler, evenings darker. We reach the AUTUMN Equinox, signifying an equal amount of light and dark hours, around 22 September and 20 March, in the different hemispheres.

Festivals in this month often relate to the harvest and the move from SUMMER into the cooler, darker side of the year. In ancient times, the year was often divided in half – the light half and the dark half. The changes in temperature and shorter daylight hours may well have taken us back indoors, around the hearth, which is perhaps why late AUTUMN is associated with a rich storytelling tradition. Across the world, it's a time when we see the harvest and ancestors being honoured. The Mid-AUTUMN Harvest Festival in China and Asia is as important as the Chinese New Year. It is thought in the Celtic tradition that Samhain is the nature festival whose roots lie behind Halloween (All Hallow's Eve) and Day of the Dead. We also have the Hindu Diwali Festival of lights to represent the rows of lamps lit to guide and lead two reunited lovers back home.

AUTUMN's changes can bring an opportunity for children to look at the winds of change, of different rhythms, a need to harvest, prepare, store, and get ready again for another cycle. With the busyness and frantic pace of modern lives and technology, AUTUMN can also help us explore themes around nature slowing down, reminding us that life is not always about constant growth. Even nature needs a rest, before bursting into life once more.

OPENING ACTIVITY: AUTUMN STROLL AND AUTUMN WORD COLLECTION		
Subject: Wellbeing **Curriculum Links:** English, PSHE	**Key Skills:** Sensation, mindfulness, observation	**Duration:** 1 hour
Resources & Creative Materials: Strips of paper in season colours, pens/pencils, a box		**Location:** Outside on a dry day Inside for Activity 2 if too windy

Learning Objectives:

- To teach mindfulness techniques and support children in mind/body wellbeing
- To introduce concepts of natural changes associated with AUTUMN
- To learn how to focus on our senses and sensations
- To create a box of AUTUMN words – sensations, emotions, natural objects, images

Introduction & Warm-Up: *15 minutes*
Introduce the idea that often we get so used to our surroundings, that we forget to look and notice all the incredible happenings in nature going on around us.

- Today we will be learning how to make our senses super strong.

Explain mindfulness and walking meditation principles behind an AUTUMN Stroll:

- A way of observing and moving through the world without judgement.
- Slowing down and allowing our bodies and minds to relax in the natural world.

Invite children first to stand in a circle outside to practice noticing through the senses

- In silence, feel ground beneath your feet and notice what is happening around you.
- What do you see and hear, what temperature do you feel on your skin?

Key Activity: *35 minutes*
Activity 1 – AUTUMN stroll – *20 minutes*

- Invite children to walk in silence in the outside space and observe their environment.
- Give attention to their senses – colours, sounds, feelings, smells.
- What are some of the signs of AUTUMN.
- What do they notice as they look around them? Changes to the trees, their leaves?
- What temperature is it? Changes to the air and wind?
- What do they see around them – any berries, leaves on the ground?
- Encourage children to find one natural object from ground – leaf, stone, feather, etc.

After some strolling in silence, invite children to stop and return to the circle.

Activity 2 – *Gathering together of AUTUMN words, images, sensations – 15 minutes*

- On a strip of paper, each child writes a few AUTUMN words/sensations and cuts out each word.
- Place these and any natural objects found in an AUTUMN box or create a display.

Sharing/Reflection: *10 minutes*
Invite participants to share their responses to the AUTUMN STROLL and share their objects. Why did they choose these particular items? What did they feel as they walked? Examples include feeling the wind on their skin, an inner calmness, or maybe giggles. Was it what they expected? Any feelings, sensations, surprises? Any objects that they picked up along the way?

Key Vocabulary/Questions: Mindfulness, senses, creativity, active noticing What kind of senses and words are unique to AUTUMN?	**Extension Activities:** AUTUMN words can be fanned out in a circle and displayed.

AUTUMN Folktale 1 from Oneida tribe, First Nation, Upstate New York, USA

A retelling of *Autumn Colour*

AUTUMN brings visual changes to the natural world, as the leaves on trees change colour and fall. Many folklore stories are told to try and make sense of the changes of nature.

Oral storytelling continues to hold an integral place in the lives of First Nation peoples, in North America. In this community, stories are made for telling and sharing, not for reading. Storytellers continue to hold an important role. These folklore legends reflect the First Nation people's deep connection with nature, as well as their interest and knowledge in astronomy.

Here is a wonderful, memorable folktale from the Oneida tribe explaining why AUTUMN leaves change colour. Even if we know the scientific reason, this natural process still appears incredible, if not magical. We can start to see that magic, story, and science are all interconnected.

Many, many years ago, a wild creature was terrorising a village, eating their livestock. A hunter discovered enormous paw prints and realised the animal was a giant bear. Desperate to stop the creature, the villagers sent out their finest warriors to find him. Following the bear tracks, the warriors caught up with the bear and tried shooting him, but their arrows could not pierce the bear's thick skin. The magnificent creature took off running, but he never went far. He'd return and circle the village, taking more and more of their food.

Three brothers fell asleep and dreamt of tracking down and killing the bear. The dreams gave them hope and courage. Taking food and provisions with them, the brothers followed the bear over mountains and across seas until they reached the end of the Earth. The great bear leapt into the heavens and the three warriors followed him.

In the AUTUMN, as the bear grew sleepy and ready for hibernation, the three hunters managed to catch up to the animal. They took a shot, but their arrows only grazed the bear's skin, not killing it. Blood dripped from the bear's paws high up in the sky and fell to the trees below, turning the leaves orange, yellow, and red.

To this day, those warriors continue to track the bear in circles around and under Earth. If you look up at the night sky, you can see the three hunters chasing the bear in the star constellation the Great Bear (also known as Ursus Major or the Big Dipper).

ACTIVITY: BRINGING THE BEAR FOLKTALE TO LIFE THROUGH DRAMA		
Subject: Performing arts **Curriculum Links:** Drama, English	**Key Skills:** Drama, oracy, storytelling Collaboration	**Duration:** 1 hour 30 minutes

Resources & Creative Materials: *Autumn Colour* folktale Percussion instruments Any colourful fabrics, ribbons, textiles	**Location:** Inside or outside

Learning Objectives:

- To learn how humans have used story to understand changes in seasons/nature
- To discover how animals were often used in First Nation legends and stories
- To learn how the names of star constellations are rooted in myth and legend
- To remember to 'look around' us and notice the changes happening in seasons
- To work collaboratively as storytellers through drama and oral storytelling

Introduction & Warm-Up: *20 minutes*
Storytelling and responses: Invite participants to share responses to the Bear Story

- What feelings are evoked in them through this story?
- What do they think about this way of explaining why leaves change colour?
- And explaining why the stars are in the shape they are?
- Which parts of the story stay with them?
- Share how important being able to track animals is in certain communities.
- Special animal *trackers* could recognise prints, but also broken branches, too!
- Share how many star constellations are rooted in ancient myth

Key Activity: *55 minutes*
Activity 1 – In *medium-sized groups of five to six participants – 35 minutes*
Each group is to bring to life the Bear Folktale through drama and oral storytelling.

- Groups can decide how they want to tell the story... either through drama or storytelling, taking turns narrating.
- Include percussion instruments and fabrics/textiles to tell the story.
- Make sure they include the animal trackers, the bear, and the warriors.
- Suggest than the bear might be made up of more than one person.
- Each piece to be no longer than three minutes, with a start, middle, and end.
- Rehearse the play, thinking about your audience.

Activity 2 – *Performance – 20 minutes*

- Invite each group to perform their drama piece.

Sharing/Reflection: *15 minutes*
Invite participants to share their responses/feedback, both to the final pieces and also their creative, collaborative process. Learnings, challenges? Did the instruments and props make a difference?

Key Vocabulary/Questions: First Nation, Oneida tribe, AUTUMN/Fall, constellations, Great Bear, Big Dipper	**Extension Activities:** Look at star constellations online as a group or individually.

ACTIVITY: CREATING A FOLKLORE LEGEND TO EXPLAIN WHY LEAVES FALL IN AUTUMN		
Subject: Performing arts **Curriculum Links:** English, Drama	**Key Skills:** Storytelling, oracy	**Duration:** 1 hour 15 minutes

Resources & Creative Materials: *Autumn Colour* folktale paper, pens/pencils	**Location:** Outside and inside

Learning Objectives:

- To learn how to personify nature and bring AUTUMN to life in oral storytelling
- To use imagination to create an original folktale around leaves falling
- To develop confidence as performers and oral storytellers

Introduction & Warm-Up: *10 minutes*

In the same way that we have heard this wonderful story about why leaves change colour, we are now going to create an original folklore legend about why leaves fall in AUTUMN.

- Let your imagination fly... you may want to use animals and birds to tell your story, or maybe a nature god/goddess or magical nature spirits or faeries.
- Think about the animals that you see in AUTUMN around you. You can make up this story any way you want. Just remember to give it a start, middle, and end.

Remember you will be sharing and reading your story aloud to the group, with each participant having a few lines.

Key Activity: *50 minutes*

Activity 1: *Devising in small groups – 30 minutes*

- As a group, come up with your own original folktale to explain why leaves fall from trees every year.
- There is no right or wrong... have fun imagining what magical and natural forces could be behind such a happening. The story doesn't have to be long – one page.

Activity 2: *Performance In small groups – 20 minutes*

- For your performance, think about how your audience can be seated – a circle/in lines.
- See how you can engage and interest the audience. Perhaps you want to use props, instruments, or have audience participation where they can become growling bears

Each group will read aloud their folktale to the rest of the participants.

Sharing/Reflection: *15 minutes*

Gain responses to the original stories and creative process. What is it like reading aloud? What is it like being an audience member? How do you engage your audience?
Were the stories similar or very different?

Key Vocabulary/Questions: Oral storytelling, oracy What difference does it make knowing that these stories are made for reading aloud, rather than reading in your head?	**Extension Activities:** Decorate folktale with cut-out coloured paper leaves.

ACTIVITY: CREATING LEAF LACING PATTERNS AND SYMBOLS		
Subject: Visual arts **Curriculum Links:** Art, science	**Key Skills:** Drawing, observation	**Duration:** 1 hour
Resources & Creative Materials: Collection of fallen different coloured AUTUMN leaves POSCA pens or acrylic/poster paint with fine-tip brush A4 paper – white or black, PVA glue		**Location:** Outside and inside

Learning Objectives:

- To learn about how to use found natural objects in creative art making
- To appreciate the different colours and shapes of leaves from trees
- To learn how a tree feeds itself from the sun
- To witness the cycle of decay and degeneration

Introduction & Warm-Up: *15 minutes*
Invite participants to pick up fallen leaves – either locally or from a journey

- Encourage participants to find flat leaves with different shapes/colours, size.
- Encourage looking at leaves... really taking notice of shapes, etc.
- Remind children they will have to be gentle with the leaves to keep them whole.
- Each child needs at least five leaves to create their leaf lacing patterns.

Explain to the group how each leaf is important because it takes the energy of the sun and turns it into food for the tree in a process called photosynthesis. The green colour of leaves is called 'chlorophyll.' When the leaves fall off the trees, it's because there is less sunlight.

Key Activity: *40 minutes*
Activity 1: *Individually – 30 minutes*

Trees have veins, just like we have inside our bodies to carry and make food. Invite participants to do this exercise slowly and mindfully, really taking their time to notice.

1. Choose a leaf to start, and look at leaf, running your fingers/hand over the surface.
2. Notice the pattern of veins/lines– try to look close up and see the details.
3. Now choose either paint or POC pen – a colour that will stand out on your leaf.
4. Take your time, and very slowly, mark the central stem/vein of your leaf.
5. Then, still slowly, start to branch out from the central stem/vein to follow other veins.
6. Try not to rush, and once you've finished, the leaf can dry while you move on to the next one.
7. After marking veins on a couple of leaves, experiment with other symbols or patterns.
8. Patterns could be swirls, circles, spirals – often the simpler the better.
9. Invite children to experiment with different colours... remembering not to paint the entire leaf, but to follow its patterns, or to create their own pattern on top.

Activity 2: *Individually – 10 minutes*
Place the leaves in a pattern, and stick down on a white or black piece of paper with glue

Sharing/Reflection: *5 minutes*
Display final images on the wall. What did the children learn about the leaves? How did they find the creative process? Take a photo and explain to participants that over the coming days/weeks we will see the leaves decay. This is a natural process – cycle of decay/regeneration.

Key Vocabulary/Questions: Photosynthesis, chlorophyll, leaf structure, veins, cycles of decay and regeneration	**Extension Activities:** Research science of falling leaves, identify tree-leaves.

ACTIVITY: CREATING A DOT-TO-DOT ANIMAL STAR CONSTELLATION		
Subject: Visual arts **Curriculum Links:** Art, astronomy, science	**Key Skills:** Drawing, observation, art making	**Duration:** 1 hour 30 minutes
Resources & Creative Materials: Examples of dot-to-dot star constellations with animals Images of animals – A4 printouts OR examples to draw A4 cartridge paper A4 card/ folded newspaper (to stop holes in the table) Compass, ruler, pencil for each child Black/blue/white ready-mix paint Little sponges, paint palettes		**Location:** Outside and inside

Learning Objectives:

- To learn how constellations of stars change with the moving planet over seasons
- To learn how constellations were often explained through story and legend
- To create our own constellation in an animal form

Introduction & Warm-Up: *15 minutes*

- Many constellations come from ancient myths, making up stories about the night sky.
- Star constellations are often the subject of myth and folklore.
- First Nation peoples were and are keen and knowledgeable astronomers. In the myth *The Tale of the Great Bear and the Hunters*, we learn how the star constellation known at The Great Bear or Ursa Major was created (this constellation is also more commonly known as The Big Dipper).
- Apparently as we move from AUTUMN to WINTER the stars rotate clockwise and change to resemble the way a bear changes its stance from a four-legged to two-legged position. When you view the constellation, it is said to resemble the body of the bear itself as well as three of the hunters...
- Show with a ball how the earth is constantly moving and the stars with it.
- Imagine if there were no electricity, no lights at all, how the stars would stand out.
- Share how constellations we see are always changing in line with the Earth's orbit.

Today we are going to make our own star constellation with our own animal.

Key Activity: *Creating an animal star constellation – 1 hour*

Step 1:

1. Use dark-coloured paints to paint a dark night sky (not stars) on A4 cartridge paper.
2. Wait for the paint to dry completely.
3. Draw an animal on a sheet of A4 OR use an A4 print-out of an animal. Make sure the animal drawing or image fills more than three quarters of the page. Thin paper is best here.
4. Place your A4 animal image **on top** of a plain sheet of card (or folded newsprint). You might want to use a paper clip to fasten the papers together so they don't move during the next step.
5. Use a small ruler to follow the shape of the animal exactly. At each change of angle make a prick with your compass (it's as if you are creating a dot-to-dot image).

Make sure holes you make with the compass go through to the underneath paper.

6. When you have finished turn the image over so all you can see are the holes you have made with the compass.
7. This design should resemble an animal constellation. Swivel the compass in each hole so that they are a little larger – careful not to tear the paper.

Step 2:

1. Place your animal constellation paper on top of the background you painted earlier.
2. Use a sponge or small brush to dab white paint through each of the holes so that the constellation appears on the background beneath.

Sharing/Reflection: *15 minutes*
What is it like to make our own constellations in this way? See what animals you can recognise in each other's work.

Key Vocabulary/Questions:	**Extension Activities:**
First Nation, astronomy, constellations, orbit	When the nights get darker, have a look to see what you can spot! Make up a story about your own constellation animal – what it is called?

AUTUMN Folktale 2 from Ireland

A retelling of *Dagda's Magic Harp – the Oak of Two blossoms*

– which can control the seasons and human emotions

In times past and present, the oak tree has held a special place for people. Across the world, this tall and beautiful tree has been seen as a symbol of strength, wisdom, and continuation of life. The name for oak in Latin is *quercus*, which means strength. Given oak trees can live for 1000 years and more, we can see why they might be known as the King of the Trees and associated with royalty as well as ancient nature gods across cultures. Sacred to Zeus, Thor, and Donar (the German equivalent of Thor), the oak is often associated with lightning. It was said in Scandinavia that acorns lined up on the windowsill could protect homes from lightning strikes. AUTUMN is when the oak tree's fruit, the acorn, ripens.

Here is a wonderful Irish Gaelic story about a magical instrument that can control the seasons and human emotions. Words/names in italic are from the ancient Irish Gaelic language.

Legend speaks of the *Dagda*, an ancient Irish nature-god of earth and sun, the leader of a race of magical people, said to have descended upon Ireland in a grey mist. The *Dadga* had many magical objects. One of which was a magical harp, carved from oak, which would fly to him if he called. Also known **as** the *Daur da Bláo*, The Oak of Two Blossoms, or sometimes the Four Angled Music, the magical harp could put the seasons in the right order, as well as make people feel certain emotions. Only the *Dagda* could make the harp play its magical music, known as the Three Noble Strains… the strains of sorrow, joy, and sleep.

There is a tale of the tribe of Fomorians, great enemies of the *Dadga* and his people, stealing the *Dagda*'s harp during a battle. The Fomorians hung up the harp like a trophy on the wall of their banquet hall, holding a huge feast in celebration.

Furious, the *Dagda* tracked down his harp with a group of warriors. Bursting through the banquet hall, he summoned his harp, and it flew across to him. First the *Dadga* played Sorrow, making the Fomorians weep. Unable to see through their tears, they tried to grab their weapons, only then the *Dagda* played a new song on his harp. The Fomorians then couldn't stop laughing and had to drop their weapons. Finally, the *Dagda* played a lullaby, the strain of sleep. As the enemy fell into a deep sleep, the *Dagda* and his warriors left, taking the magical harp with them. Never again was the harp stolen. Today in Ireland, the harp remains an important symbol, as are the Noble Strains of Music played by traditional harpers.

ACTIVITY: BRINGING *DAGDA'S MAGIC HARP* TO LIFE THROUGH DRAMA AND MUSIC		
Subject: Performing arts **Curriculum Links:** English, Drama, music, history	**Key Skills:** Drama, oracy, music	**Duration:** 1 hour 30 minutes

Resources & Creative Materials: *Magic Harp of Dagda* folktale Musical/percussion instruments – drums, cymbals, triangles, etc	Location: Inside or outside

Learning Objectives:

- To learn how for most of history, stories were spoken aloud, not read or written
- To find out how the oak was seen as a special tree and appears often in legends
- To share how aspects of nature were often turned into gods or magical objects
- To discover how nature, music and story were often connected in Irish mythology
- To work collaboratively as storytellers through drama and music

Introduction & Warm-Up: *15 minutes*
Storytelling and reflection time: Invite participants to share responses to the story

- What parts of the story stand out?
- What about these three strains of music? How do they imagine them sounding?
- In story, the harp is made from oak. What other things do we use wood from oak trees for? Furniture, ships, etc...
- Why do they think the magical harp might have made of oak wood?

Key Activity: *1 hour*
Activity 1: *In small groups – 20 minutes*
Break down the story into 6 parts with each group bringing their part to life through drama and music. Each group will create a piece no longer than five minutes.

- The *Dadga* arrives in Ireland through the magical mist – introduce the harp.
- The Fomorians steal the harp and place it on their wall, celebrating their win.
- The *Dagda* and warriors sneak up on the Fomorians and the *Dadga* calls his harp.
- The *Dadga* plays the first strain of music – Sorrow.
- The *Dadga* plays the second strain of music – Joy.
- The *Dadga* plays the third strain of music – Sleep – and leaves the Fomorians.

Activity 2: *Rehearsal in same small groups – 10 minutes*
Make sure that each drama piece is no longer than five minutes, and has some music in it.

Activity 3: *Performance – 30 minutes*
Invite each group to perform their drama piece, in order, one after the other.

Sharing/Reflection: *15 minutes*
At end of whole drama piece, invite participants to share their responses/feedback, both to the final production, and also their creative, collaborative process. Learnings, challenges?
How did they feel when the harp was playing its magical music?

Key Vocabulary/Questions: The *Dadga*, *Daur da Bláo*, Fomorians Gaelic, mythology, four angled music How did they make their music sad, joyful, sleepy?	Extension Activities: Record pieces of music. Find out other Irish legends. Listen to some Irish harp music.

CREATIVE ACTIVITY: MAKING MUSICAL INSTRUMENTS FROM NATURAL RESOURCES		
Subject: Creative arts **Curriculum Links:** Art, Design, History	**Key Skills:** Invention, making, crafting, listening, creativity, design	**Duration:** 1 hour 40 minutes

Resources & Creative Materials: Natural Materials: wooden sticks, hard skinned vegetables like squash /pumpkin, grass, seeds, dried rice, hollow sticks, large pebbles, grasses, forked branches, walnuts, acorns, shells(start collecting resources for this activity weeks before the activity to have a good variety of objects) String, glue, tape	**Location:** Inside or outside

Learning Objectives:

- To learn how musical instruments were all first made from natural materials
- To learn about 'product design' and invention
- To build our own musical instruments from natural materials

Introduction & Warm-Up: *30 minutes*

Throughout history, humans have made instruments from natural resources or nature itself depending on what was available. Give examples from across the globe.

- Maracas, also known as rumba shakers, played in Latin America and South America.
- Shakers in the Caribbean were made from turtle shells or dried calabash/ squash filled with beads, pebbles, or seeds. In Puerto Rico, this instrument is made from a native tree called a *higuera* which produces fruits with hard shells, which the Taino used to make the maracas.
- In Australia, the didgeridoo played by Aboriginal people was originally made from fallen eucalyptus branches that had been hollowed out by termites.
- In Central America, Mayan people created a similar instrument made from agave or yucca known as the Mayan trumpet.
- In parts of Africa, the thumb piano, also known as the *kalimba* or *mbira*, was made from half a coconut.
- In parts of Spain castanets were made from shells, in other parts from wood.
- The aeolian harp is an instrument 'played' by the winds. Also known as the harmonic harp or spirit harp, the aeolian harp is from Ancient Greece and named after Aeolus, the Greek god of the wind. Harps are also found in India and China.
- Wind chimes are said to have originated in South and East Asia, from Bali to Tibet, China, and Japan, and were made from seashells, bamboo, clay, glass, and stones.

There are so many more examples from across the world. You can encourage your group to research instruments made from natural resources and/or inspired by it, like the wind harp.

Key Activity: *Making instruments with natural objects*
Activity 1 (optional): *15 minutes*
Go on a nature walk and make some sounds in nature – crunch leaves, bang sticks on trees, splash in a puddle, tap stones together, blow through grass... collect how many sounds you can make and record them for future use!

Activity 2: *Musical instrument challenge working in small groups – 40 mins*

- Set each group the challenge of making an instrument from the resources you have available – the only rule being it must make an interesting sound. It does not have to be complicated; you can whistle with a blade of grass or make a dandelion trumpet!
- Encourage imaginative play, give space for the group to be inventive and creative, and experiment with sounds and noise.
- Do they want to use their breath or banging or friction as percussion?

Each group has the option of making a drum, a shaker, castanets, rain sticks, or something new. Invite each group to play with ideas. Once they have decided upon their instrument, create a new name as well.

Sharing/Reflection: *15 minutes*
In a group ask each person (or group) to make a sound with their instrument – it might be fun to record this session to play back later. Invite group to respond to different instruments/sounds. Discussion on some of the creative and design process. Any surprises, challenges in creating their own musical instruments? Invite all groups to play their musical instruments at the same time and see what happens.

Key Vocabulary/Questions:	**Extension Activities:**
Music, sound, instruments, soundscape What inspired their musical instruments?	In groups create a soundscape for a story using some of the sounds from the new instruments.

ACTIVITY: BRINGING THE AUTUMN SEASON TO LIFE THROUGH MUSIC AND ART		
Subject: Performing arts, Music **Curriculum Links:** Music, Geography	**Key Skills:** Music, collaboration, song,	**Duration:** 1 hour 20 minutes
Resources & Creative Materials: *Magic Harp of Dagda* folktale Online short sample of Vivaldi's Four Seasons – AUTUMN Paint, brushes, felt-tips, chalk-pastels, oil pastels, paper Musical instruments created from previous activity (page 49) Other instruments – drums, cymbals, triangles, recorder, voice		**Location:** Inside and outside

Learning Objectives:

- To learn how nature often inspires music
- To connect in with themes/elements of AUTUMN – how this season makes us feel
- To work collaboratively as music-makers using nature as inspiration

Introduction & Warm-Up: *20 minutes*
Like the Magical Harp in the story, music often affects our human emotions.

- Discuss how nature has inspired music across history.
- Play sample from Vivaldi Four Seasons – AUTUMN – as participants listen, make marks on the paper with art materials to capture feelings and images evoked.
- Share images made – what colours, images/elements, feelings come out?
- How do these relate to AUTUMN – changing colour of leaves, wind rustling, falling leaves, stronger winds, cooler weather, how does Vivaldi's music express this?

Key Activity: *45 minutes*
Activity 1: *In small groups – 35 minutes*
Each group to create a short three-minute music piece to bring to life AUTUMN as a season using their images as inspiration.

- Think about the different aspects of AUTUMN – falling leaves, winds, etc...
- How are we going to create the feeling of AUTUMN through instruments?
- How do we want our listeners to respond to our AUTUMN piece of music?
- Can use percussion, musical instruments, and voice (no words please!).
- Try to make your musical piece have a beginning, middle, and end.

Activity 2: *Rehearsal in same small groups – 10 minutes*
Make sure that each drama piece is no longer than three minutes, and everyone has a role in it

Sharing/Reflection: *15 minutes*
After each AUTUMN performance, invite both participants and audience to reflect on their experiences. Participants to share what it was like to create this piece, and the audience, to say how it made them feel. What aspects of AUTUMN did they feel were being expressed through music and artwork?

Key Vocabulary/ Questions The *Dadga*, *Daur da Bláo*, Three Noble Strains, Vivaldi's Four Seasons How do we capture nature in music, and how does this affect human emotions?	**Extension Activities** Perform pieces of music in class assembly, record music.

ACTIVITY: CREATING AN ACORN POEM		
Subject: Creative writing **Curriculum Links:** English, Science	**Key Skills:** Creative writing, oracy	**Duration:** 30 minutes by tree 1 hour for activity Extra time to find oak!
Resources & Creative Materials: Real acorns, acorn facts Pens and A4 orange/yellow sugar paper	**Location:** Outside for walk Inside for creative writing	

Learning Objectives:

- To learn fun facts about acorns as the fruit of the oak tree
- To put ourselves into the point of view of a growing acorn
- To connect with the oak tree through senses and poetry

Introduction & Warm-Up: *30 minutes*

If possible, go on a nature walk to find an oak, so participants can find an oak tree and acorns (best to source tree beforehand). If not possible, show a picture of an oak tree.

Invite children to observe the oak. If outside in nature, ask children to stay in silence.

Reflection time: Invite participant to share their own observations around the oak tree.

- What do they notice? If they look closer, what do they see?

Share key facts around oaks and acorns or 'oak-nuts':

- Oaks don't produce acorns until they are around 20 years old, and not every year.
- Acorns can sustain so many creatures... animals, insects, and birds.
- One in 10, 000 acorns will grow into a fully mature oak tree.
- Everything that the oak needs to grow is contained inside this tiny acorn!
- Acorns were often symbols used on flags and shields to show perseverance and growth.

Share responses to key facts and oak tree. If collecting acorns from an oak, bring them back.

Key Activity: *50 minutes*

Activity 1: *Acorn observations in small groups – 15 minutes*

Each participant to hold an acorn in their hand or have access to an acorn image.

- Invite participants to share what they notice about their acorn.
- How does it feel, what is its textures, what are the different elements to it?
- What do they imagine is inside the acorn?

Discuss together in a small group some of their thoughts and observations.

Activity 2: *Creating your poem/song lyric – individually – 35 minutes*

- Invite participants to imagine that they are the acorn.
- On an A4 piece of paper, write a poem/song lyric about the journey of their acorn...
- Write from the point of view of the acorn, imagining what's going on inside.
- Some start-phrases might be: "I see ... I hear ... I watch ... I wish ... I am ... I fall ..."
- Their poem/song can take any twist and turn – do acorns fall or get taken by a squirrel or bird? Where do they end up? How much do they grow?

Sharing/Reflection: *10 minutes*

Invite volunteers to share their poems/song lyrics and ask group for responses.

What is it like to put yourself into the point of view of an acorn, starting small?

Key Vocabulary/Questions: Oak, deciduous tree, acorn	**Extension Activities:** Decorate poems with acorn motifs.

AUTUMN Folktale 3 from Korea

A retelling of the Heungbu and Nolbu folktale
Two Brothers, a Swallow, and the Pumpkin.

In Korea, folktales used to be told through Pansori, where a singer and drummer performs the story. This style of musical storytelling dates to the 17th century. It was used to pass on rituals and spells from generation to generation, but in the 19th century it became a widespread way to entertain people. The following tale, based on Heungbu and Nolbu, is still performed today through Pansori. It covers the theme of good people getting rewarded and bad people getting punished. It was a significant story in Korea, as it challenged the notion that the first-born son is the most important in the family. The tale is about 300 years old and is still a very popular bedtime story.

Once upon a time, a father died, leaving his enormous wealth to his two sons. But the eldest brother, Nolbu, was a trickster and managed to take the land and all the money for himself. He threw the younger brother, Heungbu, out of their house.

Heungbu had nothing, but he was still kind to everyone and everything he met. One day he found a swallow with a broken wing. He took her back to his shack where he was living and made her a little home, taking time and care to make her better. Once her wing was healed, he let her go.

A few days later, the swallow flew back and gave Heungbu a seed. Planting it straight away, the younger brother watched a pumpkin start to grow. It grew bigger and bigger, and by AUTUMN, it was huge! Desperate for some food, he cut into the pumpkin and was amazed. Instead of pumpkin flesh, it was filled with treasure – gold, silver, jewels, and the finest fabrics. He shared it out among the villagers, and they celebrated a wonderful week-long harvest festival.

Nolbu was furious. He was supposed to be the richest man in the village. The following year, he saw a swallow and trapped it on purpose, hurting the little creature's wing. Nolbu built the bird a home and cared for it until it was well enough to fly away. Unbeknown to him, it was the same swallow his brother had helped.

A few days later the swallow returned with a seed and Nolbu was thrilled. He planted the seed and rubbed his hands, watching it grow bigger every day. In AUTUMN, when it was even bigger than his brother's, Nolbu cut it open eagerly. But there were no jewels or gold inside. Nor was there pumpkin flesh. Monsters of all different shapes and sizes sprang out of the pumpkin and took all of Nolbu's wealth, leaving him penniless.

Terrified and hungry, Nolbu knocked on his brother's door and begged forgiveness. Heungbu welcomed his brother inside.

ACTIVITY: A LITTLE BIRD TOLD ME – RETELLING THE STORY FROM THE SWALLOW'S POINT OF VIEW		
Subject: Performing arts **Curriculum Links:** English, PSHE, Music	**Key Skills:** Creative writing, storytelling	**Duration:** 1 hour

Resources & Creative Materials: *Two Brothers, a Swallow, and the Pumpkin* folktale Drum or anything to recreate the sound Pen/pencil and A4 paper	**Location:** Outside if possible

Learning Objectives:

- To explain the Korean way of storytelling through Pansori – a drummer and a singer perform the story
- To view characters' motives and actions from different perspectives
- To devise a folktale – taking another narrator as a starting point
- To start to think about our own relationship with nature – caring for all creatures

Introduction & Warm-Up: *15 minutes*
Invite participants to share responses to the story.

- What do you think about the two brothers?
- How do they each relate to nature differently?
- What do you think the eldest brother learnt from his younger brother?
- Which brother do we feel closest to?

Share how Pansori is a Korean way of storytelling – using a drummer and a singer/storyteller. Discuss together why this might have been effective, how drumbeats can add tension and fill pauses.

Key Activity: *40 minutes*
Activity 1: A little bird told me... In small groups, d*evise the folktale – 20 minutes*

- Explain how we are going to retell this story from another viewpoint – the swallow. Imagine you are the swallow, flying above the land, seeing the brothers' behaviours.
- In your small group, create a new story told through the eyes of the sparrow.
- You can either be the swallow, 'I', in your folktale, or tell it from the third person, 'Once there was a swallow who...'
- Tell us what the swallow sees, hears, notices, and thinks of these two brothers? In your groups, write down a short folktale story from the sparrow's point of view.

Activity 2: Rehearse in same small groups – *10 minutes*

- Make sure each folktale is no longer than five minutes and try to include everyone in the practice and reading of it. How will they incorporate the Pansori drum?

Activity 3: A Pansori Performance – *10 minutes*

- Invite each group to tell their folktale aloud to the larger group this time using a drumming technique in any way they like.

Sharing/Reflection: *5 minutes*
At end of retellings, invite participants to share responses/feedback. What elements of the story have stayed the same, or changed? Has anything new been added to the story with the change of narrator? Any new learnings? Did the drum help with the telling of the story?

Key Vocabulary/Questions: Narrator, swallow, pumpkinseed, Pansori	**Extension Activities:** Write stories neatly and display

ACTIVITY: CREATING A PICTURE BOOK ABOUT A MAGIC SEED		
Subject: Creative writing and visual arts **Curriculum Links:** Art, English	**Key Skills:** Drawing, storytelling	**Duration:** 1 hour 20 minutes

Resources & Creative Materials:	Location:
Two Brothers, a Swallow, and the Pumpkin folktale Examples of picture books Seeds (if possible) – any kind A4 pieces of paper, pencils, felt-tips, stapler	Inside

Learning Objectives:

- To engage our imaginations in creative art making and storytelling
- To make up our own folktale about a magic seed
- To learn how to tell story through images and comic strips

Introduction & Warm-Up: *10 minutes*
Re-read the story – and discuss how magic seeds appear in stories.

- Can anyone remember other stories where there have been magic seeds that have grown into extraordinary things? (Prompt *James and the Giant Peach, Jack and the Beanstalk, Thumbelina*.)
- Show a seed to the group – reflect together on how amazing everything it needs to grow into a plant/fruit and vegetable is contained inside it. Most of us will have no idea what it will grow into. So, all seeds are magic!

Key Activity: Individually create a picture book – *1 hour*
Let's imagine that we are each given a magic seed to plant somewhere. It's not going to grow into something ordinary. It's going to grow into something extraordinary. Each person is going to create a picture book to tell their story.
In your magic seed story, there needs to be a beginning, middle, and an end.

- Think about who gives you the seed and where you'd like to plant it.
- Decide what kind of plant, vegetable, or fruit it will grow into.
- What will make it so special and magical? What will happen in this story?
- What will be the end of the story?

Look at some example picture books to remind ourselves of the layout.
Draw a picture of each scene, adding a couple of lines of dialogue or narration on a separate piece of A4. When you have completed all the scenes, create a cover and a blurb. Then staple your pages together.

Sharing/Reflection: *10 minutes*
Go around the group and ask volunteers to share what their magic seeds grow into. Invite the children to read aloud their picture books.

Key Vocabulary/Questions:	Extension Activities:
Picture book, seed	Invite the children to share their books with a younger audience.

ACTIVITY: CREATING PUMPKIN LIST POEMS – EITHER JOYFUL OR SCARY		
Subject: Creative writing **Curriculum Links:** English	**Key Skills:** Poetry, metaphors, and similes	**Duration:** 1 hour

Resources & Creative Materials:	Location:
Two Brothers, a Swallow, and the Pumpkin folktale Pens/pencils, paper	Inside

Learning Objectives:

- To create a 'list-poem' including similes and metaphors
- To engage with creating our own folklore pumpkins
- To read poetry aloud, stressing certain words and including dramatic pauses

Introduction & Warm-Up: *10 minutes*

Revisit The Swallow and Pumpkinseed story, paying particular attention to the contents of each pumpkin. Imagine if you found or grew an enormous pumpkin, then cut it open.

- What might spring out or lie hidden inside?
- Would you want your pumpkin to bring joy, terror, or both? It is up to you!
- Remind the children about similes and metaphors.

Key Activity: *40 minutes*

Activity 1: Devising and inventing poems – *30 minutes*

Invite children to decide if the pumpkin in their poem is going to contain scary or joyful things, or both! They are going to write a poem listing all the contents of the pumpkin. Each item has its own line and needs to be a metaphor or a simile.

- For example:
  I cut into my pumpkin and stare in amazement
  4 red rubies glint like roses shining with due
  A waterfall of glistening gold

- Or:
  I cut into my pumpkin and my heart pounds
  Gorillas baring teeth explode from the orange flesh
  A famished hippo scrambles like me chasing chocolate

- Don't worry about the number of lines. Have fun playing with the descriptions rather than worrying about quantity. You can play with alliteration (repeating letters).

Activity 2: Rehearsal of poems – *10 minutes*

Allow children some time to practise reading their poems aloud. Explain the impact a pause can have, allowing the audience time to breathe and reflect on the words.

Sharing/Reflection: *10 minutes*

Invite the children to share their poems. What was their reason for choosing what went inside their pumpkin? What is it like to both hear and read poems aloud?

Key Vocabulary/Questions:	Extension Activities:
Pumpkin, metaphor, simile, pauses What is it like to read poetry aloud?	Draw pumpkins with exciting fillings.

ACTIVITY: DESIGNING AUTUMNAL ARTWORK FOR A PUMPKIN OR SQUASH CARVING		
Subject: Visual arts **Curriculum Links:** Art, Food	**Key Skills:** Designing	**Duration:** 50 minutes

Resources & Creative Materials: A real pumpkin and/or squash Pictures of carvings on pumpkins – leaves, trees, anything associated with nature rather than Halloween Paper, pencils, crayons	**Location:** Inside or outside

Learning Objectives:

- To learn the history of pumpkins and their culinary significance in ancient cultures
- To appreciate the beauty of pumpkins, which may be why they appear in stories!
- To develop confidence in our own creative expression

Introduction & Warm-Up: *15 minutes*

Pumpkins are one of the key foods we associate with AUTUMN. Part of the gourd and squash family, they are harvested at this time of year and play key roles in seasonal festivals, such as Samhain/Halloween and the North American Thanksgiving, rooted in the old harvest festivals of AUTUMN.

- Pumpkins are an ancient food. It's thought that they first grew in Mexico, 7000 years BCE. Nutritious, delicious, versatile, the pumpkin has travelled across the world and entered kitchens and fairy tales everywhere!
- There is a First Nation story from the Iroquois, about the Three Sisters of Agriculture, which names a pumpkin alongside green beans and maize (sweetcorn) as the three sister staples of food-farming, explaining how they can be grown well together.
- Share some of the ways that pumpkins are eaten... pumpkin pie, pumpkin soup, seeds, ground down into a flour, etc.

Key Activity: *30 minutes*

Show the children lots of different pictures of carvings on pumpkins that reflect AUTUMN scenes and aren't only Halloween type decorations.

- Draw a large outline of a squash or a pumpkin on your piece of paper.
- Decide on a design – it could be a tree, a leaf, a cloud, a flower, an AUTUMN pattern. Or perhaps you want to create a landscape.
- Remember to keep your outline simple.
- Use crayons, paint, or pens to colour in your design.

Sharing/Reflection: *5 minutes*

Create a gallery of the pumpkin/squash designs.
Which really reflect AUTUMN? Which ones were trickier or easier to carve?

Key Vocabulary/Questions: Iroquois, First Nation, pumpkin, squash, agriculture, harvest, carve, maize, *Three Sisters of Agriculture*	**Extension Activities:** Can you carve your design into a pumpkin or squash at home?

AUTUMN Folktale 4 from Baltic and Slavic regions
A retelling of *The Magic Herb and the Hedgehog*

This folktale tells the extraordinary legend about a magic plant that has very unusual magic powers. The legend of the Magic Herb crops up across many countries – Bulgaria, Poland, Servia, Croatia, Macedonia – in many different forms and with different names, such as the *earth key* or the *rainbow root*. This magic herb obviously caught the imagination of people across this region.

According to ancient legend, there is a magic herb with the ability to unlock or uncover anything that is locked or closed. No matter the size or strength of the lock, the magic herb's special powers can still open it! Just imagine.

Four-leaved and small, this magic herb, often called the Raskovnik, is notoriously difficult for humans to recognise. It is said that only certain animals can identify the magic herb. One such animal is the hedgehog, an animal often associated with AUTUMN. In some places, this magic herb is known as hedgehog grass.

Some say that if you want to find the magic herb, you need find a hedgehog to help you. First, you must lock a young hedgehog in a secure metal box. That way if the mother wants to free her young, she will have to find the Raskovnik magic herb first. As she snuffles around to find it, you must be quick! For once she has used the Raskovnik to free the little hedgehog, she will swallow it quickly after use! Grab it while you can.

Legend also says the magic herb can uncover treasures buried in the ground. In some beliefs, it can split the ground at the place where a treasure lies so it can be found.

ACTIVITY: CREATING A FOLKLORE LEGEND BASED ON *THE MAGIC HERB AND THE HEDGEHOG*		
Subject: Creative writing **Curriculum Links:** English	**Key Skills:** Creative writing, developing a story plan	**Duration:** 1 hour
Resources & Creative Materials: *The Magic Herb and the Hedgehog* folktale Paper and pens/pencils	**Location:** Inside	

Learning Objectives:

- To create a new folktale-plan based on *The Magic Herb* story
- To build confidence and flexibility in our own imaginative and storytelling abilities
- To explore how in powerful storytelling, a character always needs something!

Introduction & Warm-Up: *20 minutes*
Read the folklore of the Magical Herb and the Hedgehog, discussing the story. As a group, devise a plan for a new folklore legend using this story as a base. Imagine something really precious has been stolen from your main character. Perhaps it's gold to buy food, or their grandmother's jewels. Or maybe it's a quality – like courage or compassion!

- Your character finds where this precious thing has been taken but can't unlock it!
- They need a hedgehog for help! (Remember hedgehogs are nocturnal)
- How does your character get the hedgehog to help? Do they trick it, or ask for help?
- The hedgehog sniffs out the magic herb – what happens next?

Key Activity: *30 minutes*
Now it's the children's turn to create their own folklore about a magical herb. Here is a skeleton structure or story-plan to help with devising your folktale. It's a bit like having the bones as a central structure, and then you are going to add the flesh onto these bones.

- What's been stolen away from their character? Something so precious!
- What is locked away and where? What kind of lock?
- How do they find the hedgehog (especially because they are shy, nocturnal)?
- How do they get the hedgehog to help them?
- How does the hedgehog find the magic herb, and what happens next?
- How does the story end?
- They might wish to plan it out or they can start writing straight away.

Sharing/Reflection: *10 minutes*
Invite the children to read out their plans or stories. If it is not too cold, invite stories to be read outside.
What are responses and feedback to the stories? What are some of the most unexpected things being locked up! Are there any surprising elements in the stories?

Key Vocabulary/Questions: Herb, story plan, skeleton structure, devising, nocturnal What does your character need?	**Extension Activities:** Invite participants to write up and illustrate their stories.

ACTIVITY: CREATING STORY WHISPERS		
Subject: Performing arts **Curriculum Links:** English	**Key Skills:** Oracy, listening, imagination	**Duration:** 1 hour
Resources & Creative Materials: *The Magic Herb and the Hedgehog* folktale	**Location:** Inside or outside	

Learning Objectives:

- To create a seed of a story
- To understand how stories can change through time
- To engage in listening and whispering!

Introduction & Warm-Up: *10 minutes*

- As a whole group, sitting in a circle, play pass the smile. One person smiles at the person next to them, who smiles at the person next to them. Continue until someone decides to change the emotion to a frown. People pass on the frown. They can pass on laughter, fear etc...
- Then in the same circle, play one word or one-line stories. The first person says, "Once," the next person says, "Upon," etc... and using your imaginations you tell a short story. They can become very silly – but that's what makes them fun. Or someone says a whole sentence, before the next person continues.

Key Activity: *40 minutes*
Activity one: *Creating a new magical item – 15 minutes*

- Explain how stories often change through time, as people embellish or miss bits out.
- Together reread *The Magic Herb and the Hedgehog* folktale. In pairs, invite the children to create a new magical AUTUMNAL item.
- Ask the children to write down their item, giving it a name and its purpose. For example, a conker called the Rainbow Blob, and it makes you change colour, enabling you to blend into the background. Keep ideas hidden from other pairs.

Activity two: *Whispering a Story – 25 minutes*

- Split each pair into Team One and Team Two – to play Story Whispers.
- The Team Ones sit in a circle. The Team Twos sit in another circle. Please make sure the circles are sat as far apart as possible so they can't overhear each other.
- One person from Team One and their corresponding partner from Team Two – whisper their magical item, its name, and its purpose to the person sitting next to them in their different team circles.
- That Team One or Team Two member then whispers whatever they heard to the person next to them, and so on ... until it reaches the last person in the circle.
- The last person in each team no longer whispers but says the words aloud. Do the items, names and purposes stay the same? Compare the answers in both circles.

Sharing/Reflection: *10 minutes*
Did the words become gibberish? Did anyone guess what they were hearing and change the meaning so that it made sense? If the words changed during this short amount of time, just imagine how folklore changes over hundreds if not thousands of years.

Key Vocabulary/Questions: Why do you think people embellished or missed parts out of stories when telling a folktale?	**Extension Activities:** Play one word or one-line stories with your partner about your magical item.

ACTIVITY: CREATING AN AUTUMN TREASURE MAP		
Subject: Creative arts **Curriculum Links:** English, Geography	**Key Skills:** Map-making using elements from a story	**Duration:** 1 hour 30 minutes
Resources & Creative Materials: *The Magic Herb and the Hedgehog* folktale, examples of treasure maps Images of the four-leaved Raskovnik herb A3 paper, pens, paint, collage materials – anything required for making a treasure map	**Location:** Inside or outside	

Learning Objectives:

- To create a magical map using the folktale as a prompt
- To engage with storytelling and map-making
- To convey AUTUMN images and symbols

Introduction & Warm-Up: *20 minutes*
Revisit the Magical Herb folktale, explaining how participants are to make a treasure map to find the herb. Hedgehogs are an animal often associated with AUTUMN, so this season might be one of the best times to find these shy and nocturnal creatures!

- Create a quick example map on the board as an example.
- Discuss what needs to be included – a symbol for where the treasure is hidden, other symbols for the hedgehog (mother and child), and the Raskovnik herb.
- What else might you include to make this map feel AUTUMNAL? E.g., red/orange leafed trees, fallen leaf patterns, animals such as foxes, squirrels, deer, a cottage with a smoking chimney.
- What else might help make their map clear? Perhaps a compass or a key?
- What might help them find the shy, nocturnal hedgehog?

Key Activity: *Making their own treasure maps – 1 hour*
Invite participants to make their own AUTUMN treasure map, using the Magical Herb and the Hedgehog folklore tale as a base.

- Invite them to think about creating symbols of AUTUMN.
- What makes this season so unique?
- Try to include as many AUTUMNAL features as possible.
- Remind them to add a compass, a key, a moon…

Sharing/Reflection: *10 minutes*
Place all the maps in the middle of the floor and discuss.
How are they similar and how are they different? Invite participants to talk about their treasure.

Key Vocabulary/Questions: Treasure maps, compass, AUTUMN, magical herb, hedgehog, nocturnal	**Extension Activities:** Invite children to create an image of their treasure.

ACTIVITY: HEDGEHOG BOOK ART AROUND THEMES OF HIBERNATION		
Subject: Visual arts **Curriculum Links:** Art	**Key Skills:** 3D artmaking, upcycling, paperfolding, sculpture	**Duration:** 1 hour 30 minutes
Resources & Creative Materials: Old paperback books – one each (less than 100 pages preferably) –always recycled/second hand rather than new* Black buttons (or black paper cut into penny sized circles x 3 each) Scissors, glue, paper/pens, wooden lolly sticks *Please check that any books being used don't belong to anyone and there is permission – charity shops have many cheap paperbacks		**Location:** Inside or outside (if mild)

Learning Objectives:

- To learn skills in 3D art making and paper folding
- To explore the theme of hibernation, for animals, and us humans
- To recycle and upcycle materials for creative art making

Introduction & Warm-Up: *15 minutes*
As we enter the AUTUMN season and cooler weather arrives, many animals prepare for hibernation, and traditionally, humans have also found ways to adjust to this season.

- Group discussion on hedgehogs and process of hibernation.
- Find out which animals hibernate, and their preparations.
- Discuss how before screens and TV, humans also adjusted behaviour, moving inside to 'hibernate with a good book' and/or engage with craft-making and storytelling.

Key Activity: *Individually Making a 'Book Hedgehog' – 1 hour*

Step 1:

1 Open the book so that the cover pages are lying flat on the table.
2 Begin by folding each of the pages in the book.
   - Fold the page exactly in half.
   - Fold each of the two folded corners inwards (so you have a roof shape).
3 Repeat with all pages in the book – if you like you can fold 2/3 pages at once.
4 Your hedgehog form will soon begin to appear.
5 When all the pages are folded, you will be left with two flat cover pages sticking out.
6 Cut around them to the same shape as the folded pages.
7 Now stick on your paper or button eyes and nose and your hedgehog is ready.

Step 2:

8. Reflect on what you would need if you were to hibernate; what essential provisions would you need, and what would entertain you in moments when awake?
9. Write answers on lollypop sticks – pop these in-between pages of your hedgehog.

Sharing/Reflection: *15 minutes*
Installation of Hibernating Hedgehogs – display the book hedgehogs on a table.
Discuss all the different answers on lolly sticks – reflecting on different needs.

Key Vocabulary/Questions: Hibernation, AUTUMN preparation, recycling, upcycling What might be human's needs in AUTUMN? How might these differ to different seasons?	**Extension Activities:** Make a hedgehog book for a family member or friend

AUTUMN Folktale 5 from the West Country of England, United Kingdom

A retelling of *The Spirit-Wind Horse of AUTUMN*

Orchards are in abundance in the West Country of England, and apples in particular are celebrated. Wassailing is an ancient custom and can still be seen today. Wassail occurs on the 5th/6th of January, where people visit cider-making orchards. They sing to the trees, asking for a great harvest in the coming year. They make loud noises including firing muskets to ward off evil spirits, as well as toast the trees with cider. Then during the AUTUMN, the apples are harvested. In the past, people would try to 'scrump' (steal) the apples. It is said that the Spirit-Wind horse – sometimes known as Lazy Lawrence (although he is anything but lazy) – would find anyone 'scrumping' apples. Children complained of being nipped by an invisible horse. The following tale is a warning to anyone who is thinking of stealing a juicy apple or two.

There was an old woman who grew the most delicious apples in her orchards. Everybody loved them. Believing in the old ways, every night in AUTUMN she'd leave out a bucket of water and a bowl of thick fresh cream for Lazy Lawrence. He was the Spirit-Wind Horse that galloped through orchards protecting apples from thieves. Despite his name, there was nothing lazy about him. He ran as wild and fast as the swirling AUTUMN winds.

But the old woman had a neighbour, a wicked sorcerer. He wanted all the woman's apples but feared the Spirit-Wind Horse would stop him. So, the sorcerer built an enormous wicker basket and covered it with protection spells and made it fly. One clear AUTUMNAL night, he climbed inside and flew over the orchards. Drifting in mid-air, he used a spell, summoning apples off the trees. They filled the basket around him.

Soon he had all the apples but one. The biggest and juiciest apple was clinging onto a branch. The sorcerer should have left it but he was far too greedy. He used another more powerful spell and the apple flung through the sky towards him, hitting the man in the eye. The man fell backwards out of the basket and landed on the ground below, wailing in pain. The Spirit-Wind Horse heard the wail and galloped through the orchards. The horse glared at the man with his glowing green eyes, and instantly the sorcerer was rooted to the spot, unable to move. He begged the Spirit-Wind Horse to let him go, but the Horse simply stared at him.

The next morning, the man was finally freed, and he ran out of the orchards and out of the West Country, never to be seen again. The old woman woke up to see all her apples packed in a massive basket, the bucket of water, and the bowl of fresh cream gone. She saw a circle of hoof prints and knew that the Spirit-Wind Horse had helped her.

ACTIVITY: "WINDS" MINDFULNESS IMAGE-MAKING		
Subject: Visual arts, wellbeing **Curriculum Links:** Art, PSHE	**Key Skills:** Mindfulness, Spontaneous artmaking	**Duration:** 1 hour – plus drying time

Resources & Creative Materials: *The Spirit-Wind Horse of AUTUMN* folktale Berol fine black pens, white paper (A3) Paint brushes, cups/jars of water	**Location:** Outside on mildly windy day (Option to move inside for painting)

Learning Objectives:

- To learn how to be 'fully present' in nature
- To connect to our senses and sensation by paying attention to the 'winds'
- To learn how to trust our own creativity and be spontaneous in artmaking

Introduction & Warm-Up: *10 minutes*

Wind has always fascinated human beings. Many cultures gave names to the winds and saw them as gods. In ancient times, wind was an essential source of power, generating energy for sailboats, and for windmills (to make grain for bread). Winds could also be destructive.

- Group discussion on the positive and not so positive associations with the winds.
- E.g. on a stormy day, we need to take care *not to* walk under trees.

Today we are going to spend some time connecting and observing the winds through art.

Key Activity: *Individually – 30 minutes*

Activity 1: *Connecting to our sensations in relation to the wind – 5 minutes*

- Give participants the option of closing their eyes, and invite them to connect to their breath.
- What do they feel, hear, going on around them on a windy day?
- How does it feel to have wind going through their hair, on their cheek?

Activity 2: *Individual mark-making, following rhythm of the winds – 10 minutes*

Continuing the exercise, each child to be given an A3 sheet of white paper, and a black Berol pen.

- Following your own sensations, listening, and feeling the wind, start to draw...
- Allow yourself to really connect to the wind, and then allow your hand to move.
- Experiment with flow and how the wind seems to move around us.
- There is no right or wrong, feel free to create "wind-lines, swirls" on the page.
- Try to press down with your pen so there is enough ink on the page.

Activity 3: *Creating the flow – 15 minutes*

For this next step, we need to let go of being in control, and any idea of right and wrong!

- Take a paint brush with water, and slowly run brush along your black marks on page.
- Top tip – don't run paintbrush over lines, but along their side for maximum effect.
- You will start to see those black lines 'bleed', creating new colours and shapes.
- Follow your black marks and continue to 'water them' – noticing what happens.
- Take your time... really try to do this exercise as slowly as possible, breathing slowly.
- Allow images to dry – approx. 15–30 minutes drying time.

Sharing/Reflection: *20 minutes*

Display images in a 'Winds Gallery' in centre of a circle. Invite participants to comment on both the creative process, and images. Any feedback, responses, surprises to colours.

Key Vocabulary/Questions: The Winds, mindfulness, 'bleed' in painting What is it like to let go of being in control of art?	**Extension Activities:** Cut out shapes from wind images, to create our own 'Wind Gods'.

ACTIVITY: CREATING OUR OWN AUTUMN SPIRIT-WIND HORSE		
Subject: Visual arts, wellbeing **Curriculum Links:** Art	**Key Skills:** Artmaking	**Duration:** 1 hour

Resources & Creative Materials: *The Spirit Wind Horse of AUTUMN* folktale White paper, paper, felt-tips, paint, pastels, anything for collage material – textiles, magazine photos, tissue material, brushes, water	**Location:** Outside on a mildly windy day (Option to move inside for painting)

Learning Objectives:

- To create a mythological horse to symbolise and personify the AUTUMN winds
- To connect to nature through creativity and the arts
- To develop our own imagination and creative expression

Introduction & Warm-Up: *10 minutes*
Horses are often in legends to show the forces of nature. Lazy Lawrence is one of them.

- Why do we think horses are often given these magical roles in legend?
- What are their qualities and ways of being that might represent the wind?
- What do we imagine it would be like to ride a wild horse of the AUTUMN wind?

Group discussion on mythological horses and the powers that they personify.

Key Activity: *40 minutes*
Activity 1: *Individual artmaking – 35 minutes*

- Imagine designing your own legendary and magical horse to represent AUTUMN.
- What qualities and colours would your AUTUMN horse have?
- What special powers over the season would your horse have?
- Create your own horse outline.
- Fill in with anything from the collage material to create your horse.
- You may also want to decorate other aspects of your horse – mane, tail, hooves.
- Give your mythological horse a name.
- Try to trust yourself and not to copy anyone else around you – this is *your* horse!

Activity 2: *Home your Spirit-Wind Horse with the Winds image – 5 minutes*
Another option now is to place your spirit-wind horse in your wind image.

- Give your horse a home in your wind image.
- Where is best to place it?
- What does it look like in this environment?

Sharing/Reflection: *10 minutes*
Display images in a 'Horse Gallery' in centre of a circle. Invite participants to comment on both the creative process, and images. Any feedback, responses, surprises to horses made.
What different or shared qualities, aspects, do these mythological horses have?

Key Vocabulary/ Questions Mythology, personification How has AUTUMN come to life through horses? What do horses look like on a 'wind image' back-drop?	**Extension Activities** Research other mythological horses in legends, such as the Wind Horse for South.

ACTIVITY: CREATING ACTIONS AND MIMES TO EMBODY ASPECTS OF NATURE		
Subject: Performing arts **Curriculum Links:** English, Drama, Movement	**Key Skills:** Listening skills, drama, improvisation, concentration	**Duration:** 35 minutes
Resources & Creative Materials: *The Spirit Wind Horse of AUTUMN* folktale Our own bodies and movement		**Location:** Inside or outside

Learning Objectives:

- To mime actions to tell a story (silently)
- To learn active listening and responding to story cues
- To connect to sensations/feelings
- To embody aspects of nature

Introduction & Warm-Up: *10 minutes*
Read the story to the class, discussing the key points. Moving outside, ask them to find a space. Individually, can they improvise certain parts of the story? For example:

- being a swirling AUTUMN wind
- being an apple falling from a tree
- being a Spirit-Wind horse galloping
- being the sorcerer rooted to the spot.

What's it like to embody these aspects of nature? What helps bring these to life?

Key Activity: *20 minutes*
The children are going to improvise the whole story as the teacher/facilitator reads it aloud.

- Explain that participants need to listen for key pauses as prompts and cues to know when to perform movements.
- Repeat the process, choosing different lines for them to act, so participants have to keep listening to know their cue!

Sharing/Reflection: *5 minutes*
Share what it's like to connect to nature in this way. Discussion on favourite actions.
How did they make use of the space? How did they make use of their bodies? Any responses to how it felt to improvise, any surprises, insights, or challenges.

Key Vocabulary/Questions: Pause, improvisation, mime, embodiment	**Extension Activities:** Choose a different folktale and repeat the activity.

ACTIVITY: CREATING A RHYMING POEM – A SUMMONING SPELL		
Subject: Creative writing **Curriculum Links:** Poetry, English	**Key Skills:** Rhyming poetry	**Duration:** 1 hour
Resources & Creative Materials: *The Spirit Wind Horse of AUTUMN* folktale Paper, pens/pencils	**Location:** Inside	

Learning Objectives:

- To create a simple poem that rhymes
- To create work together in collaboration
- To perform a poem in a group

Introduction & Warm-Up: *20 minutes*
Reread the story of The Spirit Wind-Horse of AUTUMN.

- Imagine you are the sorcerer from the story.
- As a group, we are going to create a summoning spell for the apples.
- It only needs to be four lines long.
- Together, list some rhyming words with tree, yummy, red.
- Together, play with the words until you've formed a simple poem, such as:

> *Delicious apples,*
> *Come to me,*
> *I order you,*
> *Off that tree.*

- Practise saying it aloud as if you are the 'scrumping' sorcerer.

Key Activity: *30 minutes*

- In small groups, create your own summoning spell. It can have long or short lines.
- When finished, create a protection spell.
- First, list some rhyming words with horse, hide, straw etc.
- Then play with the words until you have a protection spell.

Sharing/Reflection: *10 minutes*
Chant your poems aloud to the rest of the class as if you are the greedy sorcerer.
How easy or tricky did you find creating the spells? How easy or tricky did you find it making the poems rhyme?

Key Vocabulary/Questions: Rhyming, poetry, scrumping	**Extension Activities:** Create a sorcerer's spell book.

CLOSING ACTIVITY: PERSONAL/COLLECTIVE ASSOCIATIONS WITH AUTUMN AND GIANT GROUP MANDALA		
Subject: Visual arts **Curriculum Links:** Art, Geography	**Key Skills:** Artmaking, collaboration	**Duration:** 1 hour
Resources & Creative Materials: Blank paper plate (one for each child) OR thick white paper/ card cut into a circle – plate size or larger Scissors, glue-sticks Lining paper/craft paper – masking tape Pens, paper, collage materials, fabrics, paints, chalks Any natural materials – leaves, twigs, etc		**Location:** Inside

Learning Objectives:

• To engage children in a giant creative activity to summarise the theme of AUTUMN
• To teach collaboration in a shared art-making activity such as a Mandala
• To engage children to capture their own *unique* relationship with AUTUMN

Introduction & Warm-Up: *5 minutes*

Share how the Celts and other ancient cultures saw the sun as a wheel, turning for each season. In Hindu and Buddhist cultures, they use the Mandala, a circular template, to create images and patterns to represent wholeness of the cosmos, and for human beings. Today, we are going to make our own AUTUMN mandala to focus on our own personal relationship to AUTUMN.

Invite children in silence to close their eyes and to think about the season of AUTUMN:

• When you think of AUTUMN, what comes up?
• Images, words, sounds, sensations, places, drinks, foods, activities, plants, animals.
• Spend some time really allowing yourself to think about your memories.
• Any outdoor AUTUMN scenes, festivals, important community and/or cultural events?

Key Activity: *40 minutes*

Activity 1: *Individual – create AUTUMN image – 30 minutes*

On their paper circle or plate, each participant creates their own AUTUMN image.

• Invite children to draw/write their associations with the season of AUTUMN.
• The challenge is for the children to fill in all the paper, leaving no gaps!
• If words, encourage children to decorate these in a seasonal style and colours.
• Images can be abstract, showing cold colours, patterns or a scene. It can be a collage or 2D. The choice is theirs. Encourage children to play and experiment with images and ideas.

Activity 2: *Creating a group Giant AUTUMN Mandala collage in a hall space OR outside if weather is mild – 10 minutes*

- Ask each of the children to lay their circular artworks on the floor.
- Starting in a central position (middle of the floor or playground) position the circles in a spiral starting in the middle and radiating outwards.
- You could also lay the circles out using a different formation or design or maybe try a couple of ideas before deciding on the right one.

Sharing/Reflection: *15 minutes*
Stand around the final formation on the floor and invite participants to share their responses to the AUTUMN Mandala.
Feedback also on the creative process – what is it like to contribute to the Giant Mandala?
How do they look as part of a collaborative design?
Teacher or adult helper to stand on a chair or higher point to photograph the collaborative artwork for posterity

Key Vocabulary/Questions:	**Extension Activities:**
Mandala, mindfulness, senses, creativity, collaboration What makes AUTUMN so unique?	If there is a wall space big enough the design could be stuck to a wall with white tack to be appreciated by a wider audience. At the end of term individual circles can be taken home by children to be hung up on the wall to mark the season of AUTUMN.

As we close our AUTUMN SEASON, here is one last creative exercise to try at home.

TRY THIS AT HOME: AUTUMN BINGO ON A NATURE WALK		
Subject: Wellbeing and Nature **Curriculum Links:** Science, PSHE	**Key Skills:** Observation, creativity	**Duration:** 1 hour 30 minutes
Resources & Creative Materials: AUTUMN nature bingo sheet Blank Nature Bingo sheet – see overleaf	**Location:** Outside	

Learning Objectives:

- To observe and connect to the world around you
- To look for signs of AUTUMN – seen and unseen
- To use different senses to connect to nature

Introduction & Warm-Up: *30 minutes*
This walk is so you can create your own personal AUTUMN Bingo sheet that relates to where you live. We've put examples overleaf, but they may not reflect your local area.

- Go for a walk in your local area, taking note of the nature all around you.
- Try to look for things that are both small and large, practising your observation skills.
- Remember you can include different senses, sights, smells, and sensations.
- Fill the blanks on the bingo sheet with animals, plants, and anything else from your area.
- If you are in a city, see what you can find... there may be surprises!

Key Activity: *1 hour*

- Invite a friends or members of your family to go on a Nature Bingo walk.
- Give them your own home-made Nature Bingo sheet – see overleaf.
- Can they find all the AUTUMN items in your local area?
- Circle or tick each item that they find.

Sharing/Reflection:
Did anyone manage to find all the items?
Were they able to add anything else to your own list? Any surprises?
How easy, hard was it to do this?

Key Vocabulary/Questions: Bingo, AUTUMN/FALL, observation What skills are needed to find things in nature?	**Extension Activities:** Can you create bingo sheets for the other seasons?

AUTUMN Bingo

Can you find all the items? Tick, circle, or even draw the items once you've spotted them.

Squirrel	Conker	Orange leaf	Wellies
Acorn	Spider web	Animal footprints	Pumpkin
Berries	Smell of leaves	Bare tree	Squelchy mud
Puddle	Bird (Maybe even migrating birds in a flock!)	Twig	Breeze

A Nature Bingo Walk sheet

Here are all the things I've found in my local area. Can you find them too? Try and tick them off as you find them.

WINTER

'Don't think the garden loses its ecstasy in WINTER. It's quiet, but the roots are down there riotous.'

Rumi (Sufi and Persian poet)

December, January, February in

Northern Hemisphere

June, July, August in

Southern Hemisphere

WINTER SEASON, FOLKLORE AND CREATIVE ACTIVITIES

- Introduction to WINTER

- Opening Activity – Slow WINTER Walk and Words Collection

A retelling of *Cailleach – Queen of WINTER and Storm Hag* from Scotland and Ireland

- Creating our own *Cailleach* Folktale Characters

- Creating a *Cailleach* 'WINTER Weather Drama'

- Creating an Animal Hibernation Poem

- Creating WINTER Underground 'Root Art'

A retelling of *Ameratsu, the Sun Goddess* from Japan

- Creating Ameratsu Drama Sketches

- Creating a Sunlight Mirror Portrait

- Creating a WINTER Solstice "Sun Party" Invitation

- Creating a Bare Branches Silhouette Picture

A retelling of *The Fir-Tree Spider* from Ukraine

- Creating Spider Movements and Dance

- Making Wintry Spider Webs

- Creating Kind Animal-Helper WINTER Stories

- Designing a WINTER Den or Feeder for an Animal

A retelling of *The Rainbow Crow* from Lenape tribe, First Nation, USA

- Creating a Bird's Eye View Map

- Creating a Storyboard for a Folktale (plus resources)

- Making a Totem Pole Style Art

- Exploring Our Own Strengths and Qualities in Making Rainbow Wings

- Creating a Box World Diorama

DOI: 10.4324/9781003178682-8

A retelling of *The Firefox* from Finland

- Creating a New Aurora Borealis or Northern Lights Folktale

- Creating Your Own WINTER *Haiku* (plus resources)

- Creating a Twig Photo Frame (to display a *haiku* poem)

- Creating Your Own Firefox (plus resources)

Closing exercise

- Personal/collective associations with WINTER and Giant Group Mandala

Try this at home

- Creating Natural Ornaments for a Christmas/Pine tree – Pine-cone celebration tree!

Introduction to WINTER

As leaves fall and tree-branches turn bare, WINTER in the Northern/Southern Hemisphere is a time of nature slowing down. Dark evenings draw in and cold weather arrives. Deciduous trees and plants look lifeless. Only the evergreen trees keep their leaves and green colour. Many animals slow down or retreat into hibernation. The colour palette changes in the sky and landscape, bringing grey, brown, and blue tones. As we wrap up to stay warm, our bodies physically feel that the sun is faraway.

Whether you like the cosiness of WINTER, or find the long dark nights difficult, this season has a rich history in folklore and storytelling. If we imagine a time with no electricity, no central heating, and no screens, storytelling around a fireplace must have helped people endure long nights spent indoors. As ancient people were hunters/gatherers, the sun's departure would have had a profound effect on their lives. Storytelling could help people hold hope for spring's return. As we've already seen, many characters in folktales personify natural forces and bring about seasonal change. Some of our diverse religious festivals and symbols also tap into older traditions linked with nature's rhythms building up to the shortest day and longest night – the WINTER Solstice.

In the following section, we've collected folklore characters and stories from a range of wintry places in the Northern Hemisphere. Although we've rooted folktales in specific countries, we recognise that versions of these stories will naturally migrate, cross borders, and live elsewhere in different shapes and forms.

Some stories tell how some cultures believe WINTER came about. Others explore specific wintry weather or how nature and cultural/religious rituals interconnect. In selecting our five folktales for WINTER, we tried to choose ones that are less known. At the same time, we recognise that there are so many other stories out there. We hope our stories are useful starting places that can encourage your own interest in collecting WINTER folklore tales. There is a selection of creative activities for each folklore tale; drama, creative writing, and art-making activities are offered to help children engage with different stories and their role in trying to understand the natural world.

WINTER offers children, families, and classrooms a range of creative possibilities to explore the unique qualities and rhythms of this season through storytelling, visual art making, drama, and movement. If we can connect to some of the themes of WINTER in creative and positive ways, it might help some people who find this season so difficult. Given some of the challenges working outside in cold weather during WINTER, we've offered a range of creative activities, which also enable nature to be brought inside.

ACTIVITY: SLOW WINTER WALK AND WORDS COLLECTION		
Subject: Wellbeing **Curriculum Links:** English, PSHE	**Key Skills:** Sensation, mindfulness, observation	**Duration:** 1 hour
Resources & Creative Materials: Strips of paper in seasonal colours, pens/pencils, a box	**Location:** Outside or if inside, a guided visualisation exercise on WINTER	

Learning Objectives:

- To teach mindfulness techniques and support children in mind/body wellbeing
- To help children to connect to their senses and sensations in nature
- To introduce concepts of slowing down, and hibernation in the WINTER Season
- To create a box of WINTER words, sensations, objects, and images

Introduction & Warm-Up: *15 minutes*
Explain mindfulness and walking meditation principles behind a Slow-Walk:

- A way of observing and moving through the world without judgement.
- Slowing down our heartbeat, and allowing our bodies to relax.

Invite children first to stand in a circle outside to practice noticing through the senses.

- In silence, feel the ground beneath your feet and notice what is happening.
- What do you see and hear, what temperature do you feel on your skin?
- Is there any 'smoke' or 'breath vapour' coming out of anyone's mouths?
  - Water vapour from our breath 'meets' the cold, a bit like fog!

Key Activity: *35 minutes*
Activity 1 – *Slow WINTER Walk – 20 minutes*
Explain how in WINTER, humans, animals, and plants all slow down in both growth and activity. Invite children to start to walk normally in outside space, and then to gradually slow down... observing their environment as they do so.

- Give attention to colours, sounds, senses, weather, clouds.
- What do they notice as they slow down?
- What do they see around them – any birds or trees (evergreen or not)?
- Any sounds – birdsong, wind?
- Are there any natural objects that they find on their way – a leaf, a stone, a piece of mud?

Gradually, invite children to walk as if in slow motion, until they come to a stop.
Activity 2 – *Gathering together of WINTER words, images, sensations – 15 minutes*

- On a strip of paper, each child writes a few WINTER words or sensations.
- Place these and any objects in a WINTER box or create a display.

Sharing/Reflection: *10 minutes*
Invite participants to stand/sit in a circle and share responses to their Slow WINTER Walk.
Any feelings, sensations, surprises? Any objects that they picked up along the way? What was it like to slow down? Did anyone feel bored, calmer, etc with the stillness?

Key Vocabulary/Questions: Slowing down, Imagery, Senses, Creativity, Mindfulness What kind of senses and words are unique to WINTER?	**Extension Activities:** WINTER words can be fanned out and displayed.

WINTER Folktale 1 from Scotland and Ireland
A retelling of *CAILLEACH, the Queen of WINTER and Storm Hag*

Ancient people didn't know the science behind the drastic weather of WINTER. One way to make sense of the natural world, forces, and elements was to make up stories about incredible beings with magical powers. Here is an ancient Scottish folktale about the Cailleach which explores how WINTER comes about. What makes her so interesting is how closely she is linked to specific natural sites both in Scotland and in Ireland (Hag's Head, at the Cliffs of Moher in County Clare, Ireland, and Ben Cruachan, the largest mountain in Argyll and Bute, Scotland just to name a couple).

There are many tales of the Cailleach. She is an ancient weather goddess and takes many different forms.

Some say she is an old lady, a hag. Others say she is a veiled lady, or magical old giant-ess. She is often pictured wearing a veil or a cloak and carries a magic staff. The land is said to be created by her as she makes mountains as her stepping-stones. When she lays her blanket on the ground, it becomes snow.

Using her magic hammer, she can shape the valleys and hills. Her staff will freeze the ground. In WINTER she summons the storms and the winds. She is known to herd wild deer and protect animals during the depths of WINTER. Some say that she rides a giant grey wolf.

In SPRING, it is said that she will turn to stone before her time comes again.

ACTIVITY: CREATING OUR OWN CAILLEACH FOLKTALE CHARACTERS		
Subject: Visual arts, storytelling **Curriculum Links:** Art	**Key Skills:** Artmaking, Storytelling	**Duration:** 1 hour
Resources & Creative Materials: *Cailleach, the Queen of WINTER and Storm Hag* folktale Paper, pens, paint, string/wool, natural materials	**Location:** Inside	

Learning Objectives:

- To gain confidence in our own imaginative and creative capabilities
- To bring to life the Cailleach to represent aspects of WINTER
- To practise oracy and storytelling skills

Introduction & Warm-Up: *10 minutes*

Read the folktale character of the Cailleach to children with their eyes closed, and ask the children to imagine what kind of character they see.

- What does she look/sound like? Eyes, hair, voice, clothes, colours, and wintry style?
- What might her magic staff be made of? And her hammer?

Share with children the kind of animals that would have been common in Scotland/Ireland in ancient times; deer like now, but also bears and wolves!

Reinforce that there is no right or wrong in this exercise, that Cailleach can take many forms and we all may have different versions. Also, tell the children that the Cailleach doesn't have to be beautiful, and might indeed look scary. The important part is she was powerful!

Key Activity: *Inventing our own folklore Cailleach character that brings about WINTER – 30 minutes*

- Design a picture of your own Cailleach – old, young, veiled, a giantess – any form!
- What kind of magical object/s does she use to bring about WINTER?
- Make sure that she is "doing" something in the picture to create wintry weather.
- She may also have a magical animal helper with her.
- WINTER Words, sensations, and images can be used as inspiration.
- Invite children to let their own imaginations run wild and *not to copy* each other.
- Let's see how many different Cailleachs we can have!

Sharing/Reflection: *20 minutes*

Invite participants to stand/sit in a circle and place their Cailleach inside.

This is a Cailleach Gallery – ask children what they notice.

What different forms does she take? What magical objects does she have?

What kind of powers does she have? What kind of weather does she make happen?

What landscape might she make with her magic staff and hammer?

What kind of magical animal helper might she have?

Key Vocabulary/Questions: WINTER imagery, senses, creativity, the Cailleach, Celts How to represent WINTER through magical characters Oral storytelling means tales/characters can change	**Extension Activities:** Send photos of all the Cailleachs to Folklore Scotland and Ireland organisations.

ACTIVITY: CREATING A CAILLEACH 'WINTER WEATHER DRAMA'		
Subject: Performing arts **Curriculum Links:** English, Drama, Movement	**Key Skills:** Storytelling, collaboration, drama	**Duration:** 1 hour
Resources & Creative Materials: *Cailleach, the Queen of WINTER and Storm Hag* folktale Musical instruments, any blankets, fabrics	**Location:** Inside or outside	

Learning Objectives:

- To bring the Cailleach to life through drama, movement, and sound
- To create and make up own stories about the Cailleach's magical powers
- To work in small groups to make drama pieces about making WINTER weather

Introduction & Warm-Up: *15 minutes*
Read the folktale of the Cailleach a couple of times to the children.

- Today, we are going to expand on this activity by creating short pieces of drama.
- Explore how the Cailleach might use magic powers to shape wintry weather and landscape.
- Brainstorm some ideas around how to make sounds to show weather:
  - Stamping feet as the magic hammer strikes the ground to make mountains.
  - Clapping hands as the staff calls up the winds to make stormy weather.
  - Blowing noises, as she makes ice by blowing on water.
  - Musical instruments, like triangles or drums, can bring to life the elements.
- Show how lots of people making same movements/sounds is effective.

Key Activity: *Invent a 2 min movement/drama to show Cailleach's magic at work – 25 minutes*

- In small groups, children are to create a short drama piece that tells us something about the Cailleach's powers.
- Children can personify different aspects – be it the land or the Cailleach.
- Ask them to show the magical objects that Cailleach might use to bring about WINTER and use sound/movement to bring to life characteristics such as the wind.

Sharing/Reflection: *20 minutes*
Each group performs their Cailleach piece.
Audience can be invited to comment on magical objects or magic used to create WINTER.
Audience of children give their responses and feedback at the end of all pieces.

Key Vocabulary/Questions: WINTER imagery, senses, creativity, the Cailleach How to represent WINTER through drama and sound	**Extension Activities:** Ask children to invent their own legend around the Cailleach.

ACTIVITY: CREATING AN ANIMAL HIBERNATION POEM		
Subject: Creative writing **Curriculum Links:** English	**Key Skills:** Poetry, movement, oracy	**Duration:** 1 hour
Resources & Creative Materials: Movement, mindfulness, pens, and paper		**Location:** Inside or outside

Learning Objectives:

- To connect with the theme of hibernation through mime, mindfulness, and creativity
- To use our senses to create poetry around WINTER theme
- To build confidence in our own storytelling abilities

Introduction & Warm-Up: *20 minutes*
Activity 1: *Introducing HIBERNATION – 10 minutes*
In the folktale, the Cailleach protects animals like deer.

- Introduce the idea of hibernation, how animals in WINTER move more slowly to save energy as there is less food.
- Their whole body slows down, heartbeat, blood circulation, a bit like a mindfulness and relaxation exercises!
- Share examples of animals – squirrels, bears, hedgehogs, bats – who sleep through WINTER. Once, bears lived in Scotland!

Activity 2: *Hibernation Guided Visualisation and Slow Mindfulness Walk – 10 minutes*
Invite children to choose one of the animals, and imagine they are about to enter hibernation. "We are each going to walk very slowly around the space, silently, imagining we are a bear, squirrel, hedgehog, or bat. Imagine that you are looking for a place to sleep – a den, somewhere safe. What kind of shelter are you looking for? Walk slower and slower and imagine that you are picking up items for your shelter. What do you need to survive the WINTER? What would these animals feel in their bodies as they get ready to sleep? Everyone move in slow motion until you come to a stop. Imagine your animals fall asleep, safe and cosy in their dens."

Key Activity: *30 minutes*
Divide children into groups of five to six children – it doesn't matter which animal they've chosen.

- Explain how each group will create and perform a poem on hibernating animals that will tell how their animals move, sound, what they eat; physical, emotional sensations.
- Useful to explore words and associations around sleeping – slumber, doze, yawn...
- Can each child think of two lines of poetry? Here are some examples:

This bear's heart starts slowing down
My bat yawns
Hedgehog digs underground
Squirrel picks up a thousand nuts

- Each child in group creates two lines, to make an approximately tenline hibernation poem.
- Write the group poem on one big piece of paper.

Sharing/Reflection: *10 minutes*
Invite each group to share their Animal Hibernation poem aloud – with each child reading their own two lines. Once the poem has been read, ask the group to read it backwards, starting with the last line first. Ask the other groups for responses, reflections, observations.

Key Vocabulary/Questions: Hibernation – how does it feel to slow right down?	**Extension Activities:** Children illustrate group poems.

ACTIVITY: CREATING WINTER UNDERGROUND 'ROOT ART'		
Subject: Visual arts **Curriculum Links:** Art, Science	**Key Skills:** Artmaking, imagining	**Duration:** 1 hour
Resources & Creative Materials: Child-friendly explication of 'vernalisation' Rumi quote, gentle mindfulness music Choice of creative materials – paper, paint, paint brushes, pencils, oil/chalk pastels	**Location:** Inside	

Learning Objectives:

- To learn how nature is busy in WINTER even if everything looks 'dead'
- To introduce the concept of 'vernalisation' in plants, a bit like animal hibernation
- To use artmaking and imagination to explore life in the bleak mid-WINTER
- To link in with our own 'dormant' potentials (for older children and participants)

Introduction & Warm-Up: *10 minutes*
Did you know certain plants need the cold of WINTER to kick-start their growth later in spring?
That's why gardeners/farmers store bulbs/seeds in cold/dark places before planting outside.

- Share Rumi's WINTER quote: 'Don't think the garden loses its ecstasy in WINTER. It's quiet, but the roots are down there riotous.'
- Discuss how seeds, plants, and trees lie 'dormant' in WINTER.
- This natural process is called 'vernalisation'.
- Can we imagine what kind of things might be going on underground out of sight?
- Discuss with older participants how we may also have our own potentials that might be 'asleep' or 'dormant' at certain times of our lives.
- All creative projects must start off very small, like a seed in a period of waiting.
- That's why qualities of 'patience', and 'care' are so important.
- Like nature, we can't rush... at same time, we can't leave them un-watered!

Key Activity: *30 minutes*

- Invite children to imagine what might be going on underground for roots and plants in WINTER, while it is all cold above ground.
- Draw a horizontal line 1/3 up on your page, leaving 2/3 beneath.
- In larger section, create an image of the secret life going on underground.
- Don't worry about right or wrong... let your imaginations fly.
- For older children/participants, invite them to reflect on their own lives, and what qualities, abilities, dreams might be sleeping inside, ready to wake up?
  - They can also include these in their image.

Sharing/Reflection: *20 minutes*
Invite children to place their images on the floor. What do they notice about their creations?
Feelings, responses?

Key Vocabulary/Questions: Dormancy, dormant, vernalisation, potentials How do we support our own creative potentials? What qualities are needed for our growth, creativity?	**Extension Activities:** Find out more about Rumi (a famous poet) and his work.

WINTER Folktale 2 from Japan
A retelling of *Ameratsu, The Sun Goddess*

A myth to explore how WINTER and Spring/Summer comes about.

Ancient people didn't know the science behind where the warm Summer Sun went during WINTER. They believed that the weather was ruled by gods. Gods and goddesses were their way to try to understand the seasons and why in WINTER days became much shorter, darker, and colder, before changing again to spring and summer!

Ameratsu is the Japanese goddess of the sun and her brother Susanoo is the god of the storm and winds. When Ameratsu is given power to rule over all lands, Susanoo is jealous and throws a fit of rage. He destroys Amaterasu's fields and breaks her precious necklace.

Ameratsu the sun goddess is so angry that she runs away to the mountains, and hides in the Heavenly Rock Cave, plunging the world into a freezing cold darkness.

Even when the other kami - Japanese gods/Spirits - try to tempt her out of the cave, Ameratsu refuses. With no light or warmth, all plants start to die. Eventually Omoikane, the god of wisdom, works together with the other kami to come up with a plan to tempt Ameratsu out of the cave.

Eight hundred kami gather near the cave and pretend to have a loud party. When Ameratsu calls out to ask why they are dancing and cheering, she's told there is another god who is even stronger and radiant that she is. Curious, she peeks out of the cave.

At this moment, the kami hold up a mirror. The light she sees in the mirror makes Ameratsu believe that she is seeing another god. As she tries to get a better look, the gods take her hand and bring her out of the cave, and she realises that it is her own light.

(The time Ameratsu spent in the cave was the first WINTER and, while the following WINTERs would never be as dark and cold as when Ameratsu hid in the cave, each year she dims again.)

ACTIVITY: CREATING AMERATSU DRAMA SKETCHES		
Subject: Performance Art **Curriculum Links:** English, drama, movement, music	**Key Skills:** Storytelling, drama, improvisation, oracy	**Duration:** 1 hour
Resources & creative materials: *Ameratsu, The Sun Goddess* folktale, musical instruments Any other props, fabrics	**Location:** Outside preferably or inside	

Learning Objectives:

- To explore how WINTER is said to come into being through the *Ameratsu* myth
- To support children to devise their own drama interpretation
- To encourage use movement and mime to add to drama

Introduction & Warm-Up: *10 minutes*

Read the Ameratsu story to the class, asking children for their responses to the story. Explore responses to this idea about how WINTER and summer comes into being.

Key Activity: *40 minutes*

Activity 1: *Devise and rehearse the drama – 25 minutes*

- With groups of five to six children, give each group a short section of the story to bring to life.
- Invite children to use mime and music to create their piece.
- Do they want musical instruments or sound to represent the different characters?
- How do they want to bring to life all these different nature gods/spirits?
- Each piece to last no longer than 3 minutes (make sure they time it beforehand).

Activity 2: *Performing the Ameratsu drama – 15 minutes*

- Each group brings to life their drama piece of three minutes, one after the other.

Sharing/Reflection: *10 minutes*

Invite children to respond to the whole Ameratsu myth – observations, reflections, surprises? What do they think of this way of explaining WINTER coming into being?

Key Vocabulary/ Questions	**Extension Activities**
How do we make sense of WINTER/spring? Why did ancient people create nature gods? How can sound support creating a character?	Create their own story about how WINTER came into being.

ACTIVITY: CREATING A SUNLIGHT MIRROR PORTRAIT		
Subject: Visual arts **Curriculum Links:** English, PSHE	**Key Skills:** Drawing, painting	**Duration:** 1 hour

Resources & creative materials: *Ameratsu, The Sun Goddess* folktale Small mirrors Pencils/pens, felt-tip paper, paints, wax crayons, the more choice of materials, the better!	**Location:** Inside

Learning Objectives:

- To learn about Ameratsu's light and how she needed the mirror to remind her of it
- To link this into thinking about our own 'light' and how we can forget to see it
- To learn how being outside in sunshine is essential for our health and wellbeing

Introduction & Warm-Up: *15 minutes*

- Discuss the scene when the sun goddess, Ameratsu must be tempted out of the cave.
  - In WINTER, we can also feel like we want to stay inside and not come outside.
- What do children think Ameratsu saw and felt when she looked in the mirror?
- What do we all feel when we step outside and there is sunlight on our faces?
- Do we feel other people see us differently from how we see ourselves sometimes?
- Why do we all need to feel the sunshine, even in WINTER?
- Discuss the impact that being outside in sunshine can have on our wellbeing.

(If it is a sunny WINTER day, invite children to go into the outside area to experience sun on their faces, or alternatively to find a place inside where they can feel the sun.)

Key Activity: *Draw a picture of your reflection in a mirror – 30 minutes*

- Invite each child to look at their reflection in a mirror and draw a self-portrait, incorporating the sun, sunlight, and sun rays in some way.
- Use different materials to bring to life Ameratsu's sunlight energy in the portraits.
- Help children try and explore creative ideas to show sunrays and sunlight.

Sharing/Reflection: *15 minutes*

Create a gallery of Ameratsu Light portraits as each child holds up their work.

Invite children to comment on their experience of both making and seeing portraits.

Any observations, reflections, or surprises regarding the creative process and experience?

Key Vocabulary/Questions: How do we show the sun's energy through art? How might this look different in WINTER?	**Extension Activities:** Explore different ways the sun is shown in history of art.

ACTIVITY: CREATING A WINTER SOLSTICE 'SUN PARTY' INVITATION		
Subject: Creative writing and Visual arts **Curriculum Links:** English, Science, History	**Key Skills:** Writing	**Duration:** 1 hour

Resources & creative materials: *Ameratsu, The Sun Goddess* folktale Summary of different WINTER Solstice festivals and rituals Pencils/pens, felt-tips, paper	**Location:** Inside

Learning Objectives:

- To learn about the WINTER Solstice and ancient traditions/festivals
- To think about the impact of the shortest day/longest night on us and ancient people
- To create ideas for our own Sun Party for the WINTER Solstice

Introduction & Warm-Up: *15 minutes*

- Reflect on how the gods throw a party to try to get Ameratsu to come out of the cave.
- Explore how many cultures throw parties and festivals in the depths of WINTER.
- Explain that the WINTER Solstice is the shortest day, longest night, 21/22 December.
- Discuss how we can feel when there is so little light, and long, dark nights.
- Many cultures would celebrate at this time, to welcome back the return of the sun.
  - Saturnalia for Ancient Romans was a huge party where special candles were lit.
  - Yule in ancient Europe – Celts, Anglo Saxons lit bonfires, candles, special logs.
  - It's believed the giant stones at Stonehenge in Wiltshire were used in special ceremonies around the Sun and solstices.
- Interestingly, many of religions we know today have special festivals around this time.
  - Christmas, Diwali, Passover, etc.
  - Using candles, light, fireworks, special foods to bring communities together.
  - Evergreen trees are seen as a symbol of eternal life.

Key Activity: *Inventing your own Sun Party for a WINTER solstice in ancient times – 30 minutes*

- Imagine being a tribe in ancient times – no electricity, screens, fridges, ovens!
- Imagine that you are trying to get the Sun to return in mid-WINTER.
- What party or festival would they make – what food, drink, celebrations?
  - Invite children to think about how to represent light and the sun.
- In small groups, make an invitation for your Sun party.
  - Think about how you will persuade people to come.
  - How will they feel if they come to your Sun Party?

Sharing/Reflection: *15 minutes*
Create a gallery of Sun Party images.
Invite children to present their images.
Any observations, reflections, or surprises regarding the creative process and experience?

Key Vocabulary/Questions: WINTER solstice, Yule, Saturnalia (as examples of WINTER festivals) What is the role of light, fire, in celebrating WINTER solstice?	**Extension Activities:** Invent your own WINTER solstice story.

ACTIVITY: CREATING A BARE BRANCHES SILHOUETTE PICTURE		
Subject: Visual arts **Curriculum Links:** Art	**Key Skills:** Observation, Drawing, Creativity	**Duration:** 45 minutes

Resources & Creative Materials: Twigs/branches Clip boards, plain paper for drawing Pencils, charcoal, ink pens, sticks	**Location:** Outside for research Inside for making

Learning Objectives:

- To appreciate the shapes of trees and branches in the WINTER months
- To learn that these branches aren't dead even when there are no leaves
- To learn how to notices outlines, silhouettes, and negative spaces in bare branch forms
- To bring these to life through creative arts

Introduction & Warm-Up: *15 minutes*
In WINTER, trees lose their leaves and appear lifeless. Yet behind the scenes of this apparent 'death', new life is already being regenerated.

- Outside or indoors take some moments to carefully observe an area of woodland (or a still life display) featuring bare twigs and branches. These bare branches – the structure and the skeleton of the tree – are beautiful shapes hidden in spring and summer when the leaves come. Now is the time to really appreciate them.

Warm Up prompts for careful observation:

- Look carefully at the shapes of the bare twigs and branches (silhouettes).
- Look how they aren't straight lines but go in and out and curve and bend.
- Look carefully at how many small twigs can sprout from a main branch.
- Look at the textures and patterns on the branches (if you can see that close).
- Touch and feel the twigs and branches.
- How do they feel? Are they rough or are they smooth?

Key Activity: *Drawing Activity – 20 minutes*
On paper (with a clip board if outside) draw what you see.
Drawing pointers:

- Draw what you see – there is no right or wrong. You could even try drawing without looking at the paper.
- Try and fill your whole sheet of paper with your drawings and don't draw too small.
- Look carefully at the shapes in between the branches – the negative spaces – and observe what shapes you make between the lines of the branches you have drawn.
- Encourage each person in the group to do at least two or more drawings in the 20 min slot – feel free to allow more time to the task if possible and the group are engaged.

NB: Materials – start the activity with pencil and then move onto using charcoal to explore a different technique (charcoal is made from burning wood).

Sharing/Reflection: *10 minutes*
Invite participants to stand/sit in a circle and share their drawings to the group.
Any observations, details, experiences? Any tips that they picked up during the process?
What do you like about each other's work? What have you learnt from looking at each other's drawings?

Key Vocabulary/Questions: Texture, shape, line, imagery, senses, creativity Which words are unique to WINTER?	**Extension Activities**: Try this drawing activity using sticks dipped in ink. Explore making 'ink' using found materials like berries/earth/etc.

WINTER Folktale 3 from Ukraine
A retelling of *The Fir-Tree Spider*

This story comes from Ukraine. It's said that here spider ornaments are sometimes popular on Christmas trees. Some people believe that decorating a tree with a web brings good luck for the new year. This is possibly where the idea of tinsel originates.

There was once a poor but hard-working widow. She lived in a small cottage with her children, always trying to make sure they were fed and looked after. One summer, her eldest son noticed a pinecone had fallen from a large nearby fir tree. It had started to grow, and the family were excited. They spent many hours tending to the little plant, watching it grow bigger and bigger, and that WINTER they brought it into their home. Finally, they had a Christmas tree.

Yet their tree looked bare for the family could not afford any decorations. No baubles or lights for them. The widow and children went to bed that night, feeling sad and disappointed. Little did they know that kind-hearted spiders had been watching the family. These spiders dropped down from the ceiling and spun elaborate webs all over the branches.

The following morning, the family woke up and opened the curtains. They could not believe their eyes. Rays of light streamed through the window, hitting the tree. The cobwebs glittered with gold and silver, and the family thought they had never seen anything so beautiful in all their lives.

And it has been said, that from that day on, the widow and her children always felt their lives were filled with a bit more luck and fortune.

ACTIVITY: CREATING SPIDER MOVEMENTS AND DANCE		
Subject: Performance art **Curriculum Links:** Dance and movement	**Key Skills:** Dance, mime, rhythm	**Duration:** 1 hour

Resources & Creative Materials: *The Fir-Tree Spider* folktale A piece of lyrical music (without words)	**Location:** Inside or outside

Learning Objectives:

- To learn that WINTER was a very difficult season for ancient people to endure
- To learn to choreograph in pairs
- To learn to express actions and feelings through dance
- To connect to nature – imagining you are a spider

Introduction & Warm-Up: *10 minutes*

- After reading the story, gain children's responses to the story, sharing how WINTER was often a time when people had less food and resources. It's hard for animals too.
- Move like animals around the room – a hungry cat, scared mouse, a sleepy lion.
- Invite a child to call out the next animal and its emotional state.

Key Activity: *30 minutes*

- In pairs, create a spider using your arms and legs. Back-to-back can be work well but try out what feels comfortable. Fabric such as scarves can be used as connectors.
- Think how spiders move. Scuttle across the room as if you are a spider. Listen to the music, and see how you can make your scuttling match the beat.
- In pairs – either as one spider or as two spiders, create dance sequences for:
  1) Spiders looking through the window seeing the disappointed family
  2) Spiders sneaking inside through a hole in the door
  3) Spiders spinning a web around the tree
  4) Choose your own activity for the spider as a finale.

Practise routines, moving to the music, and remember alternating moments of stillness, slowness, and speed can be powerful too.

Sharing/Reflection: *20 minutes*
Ask for volunteers to share their dances.
What was it like to try and move like a spider? What was their favourite scene to perform? Take responses, observations, and reflections from the group.

Key Vocabulary/Questions: How to express fear, delight, hunger through facial expressions, mime, and movement? How to be in a space, while being mindful of others? Times when stillness and silence is needed. How is it to work in collaboration?	**Extension Activities:** Create sound effects or music to go along with your dance. Hint: lots of fingernails tapping the ground is very effective.

ACTIVITY: MAKING WINTRY SPIDER WEBS		
Subject: Creative art **Curriculum Links:** Art, Science	**Key Skills:** Creativity, observation, artmaking	**Duration:** 1 hour 15 minutes
Resources & Creative Materials: *The Fir-Tree Spider* folktale Straight twigs, sticks, string/wool Beads, any decorative sparkly bits (encourage finding recycled materials)	**Location:** Inside for making Spider webs could be hung outside for decoration	

Learning Objectives:

- To learn about how spiders weave their webs
- To encourage children to see the beauty of the web-pattern
- To appreciate how potentially scary animals also have value in the world!
- To make a spider web with a mix of natural and man-made materials

Introduction & Warm-Up: *15 minutes*
Gain children's immediate responses to the *The Fir-Tree Spider* folktale.

- Discussion on spiders and different feelings they can evoke – fear, fascination.
- How might this story change our mind about spiders?
- Share how some people think spider webs might have been the origin of tinsel.
- Explore different times that we see spider webs – inside and outside.
  - Examples of when they look beautiful – sun shining on them, dew droplets.

Share the natural marvel of how a spider weaves a web – with 'spinnerets' on their abdomen (stomach); these are tiny organs which release silk in liquid form, but it quickly becomes solid after contacting the air (a bit like Spiderman!).

Key Activity: *Each child to make their own spider web – 45 minutes*

- Take three straight twigs/sticks and place in star pattern.
- Offer string/wool and start at the middle to create a centre…
- Wind the wool around the centre point where the twigs overlap, binding it together.
- Continue to weave the wool or string in and out between the three stick points so that a web pattern emerges.
- Encourage children to take their time and experiment with different coloured wool.
- Invite children to stick beads or sequins (recycled) to represent dewdrops or snow when the weaving is completed.

Sharing/Reflection: *15 minutes*
Ask for children to share their webs.
Were there any difficulties along the way?
How does this make everyone feel about spiders and their own spider web making skills?

Key Vocabulary/Questions: Spinnerets, silk threads How does nature inspire humans to make and create?	**Extension Activities:** Hang the webs up as a mobile installation in the classroom.

ACTIVITY: CREATING KIND ANIMAL-HELPER WINTER STORIES		
Subject: Creative writing **Curriculum Links:** English	**Key Skills:** Writing, imagination	**Duration:** 1 hour
Resources & Creative Materials: *The Fir-Tree Spider* folktale Pencils, pens, paper	**Location:** Inside	

Learning Objectives:

- To learn how animals often help people in folktale stories
- To think about how humans might have found certain aspects of WINTER difficult
- To make up our own story using a kind animal or animal helper in WINTER

Introduction & Warm-Up: *15 minutes*

- Read *The Fir-Tree* folktale aloud again, thinking about why the spiders felt moved to help the family in the story.
- Are there other fairy tales or stories where animals help the main characters?
- Explain how WINTER was a very difficult season for people to get through in older times.
- Think about other scenes when ancient humans might have run into trouble in WINTER.
  - Getting lost in the dark woods or snow, running out of food or firewood.
  - Horse running off, cart breaking down, not having enough warm clothes.
  - Water frozen, an ice-storm etc...

Key Activity: *Writing a folktale 30 minutes*

- Choose an animal that you might see in WINTER and write a short folktale about how it sees a person or people in trouble in this season.
- What touches the animal about this human that is finding WINTER difficult?
- What does the animal do to help the human?
- How does the human (and animal) feel afterwards?

Sharing/Reflection: *15 minutes*
Invite everyone to sit in a circle outside (weather permitting).
Ask for volunteers to share their folktales about animals helping people in WINTER.
Take responses from children.

Key Vocabulary/Questions: Animal helpers in mythology What do humans see of themselves in animals?	**Extension Activities:** Create a cartoon strip of the folktale.

ACTIVITY: DESIGNING A WINTER DEN OR FEEDER FOR AN ANIMAL		
Subject: Creative art **Curriculum Links:** DT, Art	**Key Skills:** Design	**Duration:** 1 hour

Resources & Creative Materials:	Location:
The Fir-Tree Spider folktale Paper and pencils/pens	Inside

Learning Objectives:

- To learn how WINTER was a hard season for ancient people and animals to endure
- To design a WINTER den or feeder for an animal in WINTER
- To learn the importance of giving something back to nature

Introduction & Warm-Up: *10 minutes*

- After rereading the story, share how WINTER was often a time when people *and* animals had less food and resources. Cosy dens were vital to keep out the cold and the wind. Bird feeders help birds. In the story, the spiders were very kind to the humans.
- How can we help animals in WINTER and give something back to nature?
- Invite the children to come up with ideas for WINTER dens. Examples include: hedgehog houses, toad sanctuaries, bug houses, spider zones, jungle gyms for squirrels, or types of feeders for birds or a different animal.

Key Activity: *Create a 2D drawing – 40 minutes*
Each child chooses a home, feeder, or adventure playground to design for a specific animal (they could have all three in their one habitat!).

- Invite children to think about their own needs in WINTER – warmth and food – and what specific animals' needs might be too.
- Give children the freedom to design their WINTER den or feeder anyway they like.
- Invite children to design their homes/feeders, labelling the different areas.

Sharing/Reflection: *10 minutes*
Ask for volunteers to share their designs.
How easy do you think it would be to actually make?

Key Vocabulary/Questions:	Extension Activities:
What does your specific animal need? How can we give back to nature?	Can they create an actual habitat or feeder that can go in a garden or a school field or forest?

WINTER Folktale 4 from Lenape tribe, First Nation, USA
A retelling of *The Rainbow Crow*

This WINTER story is often attributed to the Lenape, a First Nation tribe, indigenous to North America. However, this source is now being re-evaluated and may come from a Tsalagi (Cherokee) story. *The Rainbow Crow* story explores how an animal came to look and sound like it does as a result of weather changes in WINTER.

When it first began to snow, all the animals got excited. They played in the fluffy white flurries, but soon they grew cold and hungry. Food disappeared and water turned to ice. Yet the snow kept coming. The animals decided someone needed to visit the Creator of All Things. They needed someone to ask him for help. Rainbow Crow hopped forward, volunteering. She was such a beautiful creature with her shimmering rainbow feathers and lovely sing-song voice.

The others wished her luck and off she flew, passing the tops of trees, mountains, clouds, and the moon and stars. It took her many days, but she did not rest until she reached the Creator. Yet he did not notice her. And so, she sang as loud as she could, until at last he was drawn to her voice. She told him how the world was frozen over. He thrust a stick into the sun and gave her fire to warm up the world again. But he warned her that she must fly as quickly as she can before the fire burns all along the stick. Rainbow Crow thanked him and flew home, passing the stars and the moon. But the fire was too fast. It burned her feathers, turning them black, and when she breathed, she inhaled smoke. She could no longer sing. All she could do was, 'Caw.'

By the time she reached Earth, the snow had melted. The animals rejoiced and called Rainbow Crow a hero. Yet she was sad. No longer did she look or sound beautiful.

The Creator heard of the crow's sadness and spoke to her. 'Do not be unhappy, little one. For you will always remain free. Humans won't cage you for your voice or pluck you for your feathers.' Then he pointed at Rainbow Crow and suddenly her dull feathers turned shiny and inside each one was the glimmer of a rainbow.

ACTIVITY: CREATING A BIRD'S EYE VIEW MAP		
Subject: Creative writing **Curriculum Links:** English, Art	**Key Skills:** Art, Storytelling, Oracy	**Duration:** 1 hour 50 minutes
Resources & Creative Materials: *The Rainbow Crow* folktale, guided visualisation White A3 card or thick paper for mixed media wintry landscape Collage materials – coloured paper/tissue/magazines Found materials – cotton wool/tin foil (ask children to collect) Scissors, glue sticks/glue/felt tips/colouring materials		**Location:** Inside

Learning Objectives:

- To learn how animals were seen in ancient cultures, and the role of the shaman
- To travel and fly through the world through the eyes of a bird
- To create a wintry landscape map through art

Introduction & Warm-Up: *15 minutes*

- Gain responses to the *Rainbow Crow* story – share how animals were respected enormously in First Nation tribes and seen to communicate wisdom and unique qualities.
- It was believed that the 'shaman' – a doctor and holy man – could 'travel' with animals, seeing the world through their eyes – we find 'shamans' in many cultures.
- Animals feature in many folklore stories and are given human qualities.
- What human characteristics do we see in the animals in the *Rainbow Crow* story?

Key Activity: *45 minutes*

Activity 1: *Take the class on a guided visualisation – 10 minutes*

To start with, make yourself comfortable and close your eyes. Let your breath slow down. I'd like you to imagine that you are the rainbow crow sitting in your nest. Today you are going on a journey. As you open your wings and flap, you are lifted into the air and start to fly upwards. The land becomes smaller and smaller as you fly higher in the sky. You are riding the wind, and you are on top of the world. Imagine that you are looking down below – you can see forests, mountains, and lakes in WINTER. What does the Wintry landscape look like from up here through your eyes? Take some time enjoying flying up here, and then we are slowly going to come down, riding the wind to come closer to the ground and land gently back in our nest again.

Activity 2: *Create a Map of your Wintry landscape – 35 minutes*

- Invite children to make maps bringing to life snowy mountains, forests, ice-lakes.
- What might the world look like through the eyes of the rainbow crow?
- What might animals and trees look like from up here?
- You might want to plot your Rainbow Crow's journey on the map.

Sharing/Reflection: *15 minutes*

Share Bird's Eye View maps and experiences of the guided visualisation.
Hang up maps and explore similarities and differences.

Key Vocabulary/Questions: Shaman – discussion of the idea of 'journeying' as an animal What is it like to imagine you can see the world as an animal?	**Extension Activities:** Write a short story on what you saw as the Rainbow Crow.

ACTIVITY: CREATING A STORYBOARD FOR A FOLKTALE		
Subject: Creative writing **Curriculum Links:** English	**Key Skills:** Storytelling, storyboard, oracy	**Duration:** 1 hour

Resources & Creative Materials: *The Rainbow Crow* folktale A storyboard template Paper, pens/pencils	**Location:** Inside

Learning Objectives:

- To create a storyboard
- To show how a storyboard can be a roadmap and used as a prompt for oral storytelling
- To tell the story out loud like you are an ancient storyteller

Introduction & Warm-Up: *15 minutes*

- Read *The Rainbow Crow* as a class and decide on key moments/scenes in the story.
- Explain what a storyboard is and how directors use them in films.
- Model a storyboard – stressing how it doesn't matter about the artwork.
- Break down the *Rainbow Crow* into six scenes.

Key Activity: *30 minutes*

- As a class, brainstorm ideas for other fables. Examples include: How did the ant get so strong? How did the robin get her red breast? How did the tiger get his stripes?
- In groups, the children choose a title and come up with a story idea.
- Individually, they create a storyboard showing the key scenes.

Sharing/Reflection: *15 minutes*
Folktales were traditionally spoken aloud.
Ask for volunteers to tell their own tales using their storyboards as prompts. Encourage them to tell the story, rather than reading from their storyboard.
If weather permitting, sit outside and tell your stories to each other as if you were villagers living in the olden days, telling stories to younger generations.

Key Vocabulary/Questions: Storyboards What are the key scenes of your story? What are the pivotal moments?	**Extension Activities:** Write the story of your folktale or write your favourite key scene.

A Storyboard: _ _ _ _ _ _ _ _ _ _ _ _ _ _ _ _ _

ACTIVITY: MAKING TOTEM POLE STYLE ART		
Subject: Visual arts **Curriculum Links:** Art, History, RE	**Key Skills:** Art, storytelling, oracy	**Duration:** 1 hour 30 minutes

Resources & Creative Materials: *The Rainbow Crow* folktale Thick lining paper – 2 meters long, pencil, wax crayons/colouring equipment A3 thin white card for individual animal drawings Scissors/glue Pictures of totem poles from the Internet or books	**Location:** Inside

Learning Objectives:

- To learn about the importance of totem poles in First Nation peoples' culture
- To understand their spiritual purpose in connecting people with nature and animals
- To create a design using animals from North America
- To work together creatively and collaborate as a group and team

Introduction & Warm-Up: *15 minutes*

- Introduce how Totem poles were carved out of whole trees and held huge social and spiritual importance in First Nation peoples – some were metres high!
- These carvings could share family legends, ancestors, and religious beliefs, often showing animals important to the culture.
- Show some designs of totem poles and discuss their look and feel – their impact on us.
- Discuss how they use bold colours and lines, and capture the essence of an animal.
- What kind of animals might be on a totem pole – birds, wolves, deer, bears, etc.
- Why would particular animals be chosen?

Key Activity: *1 hour*

- In groups of fix to six children, brainstorm ideas for your artwork.
- Choose five animals to place in your artwork– each child choosing and sketching one animal.
- Work together to agree how you want to colour in each animal design.
- Each child to draw and colour their individual animal – remember to use bold, strong, contrasting colours.
- Cut out the animal carefully.
- Assemble all five animals on one large, long piece of paper – once the groups are happy with the order of the animals stick down to create the design inspired by the idea of a totem pole.

Sharing/Reflection: *15 minutes*
Hang up the totem-inspired artwork in the classroom on the walls, each group presenting their own piece.
Ask for responses, feelings – what impact does each artwork have on you?
How do they make you think about nature a bit differently?

Key Vocabulary/Questions: How does the First Nation's relationship with animals and nature differ from where you live and come from? What can we learn from the First Nation people?	**Extension Activities:** Research animal names of chiefs in First Nation tribes. What animal would you associate with?

ACTIVITY: EXPLORING OUR OWN STRENGTHS & QUALITIES IN MAKING RAINBOW WINGS		
Subject: Creative arts, wellbeing **Curriculum Links:** English, art, PSHE	**Key Skills:** Creative arts, personal reflection, emotional literacy	**Duration:** 40 minutes

Resources & creative materials: *The Rainbow Crow* folktale Coloured strips of paper/card and scissors Stapler	**Location:** Inside and outside

Learning Objectives:

- To explore different expressions of bravery and strength, and other personal qualities
- To help children appreciate different qualities in themselves and others
- To create and make two-sided feather wings

Introduction & Warm-Up: *Challenging our ideas of what strength and bravery is... 10 minutes*

- At the end of the *Rainbow Crow* story, his rainbows are hidden under his wings.
- Often when we think of bravery, we think of what we can see... climbing mountains, starting a new school, fighting a monster, scoring a penalty in a penalty shoot-out. These are indeed brave moments.
- Yet, like the hidden rainbows in the story, bravery and strengths can take different forms and are not always so obvious: patience; standing up for a friend; kindness, listening to people you don't agree with; saying no to a good friend when their actions don't feel right; speaking up in class; a sense of humour; a sensitivity for other peoples' feelings; expressing our feelings; speaking two languages; practicing our hobbies; doing our home-learning when we don't feel like it!

Key Activity: *20 minutes*

- Brainstorm in pairs the different kinds of strength and bravery we express, exploring which strengths are easy to see, and which might be more hidden. Try to find six to ten personal examples.
- Write an easy-to-see strength on one side of a piece of coloured card, and a more hidden strength/quality on the back. Choose different colours for the examples.
- Taking scissors, cut these out into a feather shape and with a stapler attach the feathers together to make a wing shape, making sure that both sides are visible.

Sharing/Reflection: *10 minutes*
In small groups, share rainbow wings and expressions of bravery.
Discuss any observations, reflections, or surprises from the exercise.
Teacher hangs the wings up from ceiling, showing different qualities everywhere!

Key Vocabulary/Questions: Strength on the outside, strength on the inside How easy is it to explore different ideas of bravery? What's most surprising expression of strength/bravery you see in yourself and friends?	**Extension Activities:** Write scenarios and short stories about some of the more unexpected forms of bravery.

ACTIVITY: CREATING A BOX WORLD DIORAMA		
Subject: Visual arts **Curriculum Links:** Art, English	**Key Skills:** Making, Drawing, Visual story telling	**Duration:** 2 hours

Resources & Creative Materials: *The Rainbow Crow* folktale A cardboard box White card cut into thin strips wider than the width of the box (3/4) White card/paper for drawing Colouring and collage materials Pritt stick/sellotape Cocktail sticks / clear string or thin cotton	**Location:** Inside

Learning Objectives:

- Mindful art making
- Storytelling
- Illustration
- 3D design thinking

Introduction & Warm-Up: *10 minutes*
Reread the story of *The Rainbow Crow* and choose a scene from the story.

Key Activity: *Creating the box world – 1–2 hours (depending on group/time/resources)*
Stage 1: *25 mins*

1. Decide what are the visual elements of your chosen scene and make a quick list. What is the background? The night skies. Daytime? Cityscape? Forest? Which characters appear in the scene? What other elements appear – trees, buildings?
2. Practise sketching some of these elements.

Stage 2: *This activity could be split into two 35-minute sessions (70 mins total time)*

1. The back of the box will be the landscape for your scene. Cut a piece of paper to the same dimensions as the back of the box.
2. Paint/draw/collage **your background scene** onto this piece of paper and stick it into the back of the box.
3. Colour three cardboard strips so they match your background (they don't have to all be the same).
4. Fold the very ends of the strips so they slide into the box and stick the folded edges to the side of the box with the coloured side facing forward.
5. Start by sticking in one at the front, one near the middle and one nearer the back.
6. Draw your characters and other elements – colour them in whatever method you like and cut them out.
7. Once you have cut them out, attach a cocktail stick to the back with a piece of tape making sure that the stick overhangs the bottom of the shape.
8. Insert your characters and elements into your box world by attaching the protruding ends of cocktail stick to the back of the paper strips so that the characters pop up over the strips into the scene.

NB: Points to ponder:

- When planning your box world, you can use as many or as few elements as you like.
- Think of scale – draw some things BIG and some SMALL.
- Use the string to hang things from the top of the box.
- Explore different colouring methods in your box; maybe the background section is painted, and the other elements are collaged or coloured in using pencil or pen?
- Use found objects/textures such as cotton wool, string, feathers, sequins etc to add interest to your world.

Sharing/Reflection: *15 minutes*
Make a gallery of all the boxes – a gallery of scenes.
Share the finished box worlds with our group – what came up in the making process? Did you decide to add anything else; did you connect more deeply to the scene? Did it help you imagine you were part of the story?
Ask the group what they can see in each other's box worlds.

Key Vocabulary/Questions:
Texture, story, imagine, sensory, creativity, illustration, presentation, mood, action, drama
Which words are unique to WINTER?

Extension Activities:
Think of sound effects for your box world and try and make a soundscape for it. Or think of a piece of music that would suit your scene? What would you say if you were narrating the scene? Film the scene using the words and music.

WINTER Folktale 5 from Finland
Retelling of *The Firefox*

Ancient people (just like people today!) marveled at the multi-colored waves of light that would light up the sky on certain nights. The Aurora Borealis, or the Northern Lights, were a mystery and different cultures had their own stories about why they existed. Here is the folktale from Finland.

There can only ever be one Firefox at a time and his name is Tulikettu. His fur is black during the day, but it twinkles with fire at night. When he runs fast, his tail brushes against the branches of trees, creating sparks which light up the night sky. This makes the Aurora Borealis, also known as revontulet – fox fires.

Many men have tried catching Tulikettu, thinking he will bring them great luck and riches, but he is far too fast and clever. He is a cunning fox.

ACTIVITY: CREATING A NEW AURORA BOREALIS OR NORTHERN LIGHTS FOLKTALE		
Subject: Creative writing **Curriculum Links:** English and storytelling	**Key Skills:** Oracy, Group Story telling	**Duration:** 1 hour

Resources & creative materials: *The Firefox* folktale Pictures of the Aurora Borealis	**Location:** Inside or outside

Learning Objectives:

- To understand how folktales often try to explain mysteries of natural world
- To use imagination to invent a new folktale to explain the Northern Lights
- To create your own name for your folktale of the Northern Lights

Introduction & Warm-Up: *15 minutes*

- Share pictures of the Northern Lights/Aurora Borealis.
- Explain how the lights are named after Aurora, the Roman goddess of the dawn, and the word borealis means northern.
- This natural light display that happens close to Earth's north and south poles captures everyone's imagination!
- Other folklore believes the lights are gods battling or gods getting married – there are so many different ideas for what causes this magnificent light-display

Key Activity: *30 minutes*

- In small groups, brainstorm other story ideas for the possible creation of the Aurora Borealis/Northern Lights, e.g. giants graffitiing the sky, cloud fairies in battle, or a party for the gods.
- In small groups, decide on your new folktale. Create a beginning, middle, and end.
- Come up with a new name for the Aurora Borealis or the Northern Lights based on your own ideas. Write down your folktale on one piece of paper.

Sharing/Reflection: *15 minutes*

Let's imagine that we are living 500 years ago looking up at the Northern Lights.

We're going to make a Story Circle. Each group takes turns to read their folktale story, standing up when it is their turn. Try and get each child in a group to read a few lines.

Invite children to respond to the different stories – what are their favourite bits in each?

Key Vocabulary/Questions: Aurora Borealis, *revontulet*, Firefox How does story bring nature to life? How does it capture our imagination?	**Extension Activities:** Research the science behind the Northern Lights! Research other foxes from myth, such as the Sky Fox.

ACTIVITY: CREATING YOUR OWN WINTER *HAIKU*		
Subject: Creative writing **Curriculum Links:** English	**Key Skills:** Poetry, storytelling	**Duration:** 1 hour

Resources & Creative Materials:	Location:
Examples of *haiku*s including the Firefox *haiku* Activity sheet: Wintry *haiku*s – Fill in the gaps Activity sheet: WINTER word bank WINTER words from walk	Inside

Learning Objectives:

- To have fun playing with language and WINTER images
- To understand a *haiku* has 17 syllables, and explore the 5, 7, 5 syllable pattern
- To create a *haiku* based on WINTER

Introduction & Warm-Up: *20 minutes*
Explain what a h*aiku* is: a short poetry style that comes from Japan.

- A *haiku* is a snapshot in time, a super-short story, based on syllables.

Make sure children understand what a syllable is.

- Clap the number of syllables in names and words as a class.
- Show how a *haiku* works, explaining the 5,7,5 syllable pattern.
- Look at various *haiku*s, starting with the one about the *Firefox*.

Create an example *haiku* together: have fun trying to make the right number of syllables.

- Speak and write line 1: Create a wintry image – thinking of senses.
- Speak and write line 2: Describe an action.
- Speak and write line 3: Have something surprising or beautiful happen.

Key Activity: *30 minutes*
Create a WINTER *haiku* of your own.

- Play with words and have fun exploring WINTER imagery and the senses.
- Give your *haiku* poem a title.

Supporting Activity 1 – 'Filling in the gaps' activity sheet.
Supporting Activity 2 – Cut out words on the sheet provided and rearrange them into a *haiku*, using any other words of your own choosing to fill in the gaps.

Sharing/Reflection: *10 minutes*
Invite participants to share their poems aloud.
How did they find writing and saying their *haiku*s? Any surprises?
What is it like to hear the different *haiku*s? Discuss responses, feelings, and observations.

Key Vocabulary/Questions:	Extension Activities:
Haiku, syllables, imagery, senses, creativity What senses have you included in your *haiku*?	Create a *haiku* on the Aurora Borealis. Illustrate your poems or create a WINTER frame for your poem.

Wintry Haikus

Colours red and green
Lighting the sky in neon
Firefox on the run

In a warm snug bed
Snoring and rolling over
Bear falls out and sulks

White tipped frosty grass
Robin hops across the field
Leaving footprints behind

Stones, hat, scarf, and snow
With a carrot for a nose
My wise snowman winks

A blanket of snow
Hiding streets, houses, and trees
A car light peers out

Wintry Haikus

Can you fill in the gaps of the *haiku* using the words below?

rosy   playing   smiles   snowmen   smiles   children

Snowballs

-------------------------------- and ----------------------------------

snow

-------------------- -------------------------- in the --------------------------------

cheeks

-------------------- -------------------------- and --------------------------------

---

Can you fill in the gaps of the *haiku* using the words below:

snowball snowflakes cheek ground white angels hits tongue snow

---

-------------------------------- on my -----------------------------------

-------------------- -------------------- on the --------------------------------

-------------------- -------------------------- my --------------------------------

---

Can you draw a picture to go with these poems?

Wintry Words for **Haiku**

Fox	Toast	Silent	Cold
Bear	Scarf	Family	Travelling
Stars	Cosy	Robin	Freezing
Crackling	Candle	Snug	Fir
Cold	Chocolate	Whispering	Snow
Fire	Holly	Mittens	Wind
Blue	Cheeks	Fog	White
Slip	Mist	Numb	Warm
Rosy	Snuggle	Deer	Gloves
Cloud	Blanket	Bells	Hug
Ringing	Bare	Bed	Lifting
Snowballs	Twigs	Footprints	Colours
Berries	Coming	Wool	Toes
Hat	Tomorrow	Grandma	Comfort
Sleep	Bright	Log	Burning
Hope	Wood	Dream	Wait
Grandpa	Red	Scuttle	Perch

ACTIVITY: CREATING A TWIG PICTURE FRAME (TO DISPLAY A *HAIKU* POEM)		
Subject: Visual arts **Curriculum Links:** Art, DT	**Key Skills:** Making, measuring	**Duration:** 1 hour

Resources & Creative Materials: Bundles of twigs / grasses (approx. 30cm long) Ribbon or string / thread Double sided tape Baking /tracing paper	**Location:** Inside

Learning Objectives:

- To create a picture frame out of natural materials
- To learn how to turn natural materials into a 3D object
- To develop our dexterity and crafting skills

Introduction & Warm-Up: *10 minutes (longer to include twig finding time!)*

- Explain how we are going to each make a picture frame to display a drawing/painting/poem.
- Talk about what you might display in your picture frame.
- Start by going outside to a wooded area and collecting individual collections of small thin twigs (about 30cm long). Eight similar sized twigs each will work.

Key Activity: *Making the Frame – 20 minutes*
Step 1:

- Separate the collection into four even bunches of twigs.
- Tie the twig bunches together with thread.
- Assemble into a square (frame shape).
- Tie the four corners together with ribbon or string.
- Use double sided sticky tape to attach a piece of baking parchment or thin paper to the back of the frame to make the backing for the work displayed to go on.
- Stick your picture in the middle of the frame.

Step 2: *20 minutes*

- When you have your frame, work out the size of paper that will fit into the frame when stuck onto the backing sheet of paper (probably a square around 20cm).
- When you have your size, cut a piece of paper to that size and write up your *haiku* poem to fit. First texture your paper by gently rubbing it over leaves or bark with a wax crayon before writing on your *haiku* OR decorate your *haiku* with drawings of images or patterns influenced by the theme.

Sharing/Reflection: *10 minutes*
Share your framed artwork with class – use to create a class display of twig-framed *haiku*s.

Key Vocabulary/Questions: Texture, shape, line, imagery, senses, creativity, illustration, presentation, framing Which words are unique to WINTER?	**Extension Activities:** Find some more twigs to make a little broom by tying a small bundle of sticks to the end of a larger stick with a piece of string. You could use this little broom to sweep away what you didn't like from the previous year or for sweeping in what you would like for the new year.

ACTIVITY: CREATING YOUR OWN FIREFOX		
Subject: Visual arts **Curriculum Links:** Arts, science	**Key Skills:** Making, drawing	**Duration:** 40 mins (not including drying time)

Resources & Creative Materials:	Location:
The Firefox folktale Heavy weight white cartridge paper (A4 or a bit bigger) Wax crayons, a selection of bright colours Black Indian Ink (important) or black acrylic Q-tips or cocktail sticks A printout/slide of star constellations or the Aurora Borealis Relaxing music playlist Fox Template (overleaf)	Inside

Learning Objectives:

- To make art using the ink scratch technique
- To learn about constellations and explore the patterns stars make in the sky
- To create a personal image of a Firefox

Introduction & Warm-Up: *5 minutes*

- Read *The Firefox* folktale together
- With the group look at images of the Aurora Borealis and discuss the colours and patterns that present within it.
- Ask the group to close their eyes and imagine Tulikettu running through the snow – what does he look like? Where is he going to?

Key Activity: *Making the Firefox – 30 mins + drying time + finishing time*
Stage 1: *Colouring and painting – music on in the background (10 mins)*

1. The aim is to leave no white spaces on the paper and use as many colours as possible.
2. Thickly colour your piece of white cartridge paper using as many colours as possible using wax crayons. Colour in any direction you like in time to the music.
3. When the paper is completely covered with crayon – paint over the whole piece with a layer of black Indian ink or black paint and leave the layer to dry. (This might be best left overnight to dry.)

Stage 2: *Scratching in the details and making the fox – 10 mins*

1. Share images of the Aurora Borealis and star constellations.
2. Scratch the patterns you can see in the images into the black surface of the paper, using a little stick to reveal the colours underneath.
3. Make as many patterns as you like.

Stage 3: *10 mins*

1. Lay the template of the fox onto your artwork, choosing a richly patterned section.
2. Draw around the template.
3. Cut out the fox outline.

Sharing/Reflection: *10 minutes*
Share the foxes in the group and talk about the patterns that were created. Imagine what Tulikettu would think of his beautiful fur!

Key Vocabulary/Questions:	Extension Activities:
Scratch art, ink, texture, night sky, Aurora Borealis, *revontulet*, Tulikettu, fire colours	Create stories about your own Firefox.

CLOSING ACTIVITY: PERSONAL/COLLECTIVE ASSOCIATIONS WITH WINTER AND GIANT GROUP MANDALA		
Subject: Visual arts **Curriculum Links:** Art	**Key Skills:** Artmaking, collaboration	**Duration:** 1 hour

Resources & Creative Materials: Blank paper plate (one for each child) OR thick white paper/card cut into a circle – plate size or larger Scissors, glue-sticks Lining paper/craft paper – masking tape Pens, paper, collage materials, fabrics, paints, chalks Any natural materials – leaves, twigs, etc	**Location:** Inside

Learning Objectives:

- To engage children in a giant creative activity to summarise theme of WINTER
- To teach collaboration in a shared art-making activity such as a mandala
- To engage children to capture their own *unique* relationship with WINTER

Introduction & Warm-Up: *5 minutes*

Share how the Celts and other ancient cultures saw the Sun as a wheel, turning for each season. In Hindu and Buddhist cultures, they use the mandala, a circular template, to create images and patterns to represent the wholeness of the cosmos and for human beings. Today we are going to make our own WINTER mandala to focus on our own personal relationship to WINTER.

Invite children in silence to close their eyes and think about the season of WINTER.

- When you think of WINTER, what comes to mind? Memories and associations?
- Images, words, sounds, sensations, places, drinks, foods, activities, plants, animals.
- Spend some time really allowing yourself to think about your memories.
- Any WINTER scenes, festivals, important community and/or cultural events?

Key Activity: *40 minutes*

Activity 1: *Individual – create a WINTER image – 30 minutes*

On the paper circle or plate, each participant creates their own WINTER image.

- Invite children to draw/write their associations with the season of WINTER.
- The challenge is for the children to fill in all the paper, leaving no gaps!
- If words, encourage children to decorate these in a seasonal style and colours.
- Images can be abstract, showing patterns, cold colours, or a scene. It can be a collage or 2D. The choice is theirs. Encourage children to play and experiment with images and ideas.

Activity 2 – Create a group *Giant WINTER Mandala collage in a hall space OR large space – 10 minutes*

- Ask each of the children to lay their circular artworks on the floor.
- Starting in a central position (middle of the floor or playground) position the circles in a spiral, starting in the middle and radiating outwards.
- You could also lay the circles out using a different formation or design or try a couple of ideas before deciding on the right one.

Sharing/Reflection: *15 minutes*
Stand around the final formation on the floor and invite participants to share their responses to the WINTER Mandala.
Feedback on the creative process – what is it like to contribute to the Giant Mandala?
How do they look as part of a collaborative design?
Teacher or adult helper to stand on a chair or higher point to photograph the collaborative artwork for posterity.

Key Vocabulary/Questions:	Extension Activities:
Mandala, mindfulness, senses, creativity, collaboration What makes WINTER so unique?	If there is a wall space big enough the design could be stuck to a wall with white tack to be appreciated by a wider audience. At the end of term individual circles can be taken home by children to be hung up on the wall to mark the season of WINTER.

As we close our WINTER SEASON, here is one last creative exercise to try at home

---

TRY THIS AT HOME: Creating Natural Ornaments for a Christmas/Pine tree – Pine-cone celebration tree!

Subject: Creative art **Curriculum Links:** Art, RE, History	**Key Skills:** Art and craft-making	**Duration:** 1 hour plus

Resources & Creative Materials: Natural materials – pinecones, corks, PVA or wood glue Different coloured wool Acrylic or thick paint, card	**Location:** Inside or outside

Learning Objectives:

- To learn about evergreen trees which keep their leaves/needles across seasons
- To learn about the history behind Christmas pine trees and the more ancient use of evergreens, such as palms, in the home across different religions
- To learn about how pine trees contain 'phytoncides'
  - Invisible chemicals which help our bodies relax and feel calm
- To connect with natural objects to make Christmas tree ornaments

Introduction & Warm-Up: *15 minutes*

- Evergreen trees and plants have been used to decorate homes since ancient times.
  - Ancient Egyptians, Romans, Vikings, Celts brought branches inside.
- As evergreen plants keep their leaves all year round, people brought them inside to remind them of everlasting life, and that the sun would return in Summer.
- Ancient people believed evergreens would keep away ghosts and illness.
- Scientists have now discovered that pine trees release 'phytoncides', invisible chemicals, proven to make us feel calm; that's why pines smell so good!
- The story of the first Christmas tree is said to have happened in Germany, when Martin Luther, a Christian, was walking home at night. Looking at the night stars through a pine forest, he brought a tree inside his home.
- With no electricity or baubles in the olden days, people had to use natural decorations for trees: home-made cakes, candles, fruit, nuts, apples etc...

Key Activity: *Pinecone trees* – *45 minutes*
Carefully glue the cork to the bottom of the pinecone to make a mini tree – use a strong glue so that this is secure.

- Carefully paint the tree to reflect celebration – bright colours or more traditional festive colours.
- Make tiny decorations from coloured card/found objects to attach to your tree.

Sharing/Reflection: *5 minutes*
Where are you going to put this mini-tree or are you going to gift it to someone? It could be placed in the home or hung on a Christmas tree.

Key Vocabulary/Questions: Phytoncides – invisible chemicals released by pine trees	**Extension Activities:** Create more trees until you have a magical forest.

SPRING

"It is SPRING again. The earth is like a child that knows poems off by heart."

Rainer Maria Rilke (Swiss poet)

March, April, May

In the Northern Hemisphere

September, October, November

In the Southern Hemisphere

SPRING SEASON, FOLKLORE, AND CREATIVE ACTIVITIES

- Introduction to SPRING

- Opening Activity – SPRING Stretch/Walk and Word Collection

A retelling of *Eostre, a Goddess of SPRING and Her Hare Messenger* from the UK and Germany

- Creating a Magical SPRING Hare Story

- Creating a Postcard to Welcome SPRING

- Creating Spring Hare Silhouette Lanterns (plus resources)

- Devising A Story - Starter About A Magic Egg

A retelling of *Baba Marta – Grandmother Spring* from Bulgaria

- Designing a Life-sized Person of SPRING using Mixed Media

- Creating Three Tableaux of *Baba Marta – Grandmother SPRING*

- Making a Traditional Martenitsa Bracelet to Welcome Spring

- Creating Animal Masks to Represent Different Emotions

A retelling of *The Red Bud Tree* from India

- Creating The Four Stages of *The Red Bud Tree*

- Performing *The Red Bud Tree* and Hot Seating

- Creating Song Lyrics for *The Red Bud Tree*

- Painting a Still Life of Blossom

A retelling of traditions associated with Beltane from the British Isles

- Creating your own Origin Story for the Green Man

- Creating a Green Man Foliate Mask

- Creating a Tree of Support Image (plus resources)

- Making Miniature Clay Tree Creatures

DOI: 10.4324/9781003178682-9

A retelling of *The Legend of the Tylwyth Teg Doorway* from Wales

- Creating a 'Magic Doorway' Folktale of Our Own

- Creating a Miniature World of the Tylwyth Teg Magical Isle

- Creating Magical, Exotic Flower Blossoms with Ink Drops

- Creating a Spring Diamante Poem (plus resources)

Closing exercise

- Personal/collective associations with SPRING and Giant Group Mandala

Try this at home

- Decorating SPRING Eggs

Introduction to SPRING

As we spot our first tree blossoms and flowers, SPRING is when we experience nature waking up. With the arrival of warmer weather and lighter evenings, SPRING shows us nature's rebirth after the long Winter months. People often say 'SPRING is in the air' or 'SPRING fever' as they hear birdsong and see an increase in animal activity and energy. Bees and butterflies start to emerge. The colour palette changes in the sky and landscape, bringing warmer and brighter tones of yellow, green, and blue. As we physically feel more sunlight, our bodies can also feel like they are waking up and have more energy. Often, SPRING brings a sense of hope and positivity. The very word 'SPRING' suggests nature bursting and SPRINGing back to life.

SPRING is an easy season to appreciate. Not too hot, not too cold, SPRING shows us the emergence of new life. However harsh the winter, SPRING always comes, bringing an array of flowers and colours. For ancient peoples, who lived with the land so closely, the return of plant-life must have been a joyous moment and a huge relief. Food could be grown again. With no central heating, the benefits of warmer weather would have been physically felt by everybody. As a result, it's not surprising then that SPRING has inspired strong traditions in folklore and storytelling across the world. Stories tell of the return of the sun and new life. Often SPRING rituals and celebrations brought people outside. As we've seen already in other seasons, many characters in folktales personify natural forces and seasonal change. Some of the world's religious festivals, symbols, and holidays also tap into older traditions linked with nature's rhythms, often tied in with the SPRING Equinox which occurs around 20 or 21 March, the astronomical start of SPRING, where the two hemispheres change over seasons. The Spring Equinox is when there are equal amounts of light and night-time hours in one day.

In the following story section, we've collected folklore characters and stories from places that celebrate SPRING in the Northern or Southern Hemispheres. Although we've rooted folktales in specific countries, versions of these stories will naturally cross borders and may live elsewhere in different shapes and forms.

Some stories tell how some cultures believe SPRING came about. Others explore specific aspects of SPRING life or how nature and cultural/religious rituals interconnect. In selecting our five folktales for SPRING, we've tried to choose lesser-known stories. Equally, we recognise that there are so many other stories out there. We hope ours are useful starting places that can encourage your own interest in collecting SPRING folklore tales. A selection of creative activities is offered for each folklore tale; drama, creative writing, and art making activities can help children engage with nature and folklore stories.

SPRING offers children, families, and classrooms a range of creative possibilities to explore the qualities and rhythms of this season through storytelling, visual art making, drama, and movement. With the milder weather associated with SPRING, there is also a real opportunity to run creative sessions outside, and have children and adults enjoy the natural world.

ACTIVITY: SPRING STRETCH/WALK AND WORD COLLECTION		
Subject: Wellbeing **Curriculum Links:** English, PSHE	**Key Skills:** Sensation, mindfulness, observation	**Duration:** 1 hour

Resources & Creative Materials:	Location:
Our senses and sensations Strips of paper in seasonal colours, pens/pencils, a box	Outside

Learning Objectives:

- To teach mindfulness techniques and support children in mind/body wellbeing
- To introduce concepts of waking up, new life, and rebirth in the SPRING season
- To create a box of SPRING words, sensations, objects, and images

Introduction & Warm-Up: *15 minutes*
Explain mindfulness and walking meditation principles behind a SPRING stretch/walk:

- A way of observing and moving through the world without judgement.
- Slowing down and allowing our bodies and minds to relax.

Invite children first to stand in a circle outside to practice noticing through the senses.

- In silence, feel the ground beneath your feet and notice what is happening around you.
- What do you see and hear, what temperature do you feel on your skin?

Key Activity: *35 minutes*
Activity 1 –*SPRING Stretch & Walk – 20 minutes*

- Explain how in SPRING, animals, plants, humans... all start to slowly wake up
- It's a time of new life – when seeds grow, and animals start to have babies.
- Invite children to walk slowly in outside space, and then to yawn and stretch... and then they can move at their normal pace, observing their environment.
  - Give attention to their senses – colours, sounds, feelings
  - What do they notice as they look around them? Weather, clouds, sky?
  - What do they see around them – any new leaves on the trees, birds, buds?
  - Any sounds – birdsong, wind?
  - Are there any natural objects that they find on their way – leaf, stone, etc?

Invite children to walk in a SPRINGY, bouncy way... and then gradually come to a stop.

Activity 2 – *Gathering together of winter words, images, sensations – 15 minutes*

- On a strip of paper, each child writes a few SPRING words or sensations.
- Place these and any objects in a SPRING box or create a display.

Sharing/Reflection: *10 minutes*
Invite participants to stand/sit in a circle and share their responses to the SPRING Walk.
Any feelings, sensations, surprises? Any objects that they picked up along the way? How did they feel on their SPRING walk?

Key Vocabulary/Questions:	Extension Activities:
Rebirth, new life, mindfulness, imagery, senses What kind of senses and words are unique to SPRING?	SPRING words can be fanned out and displayed.

SPRING Folktale 1 from the British Isles and Germany

A retelling of *Eostre, a goddess of SPRING and her Hare messenger* folktale

Some say that Eostre is an ancient Anglo-Saxon goddess of the SPRING, associated with new life and the dawn, and maybe the root of the name 'Easter'. It is said that Eostre would change into a hare every full moon. Serving as messengers, Hares were special to her. Sometimes, Eostre is depicted as having a hare's head and shoulders.

When Eostre, goddess of the Dawn, was trying to bring light and warmth into the world, it's said that she had a bird as a messenger. The bird was too small and light to travel in all climates and weathers, and so Eostre transformed it into a hare…

This hare was a quick-footed, furry companion who could leap to great heights and help carry the lights of SPRING. That way, the hare could help summon forth the return of SPRING from even the coldest and most frozen of temperatures.

In memory of the hare once being a bird, Eostre rewarded it by giving it the gift of laying brightly coloured eggs once a year at Easter, as the egg is a symbol of the awakening of earth and the renewal of life.

ACTIVITY: CREATING A MAGICAL SPRING HARE STORY		
Subject: Wellbeing **Curriculum Links:** English, PSHE	**Key Skills:** Storytelling, creative writing, oracy	**Duration:** 1 hour
Resources & Creative Materials: Paper, pencils, and pens Synopses of Hare stories (below)		**Location:** Inside or outside

Learning Objectives:

- To teach children about the Hare, and mythology it has inspired in many countries
- To introduce idea of using animals as metaphors in folklore and storytelling
- To create our own Hare folktale

Introduction & Warm-Up: *15 minutes*

In the Eostre folktale, the Hare plays an important role of bringing the light of SPRING. Ancient peoples across the world thought that the Hare was a magical creature. Like a rabbit, but with much longer ears, and legs, the hare can do lots of special things...

- The Hare can reach speeds of 72 kilometres/45 miles an hour and jump up to ten feet/three metres in the air! Hares are known for their boxing and aerial acrobatics!
- Hares are found all over the world except Antarctica. There is a white Arctic Hare. The Hare is native to the British Isles... the Rabbit was brought later by the Romans.
- Boudicca the warrior queen, kept a hare inside her tunic when she went into battle!
- Maybe that's why there are so many folklore stories about Hares across the world.

Key Activity: *30 minutes*

Activity 1: *Share examples of Hare Folklore stories from across the world – 10 minutes*

- The Algonquin Great Hare in North America brought summer to defeat winter.
- The hare from Ceylon/Sri Lanka threw himself into the fire to feed Buddha and was rewarded by being placed on the moon.
- The African trickster hare tricked a lion into fighting his own reflection to save himself.
- An Irish hare is injured by the great warrior, Oisin. When Oisin follows the hare down to an underground hall, he finds an injured woman on a throne!
- Gwion transforms into a Welsh hare to escape Ceridwen after he accidentally stole the wisdom she was brewing for her son.

Activity 2: *Creating our own Hare SPRING folktale – 20 minutes*

- On a piece of paper, each group writes a short folktale about a magical Hare bringing SPRING to the world, deciding where you'd like your Hare to come from – which country?
- Let your imaginations run wild to create your story. Here are some questions as aids: What role might your Hare play in the bringing of SPRING? What magic powers does your Hare have? How might the light and warmth of SPRING be brought by your Hare?

Reflection/Sharing: *20 minutes*

Invite participants to stand/sit in a circle and share their short stories about the Hare.
What was it like to create this story, and listen to others' stories?

Key Vocabulary/Questions: Algonquin Great Hare, Eostre, Oisin, African trickster, Boudicca, Gwion, Ceridwen Why do you think people were inspired by the Hare?	**Extension Activities:** Act out the story as a drama. Find African hare trickster stories.

ACTIVITY: CREATING A POSTCARD TO WELCOME SPRING		
Subject: Visual arts, Creative writing **Curriculum Links:** Art, Writing	**Key Skills:** Drawing, print making, writing	**Duration:** 1 hour 10 minutes
Resources & Creative Materials: (per child) *Eostre* folktale White card postcards – A5 size White paper, notebooks, scrap paper Pencils, drawing boards or clip boards (if outside) Leaves, feathers (or children can collect them as part of the lesson), rollers, block printing ink – shades of green		**Location:** Inside or outside Preferably outdoors if possible

Learning Objectives:

- To learn how to use printmaking with natural objects
- To think about the unique characteristics of SPRING as a season
- To use our senses to help us write a postcard to SPRING

Introduction & Warm-Up: *5 minutes*

- If outdoors begin by sitting quietly on the ground observing what you can see, smell, hear (can also collect a few leaves or feathers from the ground).
- If indoors sit quietly with eyes closed imagining a sunny SPRING Day.

Key Activity: *55 minutes*
Activity 1: *Writing and Illustrating the post card – 35 minutes*
Stage 1: Decorating the SPRING postcard (Small groups outside at a table) 20 mins p/group

1. Carefully roll a small amount of ink into a paint tray.
2. Use the inky roller to roll ink onto the textured sides of leaves or feathers on a piece of newspaper/newsprint (when this gets very inky change it).
3. Carefully place the leaf *ink side down* onto the postcard and gently roll with a CLEAN roller – peel off the leaf to reveal a leaf print.
4. Keep printing leaves / feathers onto the postcard until you have no more space left (If time each child could print more than one postcard).
5. Peg the finished postcards onto a washing line outside to dry.

Activity 2: *Writing postcard– write on the actual postcards when they are dry – 20 minutes*
On a rough piece of paper begin writing the words for your postcard to SPRING.
Begin with 'Dear SPRING, I have missed... warm days, playing outside etc.
Encourage children to have their own ideas from their own unique experiences – first draft can be a brainstorm!
Once children are happy with what they have written – ask them to neatly write on the back of the postcard in whatever colours they like.

Sharing/Reflection: *10 minutes*
Invite the class to share their postcards to SPRING. Discuss who they would send their SPRING postcards to. Who would deliver it? Animal or human or other?

Key Vocabulary/Questions: Colour, print, texture, ink, natural forms	**Extension Activities:** Add SPRING symbols to postcard – eggs, hares, rabbits, flowers. Send as an Easter Card.

ACTIVITY: CREATING SPRING HARE SILHOUETTE LANTERNS		
Subject: Creative arts **Curriculum Links:** Art, design	**Key Skills:** Design/technology, paper art	**Duration:** 1 hour (not including prep time)

Resources & Creative Materials: (per child) Hare template Three Hare image (page overleaf) 2 litre recycled plastic bottle – labels removed and empty Sharp knife or scissors (adults to use) Coloured masking tape, single hole punch Coloured tissue paper (SPRING Colours scheme) Glue / Pritt sticks Battery pack fairy lights (optional) Coloured cord / string A5 templates of a hare (hare smaller than A5) Pencils, Scissors	**Location:** Inside

Learning Objectives:

- To learn skills in 3D artmaking
- To find out about the universal motif of the hare in different cultures
- To experiment with leaf design

Introduction & Warm-Up: *5 minutes*

- Explain how the three hares is an international motif that appears on cultural artifacts from England, France, Germany, China, and other places.
- This common motif shows three hares running in a circle – each hare shares one ear as you can see in our example on page x, to complete the whole.

Key Activity: *Making the Hare Lantern – 5 minutes*
Stage 1: Preparing the lantern shapes (**this should be done by an adult in advance of the session** – or with older children carefully supervised)

1. Carefully cut away the top part of the plastic bottle so you are left with a long plastic cylinder shape with a solid base. You might like to mark the line where you cut first to make it easier.
2. Carefully run a piece of tape around the cut edge, overlapping it as it may be sharp to the touch.
3. Use the hole punch to make two holes directly opposite each other in the top of the cylinder.

Stage 2: *Decorating the lanterns – 30 minutes*

1. Using the template draw and cut out at least three different coloured hare shapes from the tissue paper – discuss what SPRING colours are before inviting children to choose their own colours from a selection.
2. Ask children to also cut out different patterns like leaves/stars/circles/from the coloured tissue paper and make as many as you like.
3. Carefully examine your plastic container and decide where to place your hares and patterns on it to create a design. This design could be drawn on paper first.
4. Very carefully stick the tissue shapes onto the plastic bottle – don't worry about overlapping shapes, this can look visually interesting as the tissue is transparent and colours will blend.
5. **Avoid covering the two holes in the sides with tissue** – feel free to cover the tape!

Stage 3: *10 minutes*

1. Thread a long piece of cord or string through the two holes at the top of the container and tie at each end to create a handle.
2. A small fairy lights battery pack can be placed inside the lantern at the bottom and switched on when it's dark.
3. All the lanterns could also be hung on a line in the classroom to create a SPRING light display OR attached to short garden sticks for a SPRING Parade outside!

Sharing/Reflection: *10 minutes*
Share the SPRING Hare Lanterns in the group and talk about the patterns that were created.

Key Vocabulary/Questions:	**Extension Activities:**
Colour, pattern, design, recycle, motif, hare	Have a procession with the children carrying their lanterns. Investigate the three-hare motif and look at where it appears in the world.

ACTIVITY: DEVISING A STORY-STARTER ABOUT A MAGIC EGG		
Subject: Creative writing **Curriculum Links:** English, science	**Key Skills:** Writing	**Duration:** 1 hour

Resources & Creative Materials: *Eostre* folktale An egg with strange markings (you can use paint or pens to decorate a boiled egg)	**Location:** Inside and outside

Learning Objectives:

- To learn how to treat animals in nature
- To identify what eggs and animals might need
- To create an intriguing and exciting beginning to a story

Introduction & Warm-Up: *10 minutes*

- Eggs are the symbol of new life so often are the symbol of SPRING.
- Reveal your strange looking egg that you prepared earlier.
- Explain how you found it on your way to school. You looked for a mother bird, but no one came.
- What could be inside the egg? Can the children use their imaginations so it's something unexpected? It could be a magical being or a normal creature you wouldn't expect – like a puppy or a pony.
- How do you think we should look after it now? If we made it a nest, what could we use? Eggs need to be incubated – so it needs to be warm at all times.

Key Activity: *35 minutes*

The children are going to write the start of a story, and here are some ideas to help them plan it. Imagine you discover an egg somewhere in nature.

- Where do you find it? Perhaps at the bottom of a tree or in a hedge? You wait, but it looks like it's been abandoned. So, you pick it up and bring it home.
- Where do you put it? Do you make a nest in your sock drawer, or do you bring in straw and leaves from outside?
- How does it open?
- What creature is inside? Is there tapping, followed by a crack? Or does it open like the petals on a flower? Perhaps it is an alien egg?
- How do you provide for it now? How do you make sure it is well looked after?
- Can you leave the story on a cliff hanger? Perhaps you are keeping the creature a secret and your parent/guardian comes in? Or perhaps your creature breathes fire? Or perhaps the parent/guardian of the new creature comes in breathing fire?

Once you have come up with some ideas, write the beginning of your story.

Sharing/Reflection: *15 minutes*

Invite the children to read their stories aloud.
Think about how an egg is a little seed of life, and out of it comes something extraordinary.
Discuss whether wild animals should ever be pets.

Key Vocabulary/Questions: Eostre, new life, nurture, incubate	**Extension Activities:** Invite the children to draw their creature. Can they write the next chapter in their stories?

SPRING Folktale 2 from Bulgaria
A retelling of *Baba Marta – Grandmother Spring*

In Bulgaria, many people celebrate a festival where Baba Marta personifies SPRING. On 1 March (Grandmother March Day), it is said that she brings SPRING to the world, ending the cold months of winter. However, as weather in March is often erratic, Baba Marta is portrayed as being feisty and having big mood swings.

On the day of the festival, people give each other a Martenitsa – red and white woven threads – to be worn around the wrist, or sometimes made into dolls. They offer health and happiness. People wear them until they see the first signs of SPRING – such as a blossom, swallow, or crane. They then tie them onto the first blossoming fruit tree they see.

Once upon a time there lived a feisty old woman named Baba Marta (Grandmother March).

On 1 March, she started her spring cleaning. She shook out her mattress and all the feathers poured out of it, creating the last snowfall on earth. Baba Marta felt happy and content. She smiled a big smile, and the sun came out. The skies grew clear, the air warmed, and nature reawakened. Flowers began to bloom. Young bears, wolves, hedgehogs, and foxes came out to play. And everyone felt happy…

Until Baba Marta's troublesome brothers caused trouble. Big Sechko (known as January) and Small Sechko (known as February) stole her favourite drink that she'd been saving, and they made an absolute mess in the house at the top of the mountains where they all lived. Baba Marta was furious. How dare they! Especially after all her spring cleaning! Her smile turned cold, and she stamped her feet. The sun vanished, instantly replaced by cold winds, rain, and snow.

Her brothers begged forgiveness. Baba Marta folded her arms, but after a short while she decided to forgive them. She smiled lovingly and the sun reappeared, bringing warm air and clear skies. It felt like SPRING again.

ACTIVITY: DESIGNING A LIFE-SIZED PERSON OF SPRING USING MIXED MEDIA		
Subject: Visual arts **Curriculum Links:** Art	**Key Skills:** Personification, artmaking collage, mixed media skills collaboration	**Duration:** 1 hour 20 minutes
Resources & Creative Materials: *Baba Marta – Grandmother SPRING* folktale Large rolls of paper, possibly wallpaper or lining paper Paints, art, and craft materials Leaves or flowers found on the ground		**Location:** Inside

Learning Objectives:

- To create a life size personification of SPRING
- To think about the different natural elements that would bring SPRING to life
- To collaborate in groups in artmaking

Introduction & Warm-Up: *10 minutes*

- Together, read *Baba Marta – Grandmother SPRING.*
- Discuss how her moods bring the erratic weather we get at SPRINGTIME. Sunny one day, rain the next etc.
- What do you imagine Baba Marta looks like?
- We are going to create our own personification of SPRING – either male, female or non-binary.
- How do you imagine Spring to look? For you personally, would she be older like Baba Marta or a younger person?
- Brainstorm how the season could be interpreted – for example a skirt made from clouds, hair made from sunbeams, a beard made from sheep.

Key Activity: *1 hour*

- In groups, choose to create either a male, female or non-binary SPRING, old or young.
- Draw around someone in your group to use as a human template.
- Use paints or other art and crafts to incorporate as much of SPRING into your person. Ideas include blossoming trees and flowers, the weather, the animals.

Sharing/Reflection: *10 minutes*
Wander around each person. Explore the different expression of SPRING? What were the reasons for showing SPRING in this way? Are the interpretations similar or different? How did they find working collaboratively?

Key Vocabulary/ Questions: Personification, interpretation, collaboration Why have you chosen these media?	**Extension Activities:** Create a poem based on your SPRING person.

ACTIVITY: CREATING THREE TABLEAUX OF *BABA MARTA – GRANDMOTHER SPRING*		
Subject: Performance art **Curriculum Links:** English	**Key Skills:** Splitting of scenes Creating a tableau Collaboration	**Duration:** 35 minutes

Resources & Creative Materials:
Baba Marta – Grandmother SPRING folktale
A device to take photos

Location:
Inside or outside

Learning Objectives:

- To use your body to create an image
- To work together to create a tableau
- To use your imagination to fill in the blank of a story
- To embody a cold and warm scene

Introduction & Warm-Up: *5 minutes*
Explain to the children that they are going to use their bodies to sculpt something out of the story and nature. Working in groups, they have 30 seconds to become a shape. They can be separate or physically connected. Examples include:

- A tree
- A wolf
- A mountain
- Warm sun
- Cold wind

Key Activity: *20 minutes*

- Explain how a tableau is a technique where actors freeze in poses that capture a picture of an important moment in a play.
- In the same groups, ask them to create 3 tableaux of:
  a. Baba Marta happy and smiling. Other members of the group could be trees, animals, the weather. Perhaps she is SPRING cleaning.
  b. The brothers Big Sechko (January) and Small Sechko (February) doing something really annoying. It can be anything. Let your imaginations go wild. Are some animals watching on in horror? Is Baba Marta there?
  c. Baba Marta scowling and stamping her foot. What is the weather, the brothers, the animals doing now?

Sharing/Reflection: *10 minutes*
Share your tableau with the other groups and have someone take a photograph of each scene. Can you work out what the brothers are doing that is so annoying?

Key Vocabulary/Questions: Tableau, scene What happens next?	**Extension Activities:** Create a comic on Baba Marta using your tableau as inspiration.

ACTIVITY: MAKING A TRADITIONAL MARTENITSA BRACELET TO WELCOME SPRING		
Subject: Visual arts **Curriculum Links:** Arts, Geography	**Key Skills:** Making, crafting	**Duration:** 40 minutes

Resources & Creative Materials:	Location:
Martenitsa red and white colour thread Yellow and green thread (often used in traditional embroidery), scissors	Inside or outside if a mild day

Learning Objectives:

- To learn how to use plaiting threads as in the art-making of the Martenitsa
- To find out about colour meanings in traditional craft
- To find out about the symbolic nature of this Bulgarian cultural tradition in SPRING

Introduction & Warm-Up: *5 minutes*
We are going to making a bracelet to welcome SPRING inspired by the Bulgarian tradition of a Martenitsa. They will look a bit familiar, because they look like our friendship bracelets.

- It's traditionally a red and white bracelet (or sometimes a woollen doll) which is traditionally worn from 1 March until you see a stork, swallow, or a blossoming tree.
- The colours are thought to represent the coming of SPRING and hope for the end of WINTER and is used to celebrate nature.
- Once taken off, the Martenitsa is then attached to the first blossoming fruit tree people see.
- We are also offering a choice of extra colours – green and yellow – which are traditional in Bulgarian embroidery – very SPRING-like, sun and grass...

Key Activity: *25 minutes*
There are lots of videos on YouTube to show how to make the traditional Martenitsa woven bracelets. Here is a simple method to make our bracelets to welcome SPRING.

- Cut 12 lengths of thread to 30 cm length(use a mix of colours).
- Divide cut pieces of thread into **three sections** of **four** strands and lie flat on a table.
- Gather all 12 strands at the end and tie in a knot.
- Separate the three sections again and lie flat again.
- Slowly plait the three sections together – overlapping from the outside in.*
- When you have finished plaiting the whole length – carefully knot the end.

*NB: if your group have not plaited before it would be good to practise first.

Reflection/Sharing: *10 minutes*

- Encourage the group to wear their bracelets until they see a swallow or tree in blossom (or stork) to mark the arrival of SPRING (or a sign relevant to where you are located).
- As the colour red is also seen as a colour to symbolise warmth, companionship, and mutual affection suggest that the group swap bracelets with each other OR keep their own if they want to. *Once decided carefully tie the woven strands to wrists.*

Traditionally, at the first sign of SPRING a Martenitsa bracelet is hung on a fruit tree or placed beneath a stone – request the group report back if they notice any of the first signs of Spring – discuss what you could do with the bracelets in the context of where you live.

Key Vocabulary/Questions:	Extension Activities:
Weave, colour, textures, Martenitsa What SPRING traditions do you have in your culture?	Research Martenitsa tradition. Make other friendship bracelets.

ACTIVITY: CREATING ANIMAL MASKS TO REPRESENT DIFFERENT EMOTIONS		
Subject: Creative arts, wellbeing, performing arts **Curriculum Links:** Art, English, Drama, PSHE	**Key Skills:** Art, drama, oracy	**Duration:** 1 hour and 50 minutes

Resources & Creative Materials: *Baba Marta – Grandmother SPRING* folktale Paper plates, cardboard (recycled), paint, paint brushes, oil pastels, sugar paper, tissue paper, string Natural materials, feathers, leaves (found on ground)	**Location:** Inside or outside (on mild day)

Learning Objectives:

- To explore our moods and feelings through the metaphor of animals
- To use personification and mask-making to bring different characteristics to life
- To create dialogues between different animals

Introduction & Warm-Up: *15 minutes*
In the *Grandmother SPRING* folktale, Baba Marta's moods dictate the weather.

- Discuss how different animals can represent certain qualities and emotions
- Which animals do we associate with anger, shyness, kindness, speed, slowness?
- In a circle, invite children to enact sounds/gestures for different animals:
  - Tiger, mouse, hedgehog, bird, etc
  - How can we tell what these animals are feeling and communicating?

Key Activity: *1 hour*
Activity 1: *Mask making – 45 minutes*
Create a mask for an animal that represents a certain quality, feeling, or emotion. You can choose an animal that you feel represents a side of you, or maybe you'd like to choose a creature that is very different – if you are naturally noisy, you might want to choose a shy, quieter animal, or if you are a bit quiet, one that is louder.

- Choose creative materials to bring your animal mask to life.
- Think about how you want to communicate the qualities of your chosen animal.
- If you like, you can give each animal a name.

Activity 2: *Creating a drama dialogue – 15 minutes – in pairs*
Find a partner – preferably someone who has a very different animal to yours and spend some time creating a dialogue between the different animals.

- Starter phrases can be "I feel…, I want…, I need…, I wish…, I care about…" and then complete the sentence.
- Swap the masks with a partner to experiment with different animal personalities.

Sharing/Reflection: *20 minutes*
Invite volunteers to come forward to perform a drama dialogue with their masks.
Invite children to feedback on process. What was it like to swap masks?
What did they learn about themselves and their own nature in this exercise?

Key Vocabulary/Questions: Personification, metaphor How do animals represent different sides of ourselves?	**Extension Activities:** Capture the dialogue and drama through writing it down.

SPRING Folktale 3 from India
A retelling of *The Red Bud Tree* Folktale

The Red Bud Tree is a folktale that comes from India, part of the Jataka tales, with messages of how nature can teach us valuable learnings about life. This story is based in the time when King Bramadutta ruled the city of Banaras.

Once four young princes heard the legend of a very special tree - the Red Bud Tree. As they'd never seen one before, each prince wished to visit it. The eldest son asked the king's charioteer to take him into the woods where this tree grew.

On finding it, the eldest son was disappointed. Given it was so early in SPRINGTIME, the tree had no leaves or buds, only bare branches. Later in the SPRING, the next son went with the king's charioteer to visit the tree, to find it covered in red buds, even more beautiful than he could have imagined. When the third son went later to see it, it flourished with green leaves. When the youngest prince asked to see the Red Bud Tree even later, it had grown little bean-pods all over. When the youngest came back he ran to his brothers in dismay, calling out:

"I've seen the Red Bud Tree, but it had no redbuds, only little bean-pods!"
"No, I didn't see that," said the eldest prince. "It looked bare … almost dead."
"Oh no, you are mistaken," cried the second son. "The tree has so many red buds, vibrant and blossoming, all over."
The third prince shook his head: "You're mistaken, there were only green leaves."

The king overheard their conversation. Once the four princes had stopped arguing, he cried out: "My dear boys, you have each seen the same tree, just at a different time of the year!"

ACTIVITY: CREATING THE FOUR STAGES OF THE RED BUD TREE		
Subject: Visual arts **Curriculum Links:** Art	**Key Skills:** Drawing, designing, tree rubbing	**Duration:** 1 hour 40 minutes

Resources & Creative Materials: (per child)	Location: Inside or outside*
The Red Bud Tree folktale White A4 paper, pencils, wax crayons Scissors, glue sticks Colouring equipment pencils/crayons/felt tips Sellotape (to share) Images of the *butea frondose*, which is the Red Bud Tree Examples of blossom trees at different stages	*It would be great if you were able to access a blossom tree during the SPRING Season and notice the stages from bare branches to bloom.

Learning Objectives:

- To learn to recognise changes in nature across the seasons
- To appreciate and connect with trees – their texture and unique nature
- To learn how to make a tree rubbing

Introduction & Warm-Up: *15 minutes*
Outside, read the story of *The Red Bud Tree*, discussing what each of the four Princes saw when they visited the Red Bud Tree.

- Identify what the tree looked like in the four stages: Bare/Bud and blossom/ Leaves/Bean Pods (fruit).

Key Activity: *1 hour and 5 minutes*
Stage 1: *Tree rubbing – 20 minutes.* Ask each child to make a rubbing from the trunk of the tree by placing a piece of paper against the side of the tree and gently rubbing on top with the **side** of a wax crayon until the texture is revealed:

- Make sure to cover the whole side of A4 paper.
- Repeat this on four different trees on four different pieces of paper.
- Outcome = four pieces of A4 with rubbings on per child.
- Whilst outside discuss and compare the different textures and how you found the process.

Stage 2: *Indoors OR at an outside table if possible – 15 minutes*

1. Each child to stretch/extend their fingers and lay flat onto one of the tree rubbings pages – each child to draw around their hand and a bit of their arm to create a 'tree' outline.
2. Repeat on all four of the rubbing pages.
3. Cut out all four hand shapes.
4. Stick each hand onto a separate piece of white paper with a glue stick – you now have four tree shapes.
5. Label each paper 1/2/3/4 lightly with a pencil.

Stage 3: *30 minutes*

1. Illustrate the four stages of The Red Bud story on each page. Start with pencil.
2. Page 1 is already the bare branches, but you could add a few twig details if you like...
3. Specifically draw what is happening to the **TREE** at each stage but feel free to add other details – animals/birds/moss.
4. Once you are happy with all four images in pencil – colour them in using whatever media you like.
5. Once all four pages are finished attach them together in order (1–4) using tape or a hole punch and string along the spine.

Sharing/Reflection: *10 minutes*
Share your Red Bud Tree books with the class, noticing similarities and differences.

Key Vocabulary/Questions:	**Extension Activities:**
Colour, mixed media, texture, collage, natural forms	You will have blank pages in your books – write a poem inspired by the four stages of SPRING and write it into the book. You could write more than one!

ACTIVITY: PERFORMING *THE RED BUD TREE* FOLKTALE AND HOT SEATING		
Subject: Performing arts **Curriculum Links:** English, Music, Drama	**Key Skills:** Drama, Oracy, Improvisation	**Duration:** 1 hour

Resources & Creative Materials: *The Red Bud Tree* folktale Props for the play – such as tissue paper and twigs	**Location:** Inside or outside

Learning Objectives:

- To embody a character and improvise their history and experience
- To enact out a story through oracy
- To consider the needs of the audience in your performance

Introduction & Warm-Up: *10 minutes*

- Reread *The Red Bud Tree*.
- Play Hot seating:
  1. Ask for a volunteer to pretend to be the first prince.
  2. He/she sits in the centre of the circle, while the children ask the 'prince' questions.
  3. They can ask him what he saw when he looked at the tree, as well as questions about his hobbies and his life in the palace.
  4. Using his/her imagination, the child makes up the answers on the spot. There are no right or wrong answers.
- Repeat with the next three princes, the king, and most importantly, the tree.

Key Activity: *30 minutes*

- In groups of five/six, the children are going to create a play for *The Red Bud Tree*.
- They can add their own creative flair. Someone could be the tree – perhaps rolling their eyes at the princes' mistaken ideas.
- When they rehearse, remind the children that they will have an audience. They need to speak loudly and ensure they face the audience.
- They can include props, such as twigs for the bare branches and tissue paper for the blossoms etc.

Sharing/Reflection: *20 minutes*
Invite the groups to perform their plays. How were they similar and how did they differ? Were there any surprising interpretations?

Key Vocabulary/Questions: Hot-seating, embodiment What is it like to step into the tree or any of the other characters?	**Extension Activities:** Invite the children to write their scripts as if they were creating a screen play

ACTIVITY: CREATING SONG LYRICS FOR *THE RED BUD TREE*		
Subject: Performing arts and creative writing **Curriculum Links:** English, Music Geography	**Key Skills:** Creative writing, singing, oracy	**Duration:** 1 hour 10 minutes
Resources & Creative Materials: *The Red Bud Tree* folktale Paper, pencils, and pens	**Location:** Inside or outside if possible	

Learning Objectives:

- To engage children with the different stages of development in the SPRING season
- To use personification and metaphor in devising song lyrics around tree growth
- To experiment with different musical and rhythmic styles

Introduction & Warm-Up: *10 minutes*
In *The Red Bud Tree* story, each prince witnesses a different stage of growth.

- Discuss the different phases with trees in SPRING and then summer:
  - Buds, the blossoms, the fresh leaves, the leaves, and fruit.
- Look around in the outside area (if possible) for any visual evidence of tree growth and discuss any other trees children know that are in blossom around them.
- What feelings do we have when we see trees in blossom in SPRING?

Key Activity: *40 minutes*
Activity 1: *In small groups, devise song lyrics for The* Red Bud Tree *in SPRING – 30 minutes*

- Decide which point of view you'd like to take, *The Red Bud Tree* or the princes, or both!
- Ideas... you could be the Red Bud Tree experiencing its own growth, or the princes witnessing this growth, or you could create a dialogue between the Red Tree and the princes...
- Create four verses to bring to life the different phases of buds, blossoms, flowers, fruit.
- Decide the music style you sing in... pop, classical, RAP (Rhythm and Poetry), other.

Activity 2: *Rehearse your song – 10 minutes*

Sharing/Reflection: *20 minutes*
Invite participants to stand/sit in a circle and perform their music pieces in small groups.
What was it like to create this story and listen to others' stories?

Key Vocabulary/Questions: Different phases of growth in SPRING, blossoms, personification RAP – Rhythm and Poetry Which music style is most effective?	**Extension Activities:** Create percussion and sound effects for the music pieces.

ACTIVITY: PAINTING A STILL LIFE OF BLOSSOM		
Subject: Visual Arts **Curriculum Links:** Art, Science	**Key Skills:** Making, drawing, painting, creating	**Duration:** 45 minutes

Resources & Creative Materials: (per child) SPRING flowers or blossom branches: Cut flowers/branches in a vase if indoors or at a table outside Wildflowers, SPRING flowers, blossom growing wild – if painting outside at an easel or with a drawing board Painting equipment/watercolour or acrylic paint Brushes Water pots Aprons/drawing boards (if outside) A3 white cartridge paper	**Location:** Inside or outside

Learning Objectives:

- To learn about the importance of blossom in cultures across the world
- To appreciate the ephemeral beauty of blossoming flowers
- To see how blossoms are connected to SPRING
- To learn practical techniques in painting flowers

Introduction & Warm-Up: *5 minutes*

Blossom and flowers are synonymous with SPRING in cultures across the world. In Japan cherry blossoms are called *sakura*, a special flower for the people and the country. Cherry blossoms are a symbolic flower of the SPRING, a time of renewal, and the fleeting nature of life. Given the blossoms start to decay and fall after two weeks, their life is very brief. (By human standards!) During this season in Japan, people have cherry blossom parties with friends and family. They enjoy eating, drinking, and barbecuing underneath the cherry blossoms. They call this custom *hanami*. Hanami means 'blossom watching', and the tradition can be dated back to a thousand years.

An old SPRING tradition in the UK is the May Day Festival celebrated on the 1st of May every year. Its roots can be dated back to pre-Christian times, to the Floralia, an ancient festival that honoured the Roman goddess of flowers, who was known as Floralia. This festival celebrated the richness of nature – the land, the livestock, and the crops.

Key Activity: *Still Life Floralia Painting – 30 minutes*
Set up the flower still life OR painting equipment in a suitable outside location.

1. Ask each child to spend a few moments quietly observing the SPRING flowers; the details, the colours, the shapes, the textures.
2. Ask each child to 'be an artist'; to work quietly and mindfully whilst painting what they see in front of them.
3. Encourage children to fill the page and really focus on the details they can see.
4. It would be a good idea to have a few different size paint brushes available; large for washes of colour and small for details.

Sharing/Reflection: *10 minutes*

- Discuss how they found the observational painting experience.
- Create a flower wall of paintings to celebrate SPRING!
- Display some SPRING flowers with the paintings.
- Invite other groups to view them.
- Let the children take a selfie in front of the flower wall as the season of SPRING flowers is such a short moment in time and needs celebrating.

Key Vocabulary/Questions:	Extension Activities:
Colour, painting, flowers, ephemeral, petals, leaves, blossom, detail, nature's beauty, *hanami,* Floralia, sakura, May Day	Continue flower painting from observation in a sketchbook – it's a very good discipline to improve art skills. Create a flower journal to capture images of flowers you see across SPRING.

Folktale 4 and Beltane traditions from the British Isles
A retelling of Traditions Associated with Beltane

Beltane is the Gaelic May Day festival, most commonly held on 1 May. Historically, it was observed through Ireland, Scotland, and the Isle of Man.

Beltane was a time to mark and honour SPRING waking up and turning warmer, as plants and animals came to life, and people could benefit from growing and harvesting plants again. It was a time to reconnect to the sun's warmth, which is perhaps why ancient peoples lit multiple bonfires and drove their cattle between the fires, as an act of protection.

There are other rituals associated with Beltane, such as a decoration of the May Bush, a small tree or branch – typically hawthorn, rowan, holly, or sycamore – decorated with bright flowers, ribbons, and painted shells. Folklorists believe that these traditions may have come from an older tree-worship where ancient peoples believed in the spirits of trees. The Green Man, a mysterious leafy figurehead that appears all over in churches and cathedrals in the UK, may be part of this tradition. Some folklorists think that the Green Man might have been part of May Day celebrations throughout Northern and Central Europe. As the Green Man is also shown with acorns and hawthorn leaves, symbols of new life, it may indeed have been associated with SPRING.

In England, you can also see traditions of the May Pole continuing today with dancing around a pole (originally a tree branch), and the Jack of the Green, where someone dresses up in leafy branches.

ACTIVITY: CREATING YOUR OWN ORIGIN STORY FOR THE GREEN MAN		
Subject: Performing arts **Curriculum Links:** English, History	**Key Skills:** Imagination and drama	**Duration:** 1 hour
Resources & Creative Materials: 'Traditions Associated with Beltane' Pictures of the Green Man found on churches, ancient buildings, and more modern drawings		**Location:** Inside or outside

Learning Objectives:

- To learn about characters in folklore personifying aspects of nature across the world
- To create your own original folktale
- To perform a folktale in a group setting

Introduction & Warm-Up: *10 minutes*
Show pictures of the Green Man on churches, ancient ruins, and more modern pictures.
Explain how there are signs of the Green Man all over the world, but no one knows his real origin story. Some people believe that the sculptures of him date back to Rome.

- A leaf clad statue of Dionysus/Pan in Italy dates back to 420BC – he is thought to be the first Green Man.
- In Iraq, one dates back to 300BC.
- There's a Green Man from the 8th century in India.
- From the 11th century, he is found all over Europe.

He is associated with the heralding of the SPRING, and it is thought he is a nature god.

Key Activity: *40 minutes*
As no one knows his story, can you make up a folktale of your own explaining the Green Man's origin, a story that can be passed down for generations? Remind the children that he is interlinked with the natural world, so nature needs to play a large part in the story.
In groups, create a play.

- Could he be a wizard conjuring up the SPRING?
- Is he a prince fighting the King of Winter?
- Is he a man that was trapped in a tree by an evil sorcerer?
- Is he a god that emerged from a tree, helping new life grow?
- Or is he a member of the Fae – a human sized fairy – who watches over SPRING?

Enjoy playing with ideas.

Sharing/Reflection: *10 minutes*
Invite groups to perform their folktales.
Are there any similarities or do the stories vary greatly?
How easy is it to create a folktale or a legend?

Key Vocabulary/ Questions: Where do you think the Green Man came from? Origin story, Pan, Dionysus, personification of nature	**Extension Activities:** Using your play as a guide, create a written story that could be passed down for generations. These can be displayed along with the foliate masks (see next activity).

ACTIVITY: CREATING A GREEN MAN FOLIATE MASK		
Subject: English, Music, History **Curriculum Links:** Art, drama	**Key Skills:** Artmaking, creativity	**Duration:** 1 hour 35 minutes
Resources & Creative Materials: A3 cardboard (could be recycled from boxes/cereal packets), sturdy card is better Newspaper, glue Lots of different real leaves – a variety of shapes and sizes is important – found on the ground (Could go on a leaf walk to a green space with a group and collect lots of different leaves) Coloured paper different textures (tissue / sugar / cartridge/ wrapping paper) in shades of green Green garden sticks		**Location:** Inside or outside

Learning Objectives:

- To use our imaginations to connect with nature
- To imagine how ancient people might have related to nature
- To create our own Green Man, Woman or Non-Binary mask

Introduction & Warm-Up: *15 minutes*

No-one knows where The Green Man figure comes from. The mask takes many forms and is found in many ancient cultures from around the world. It's thought The Green Man image might relate to 'Nature gods' or 'Nature goddesses' which embody the natural cycle of life, and the season of SPRING following WINTER. It is seen to represent the cycle of growth and rebirth that happens each SPRING. The 'Foliate Mask' has a long tradition of appearing on sculptures, drawings, and pub signs in many different places. It's often carved out of wood or stone.

Key Activity: *1 hour*

Lay out all the different leaves on a table for children to select from.

Step 1:

1. Cut out a face shape from the stiffer card.
2. Draw where the eyes / nose / mouth go (no detail necessary).
3. Build up the nose/cheeks/lips areas by gluing screwed-up newspaper onto the face shape.

Step 2:

1. Choose a few different leaf shapes and a selection of coloured papers.
2. Draw around the leaf shapes onto the coloured papers – repeat until you have lots of different shapes on different shades of green.
3. Cut out all the leaf shapes, Top tip: cut 3–4 leaves out at the same time.
4. You should now have a collection of different paper leaves in various shades of green.

Step 3:

1. Begin to place the leaves on your face template so that they radiate outwards from the eyes/nose/mouth area.
2. When you are happy with the layout stick the leaves down – it's fine to just stick the tip of the leaves down so that they can overlap each other.
3. When all the leaves are stuck down and your mask is finished – use a piece of tape to attach a gardening stick to the back of the mask.
4. Hold the mask in front of your face.

Sharing/reflection: *20 minutes*
Invite children to group together with their masks. What are their responses, feedback to the exercises? Any surprises. Take a group picture of everyone holding their masks in front of their faces – do they look like a forest of trees?
Think of animals/characters that disguise themselves by blending into the background using camouflage.

Key Vocabulary/Questions:
The Green Man, SPRING as a symbol of rebirth and new life, Foliate
Fun fact: Camouflage – to disguise – comes from the French word and only entered the English language in WW1. Before then, the British navy called camouflage dazzle painting!

Extension Activities:
Try this outdoors in nature by collecting leaves and making leaf masks on the ground – maybe you could make a whole leaf person! Take photos of your creations before they disappear back into nature...

ACTIVITY: CREATING A TREE OF SUPPORT IMAGE		
Subject: Wellbeing, Visual arts **Curriculum Links:** Art, PSHE	**Key Skills:** Mindfulness, image-making	**Duration:** 1 hour 15 minutes

Resources & Creative Materials:	Location:
Mindfulness, guided visualisation, a green or nature area Oil pastels, felt-tips, paints, tissue paper, textiles Guided Visualisation overleaf	Inside or outside

Learning Objectives:

- To learn about how trees have been important for many different cultures
- To learn about the concept of *viriditas* – greening power, growth, and life force
- To find out about some of the practices of 'forest bathing' as a tool for mindfulness
- To help children go into their own imagination for self-support
- To create an image of a personal Tree of Support

Introduction & Warm-Up: *15 minutes*

Humans have a long tradition of valuing trees. Often people believed trees had spirits inside them. Germany is a country with a rich history in appreciating tree-life.

- One thousand years ago, there was a German abbess who was a composer, philosopher, a writer, and a lover of nature called Hildegard of Bingen. Inspired by how trees and plants could regenerate themselves across the season, she believed that humans also had a life force inside them that could help them grow in healthy and meaningful ways in life. She named this life force *viriditas*, a 'greening power' that was inside us all.

Japan is another country with its own unique way of relating to trees.

- The Japanese tradition of *shinrin-yoku*, forest bathing, of mindfulness in the forest, is becoming more widely known. This is the practice of being mindful and attentive in the forest, giving attention to our senses and connecting with trees and nature.

Discuss with children how we can feel being around trees... Trees can give us strength, calm, stillness, a place to lean against, a climbing frame, and a sense of feeling grounded.

Key Activity: *40 minutes*
Activity 1: *Tree guided visualisation outside or inside – 10 minutes*
Invite children to sit down, and imagine that they are walking through a special, magical forest full of beauty and calm. Invite children to imagine they find a special tree there just for them, which will be their very own personal Tree of Support.

• Read the Guided Visualisation exercise overleaf.

Activity 2: *Create an image of your Magical Tree of Support – 30 minutes*
Invite each child to take their time and make an image of their Tree of Support.

• Encourage them to experiment with different materials to bring it to life.
• Encourage them to follow their hands and use the materials freely to let the tree take shape,To bring its roots and branches to life in whatever way they'd like.
• Encourage children to make the tree in any way they like and follow their imagination (it doesn't have to look like any recognisable tree!).

Sharing/Reflection: *20 minutes*
Create a gallery of trees in the centre, a forest of Trees of Support.
Invite children to stand in a circle around the trees, and ask for feedback on their experience.
What was it like to enter this forest in their imagination, and make their own unique trees?
What do they notice about the forest of trees before them?

Key Vocabulary/Questions:	**Extension Activities:**
Viriditas, Hildegard of Bingen, *shinrin-yoku*, forest bathing	Find a safe space to observe nature either sitting outside or looking out of a window. Try to use your different senses to notice what is going on. This place is sometimes called a 'Sit Spot'.
Feeling grounded – what is this, and why is it important?	
How does the forest of trees make them feel?	

Example of guided visualisation for Tree of Support and nature self-reflection exercise

A guided visualisation can be used to help children relax and enter their imaginations. In reading it, try to pace it slowly and gently, leaving lots of pauses, so that children can use their imagination to fill in the gaps and paint the story in their imagination. You may need to adapt the wording accordingly depending on whether you are inside or outside.

Today we are going on a journey in our imagination. I'm going to invite you to shut your eyes, and to sit comfortably, to feel the chair/ground underneath. You may hear sounds outside. You may need to yawn, or wriggle to find a comfortable position. Now I'm going to invite you to tune into your breath, to take a few breaths, slowly, and blow out slowly too.

I'd like you to imagine that you are walking through a beautiful wood, where there is a gentle breeze and sunshine coming through the leaves. You walk slowly along a lovely path. All around you are the most incredible trees. You may decide to stay on the path, or you may wander off it. In the distance, you see a magical tree waiting for you, a special tree of support.

Spend some time noticing what your tree looks like. What kind of trunk, what kind of branches, what kind of leaves? What makes your tree so special and magical? Now it's time to be with your tree and get to know it. It may be that you are up in the branches somehow, or down by the roots. Wherever you are, your tree is going to be there for you as a personal support. Take your time just being with your tree and getting to know it.

As we need to start thinking about leaving, find a way to say goodbye to your tree. Also, your tree is going to give you a gift to take back with you. It can be anything! In a few moments, we are going to take some steps away, and you will return along the path you came along. You will retrace your steps. When you are ready, take your time, open your eyes, and come back to the group. You may need to yawn or have a stretch, because you really have been on a trip... in your imagination!

ACTIVITY: MAKING MINIATURE CLAY TREE CREATURES		
Subject: Visual arts, sculpture **Curriculum Links:** Art	**Key Skills:** Crafting, clay-making, observation, coordination	**Duration:** 1 hour

Resources & Creative Materials:	Location:
Clay – a 'cricket ball' size for each participant A real tree if possible – to display clay animals	Outside by a tree if possible

Learning Objectives:

- To learn about and connect to animals living in the ecosystem of a forest
- To sculpt our own tree creatures relevant to our local habitat
- To create our own community of clay tree creatures

Introduction & Warm-Up: *15 minutes*

Given the huge amount of life that trees support, and how they can regenerate in SPRING, we can see why ancient and modern peoples have such a lot of respect for their tree communities. Trees are an important ecosystem, and scientists are finding out that they may even communicate through roots! Animals also spring to life when trees do. Trees provide important shelter or hiding places for wild animals, who tend to be shy of humans.

- Today we are going to explore some of our local animals living from trees.
- Generate ideas for the different creatures that find shelter around or up trees across different cultures, for example, cats, squirrels, birds (owls, woodpeckers, or the more tropical toucans), chipmunks, sloths, leopards, snakes, etc.
- We are each going to make our own tree creatures from clay.

Introduction to the clay, inviting participants to get used to their clay, warming up the clay in their own hands. Invite participants to see what kind of simple shapes come up spontaneously from playing with clay – be it bowls, balls, snakes, etc. Share with the group how all these shapes can be the basis for making clay creatures.

Key Activity: *30 minutes*
Individual clay-making exercise

- Each child decides which animal they want to make – from anywhere in the world.
- Invite people to take time crafting their creature, letting them emerge from the clay.
- Allow time to finish off the animal texture, be it feathers, fur, scales, or other.

If possible, have water available to help with smoothing or texture. Encourage participants to find twigs from the ground if they need sculpting tools.

Sharing/Reflection: *15 minutes*

Invite each participant to place their clay creature anywhere in the tree, be it tucked safely on a branch, or in the roots, wherever feels a safe place.
As a group, look at the animal display, and invite children to introduce their clay creatures. Discuss together what the tree gives their animals, and what makes them feel safe.

Key Vocabulary/Questions:	Extension Activities:
Clay-making, sculpting, ecosystem, roots Exotic animals – such as sloth, toucan, jaguar	Display clay creatures in the group-room. Write a short story from your creature's point of view.

SPRING Folktale 5 from Wales, UK
A retelling of *The Legend of The Tylwyth Teg Doorway*

Here is a folktale that is based very specifically around a small lake in Wales, in the Brecon Beacons, an area of natural beauty, with mountains and waterfalls. This lake is called Llyn Cwm Llwch which roughly translates as Dust Valley Lake.

There is a legend that tells of a magical, enchanted island, invisible to the human eye, that lies in the middle of the lake Llyn Cwm Llwch.

It's said that a doorway between a rock on the shore and the island would magically appear on May Day in SPRING each year. Any person who dared to pass through the doorway would arrive at a secret garden on the island, where they would see faeries and beautiful creatures, and sights never seen before. These faery folk were known as the Tylwyth Teg.

The Tylwyth Teg would play merry music, tell stories, and share the most incredible SPRING flowers and fruit. Everything would be bursting into life. Visitors would see giant dragonflies, incredible blossoming flowers, and hear the most enchanting song-birds. In return for all the Tylwyth Teg's warmth and hospitality, the guests were asked for one thing: don't take anything away from the island, anything at all.

Only one May Day, a visitor was tempted. Instead of giving back the beautiful flower that he had been shown, he plucked it from a bush, and hid it away in his pocket. When he returned from the island to the rock, the flower had vanished from his pocket, and the visitor had lost all his memory.

From that moment on, despite the best efforts of many different visitors, the magical doorway to the island and the Tylwyth Teg has never opened again.

ACTIVITY: CREATING A 'MAGIC DOORWAY' FOLKTALE OF OUR OWN		
Subject: Creative writing **Curriculum Links:** English	**Key Skills:** Creative writing, drama, oracy	**Duration:** 1 hour

Resources & Creative Materials: *The Tylwyth Teg Doorway* folktale Pens and paper	**Location:** Inside or outside

Learning Objectives:

- To create our own folktale inspired by the *Tylwyth Teg Doorway*
- To harness the imagination to create our own folktales
- To build confidence in our own storytelling abilities

Introduction & Warm-Up: *15 minutes*
Reread the *Tylwyth Teg Doorway* folktale, focussing on the rock that serves as a magic doorway that leads to the island. Discuss together other stories that talk about magic doorways, or openings to other worlds.

- What are some other names/words for magic doorways? Portals, gateways, etc.
- Ask children to name some from their favourite legends, books, TV series or films.
- Brainstorm where we might find openings – a cave, a tree root, under a lake, anywhere.
- Discuss together what kind of magic worlds can be found on the other side!

Key Activity: *30 minutes*
Individually, each participant is going to create their own folktale, inspired by *The Tylwyth Teg Doorway* tale, about their own magic doorway leading to another world. Try to include:

- A beginning when you discover the gateway – where is this, how do you find it?
- A middle about what kind of world you find on the other side. What happens there?
- An ending – how do you get back? Any dangers or threats to coming home?

Try to let your imagination run free and see where it takes you...

Sharing/Reflection: *10 minutes*
Ask children to share what they used as doorways to other worlds. Invite volunteers to share their beginnings, middles, and endings of folktales. What was it like to be given complete creative freedom to create their own story? Any challenges, surprises?

Key Vocabulary/ Questions Tylwyth Teg, magic doorways, portals Why do we think so many stories use doorways?	**Extension Activities** Design your own magic doorway through illustration and art.

ACTIVITY: CREATING A MINIATURE WORLD OF THE TYLWYTH TEG MAGICAL ISLE		
Subject: Visual arts **Curriculum Links:** English, Art	**Key Skills:** Interpreting a story through art, 3D art	**Duration:** 1 hour 20 minutes, plus extra time to allow paint to dry

Resources & Creative Materials:
The Tylwyth Teg Doorway folktale
Shoe boxes or other boxes of a similar size
Choose a selection of natural materials such grass, leaves, pinecones, feathers, as well as any art and craft materials such as tinfoil, tissue paper, cotton wool, clay, paper, and colouring equipment, anything recycled
Glue, glue sticks, string or wool, scissors

Location:
Inside or outside

Learning Objectives:

- To create our own miniature world of an imaginary place
- To learn how to play with perspective
- To create different landscapes using natural materials

Introduction & Warm-Up: *10 minutes*

- Reread *The Tylwyth Teg Doorway*.
- Explain how each child will turn their box into a world of *The Tylwyth Teg Doorway*.
- It is their interpretation, so they can use any elements of the story – such as the rock doorway, magical creatures, special flowers, food, or faeries. It is entirely up to them.

Key Activity: *1 hour – individually*
Think about what you want the *Tylwyth Teg* isle to look like. Which elements engage you?

- Turn the box onto its side so you have a base, back panel, and three sides to decorate OR keep it as a box that you look down into.
- Create the ground in your box with sand/grass/soil (nothing too wet) or line the box with tissue paper. Perhaps you want to paint it.
- How are you going to make your flowers, creatures, etc? You can draw pictures on paper and add them to the sides of your box OR you can use twigs, cardboard, plasticine, pinecones, or draw onto stones. Tinfoil could be the lake or perhaps you could use a little plastic dish. *Let your imaginations go wild as you create the magic isle.*

You can also hang elements from the top of sides of your box by making holes with a hole punch and hanging things with string or wool.

Sharing/Reflection: *10 minutes*
Create a gallery of the Miniature Worlds or Magical Isles and invite everyone to look at each other's creative work. Explore how different people brought the landscapes and story elements to life. Invite a conversation on the creative process – any surprises?

Key Vocabulary/ Questions The Tylwyth Teg doorway, interpretation, miniature world Which part of the box are you most proud of? Why did you choose to represent the isle like this?	**Extension Activities** Decorate the outside of your box. Tell a story with your box.

ACTIVITY: CREATING MAGICAL, EXOTIC FLOWER BLOSSOMS WITH INK DROPS		
Subject: Visual arts **Curriculum Links:** Art, Science	**Key Skills:** Painting	**Duration:** 45 minutes

Resources & Creative Materials:	Location:
The Tylwyth Teg Doorway folktale White/cream watercolour paper (soft absorbent paper works best) White kitchen roll to practise on Pipettes (small liquid droppers) Liquid watercolour or ink (vibrant colours) Small glass jars for each colour (recycled) Table covering/paint aprons	Inside or outside* *Works well on a table outdoors on a dry and not windy day

Learning Objectives:

- To learn how to create an ink drop painting
- To create abstract art based on folktale elements
- To let go and surrender to the creative process, rather than being in control

Introduction & Warm-Up: *5 minutes*

- Reread the *Tylwyth Teg Doorway* folktale.
- Explain that this creative exercise is going to bring to life visually the magical plants and blossoming flowers that live on this magical island.
- Brainstorm as a group some of the colours we imagine on this magic island.

Key Activity: *30 minutes*
Stage 1: *Set Up – 10 minutes*

1. Cover the painting table with a table covering as there will be drips!
2. Place a different coloured ink/paint in each of the glass jars – aim for at least 3 primary colours; yellow, blue, red – the more colours the better – pink, green, orange etc
   (avoid black for this activity as it will affect the other colours).
3. Arrange the glass jars of ink down the middle of the table and have a separate pipette in each one – also have a glass jar with plain water and a pipette available.
4. Each child to have a practise piece of paper and then at least two/three A4 pieces of paper to create on if time.

NB: This activity could also be collaborative by having one long piece of paper down the centre of the table and encouraging children to work together on it.

Stage 2: *Painting & Play – 20 minutes*

1. Let the children practise using the pipettes to drop colour on the paper.
2. Encourage putting the pipette back into the right colour so the colours in the jars stay clean.
3. Let the children play using the pipettes to drop colour on the paper – lifting the paper to let the drops run in different directions – overlap different colours on top of each other.
4. Encourage the children to observe the drops growing – blooming on the paper like blossoming flowers.
5. Encourage children to use the plain water dropper on their paintings to see what happens.
6. Leave the finished paintings to dry in a sunny area OR on a drying rack – they will be quite wet!

Sharing/Reflection: *10 minutes*

1. Place the paintings on a table or floor so that everyone can see them (if dry clip them onto a line or display on a wall).
2. Encourage children to comment on and discuss the paintings, their own and each other's.

   - Notice how many *new colours* have been created by overlapping colours.
   - What shapes can they see in the paintings?
   - What has grown on the page from the simple act of dropping watery paint?
   - What effects do they like or dislike?
   - SPRING brings an abundance of colour to the land – what are the similarities in this process?

Key Vocabulary/ Questions:	**Extension Activities:**
Colour, experiment, play, ink, bloom, drip, drop, pipette	Using this painting process and a pen or pencil see if you can create one of giant dragonflies or a magical songbird from the island of Tylwyth Teg.

ACTIVITY: CREATING A SPRING DIAMANTE POEM		
Subject: Creative writing **Curriculum Links:** English	**Key Skills:** Poetry, Diamante format, performance	**Duration:** 1 hour
Resources & Creative Materials: *Tylwyth Teg* folktale Examples of Diamante poems, paper, pens/pencils Words collected in SPRING box	**Location:** Inside or outside	

Learning Objectives:

- To have fun playing with language and SPRING images
- To understand the diamante poem structure
- To create a diamante poem based on SPRING

Introduction & Warm-Up: *20 minutes*

- Reread the *Tylwyth Teg* story and think of the scenes of SPRING it conjures
- Close your eyes and visualise SPRING. What images do you think of?
- Explain what a Diamante poem is and how it works.

Noun,

Adjective, Adjective,

Verb,   verb,   verb,

Noun, noun, noun, noun, or a short phrase

Verb,   verb,   verb

Adjective, Adjective

Noun

- Remind the children what nouns, adjectives and verbs are.
- Show the children examples from the sheet given.
- Create a small word bank for SPRING nouns, adjectives, and verbs. Then together put them into a SPRING diamante poem.

NB: instead of nouns in the middle line, there can be a short phrase. You just need to try to keep the diamond shape. Verbs don't need to end in 'ing' but that often helps with the diamond shape.

Key Activity: *30 minutes*

- Allow the children some time to create bigger word banks based on SPRING, making sure they have three categories: nouns, adjectives, and verbs. They can also use the words they collected in their SPRING box.
- Let them play with the positioning of the words. If it helps, they can cut them out so they can keep rearranging them.
- Create a SPRING diamante poem of their own.

Sharing/Reflection: *10 minutes*
Invite each child to read their poems aloud. How are these poems effective? Do they make us think of SPRING? Were they easy or hard to create?

Key Vocabulary/Questions: Diamante, nouns, verbs, adjectives, phrases	**Extension Activities:** Write the poems in SPRING colours. Mount them on card, then cut out the diamond shape. You can draw a picture of SPRING on the other side.

Examples of Diamante poems on the theme of Spring

The Structure

Noun,
Adjective, Adjective,
Verb, verb, verb,
Noun, noun, noun, noun, or a short phrase
Verb, verb, verb,
Adjective, Adjective,
Noun

SPRING

Season,
Warm, Sunny,
Gambolling, Leaping, Trotting,
Lambs, Leverets, Fawns, Calves,
Nibbling, Munching, Gulping,
New, Young,
SPRING

Nature

Flowers,
Yellow, Orange,
Growing, Swaying, Dreaming,
Daffodils, Tulips, Magnolia, Hawthorn,
Blossoming, Reaching, Watching,
Green, Brown,
Trees

SPRING Weather

Sun,
Warm, Dry,
Playing, Gardening, Smiling,
Weather, Outside, Inside, SPRING,
Watching, Waiting, Frowning,
Cold, Annoyed,
Rain

CLOSING ACTIVITY: PERSONAL/COLLECTIVE ASSOCIATIONS WITH SPRING AND GIANT GROUP MANDALA		
Subject: Visual arts **Curriculum Links:** Art	**Key Skills:** Artmaking, collaboration	**Duration:** 1 hour

Resources & Creative Materials: Blank paper plate (one for each child) OR thick white paper/card cut into a circle – plate size or larger Scissors, glue-sticks Lining paper/craft paper – masking tape Pens, paper, collage materials, fabrics, paints, chalks Any natural materials – leaves, twigs, fallen flowers, etc	**Location:** Inside or outside

Learning Objectives:

- To engage children in a giant creative activity to summarise the theme of SPRING
- To teach collaboration in a shared art-making activity such as a Mandala
- To engage children to capture their own *unique* relationship with SPRING

Introduction & Warm-Up: *5 minutes*

Share how the Celts and other ancient cultures saw the Sun as a wheel, turning for each season. In Hindu and Buddhist cultures, they use the Mandala, a circular template, to create images and patterns to represent the wholeness of the cosmos and for human beings. Today we are going to make our own SPRING mandala to focus on our own personal relationship to SPRING.

Invite children in silence to close their eyes and think about the season of SPRING:

- When you think of SPRING, what comes up? Memories and associations?
- Images, words, sounds, sensations, places, drinks, foods, activities, plants, animals.
- Spend some time really allowing yourself to think about your memories.
- Any SPRING scenes, festivals, important community and/or cultural events?

Key Activity: *40 minutes*

Activity 1: *Individual – create a SPRING image – 30 minutes*

On the paper circle or plate, each participant creates their own SPRING image.

- Invite children to draw/write their associations with the season of SPRING.
- The challenge is for the children to fill in all the paper, leaving no gaps!
- If words, encourage children to decorate these in a seasonal style and colours.
- Images can be abstract, showing warm colours, patterns or a scene. It can be a collage or 2D. The choice is theirs. Encourage children to play and experiment with images and ideas.

Activity 2: *Create a group Giant SPRING Mandala collage in a hall space OR large space – 10 minutes*

- Ask each of the children to lay their circular artworks on the floor.
- Starting in a central position (middle of the floor or playground), position the circles in a spiral starting in the middle and radiating outwards.
- You could also lay the circles out using a different formation or design and try a couple of ideas before deciding on the right one.

Sharing/Reflection: *15 minutes*

Stand around the final formation on the floor and invite participants to share their responses to the SPRING Mandala.

Feedback on the creative process – what is it like to contribute to the Giant Mandala?

How do they look as part of a collaborative design?

Teacher or adult helper to stand on a chair or higher point to photograph the collaborative artwork for posterity.

Key Vocabulary/Questions:	**Extension Activities:**
Mandala, mindfulness, senses, creativity, collaboration What makes SPRING so unique?	If there is a wall space big enough the design could be stuck to a wall with white tack to be appreciated by a wider audience. At the end of term individual circles can be taken home by children to be hung up on the wall to mark the season of SPRING.

As we close our SPRING SEASON, here is one last creative exercise to try at home.

TRY THIS AT HOME: Decorating SPRING Eggs		
Subject: Visual arts **Curriculum Links:** Art	**Key Skills:** Art and craft-making	**Duration:** 1 hour plus

Resources & Creative Materials:	Location:
Eggs – white or as pale as possible Paper napkins with a nice design following a SPRING feel – could be flowers, rabbits, chicks, etc Egg white (as glue) and a clean paint or basting brush	Home – inside or outside on a nice day

Learning Objectives:

- To learn about how eggs have been decorated across cultures in the world
- To use natural ways to decorate eggs
- To use napkins as 'transfers' and egg white as glue
- To create our own design in the Eastern European and Russian style

Introduction & Warm-Up: *10 minutes*

Eggs have been decorated across history. A symbol of new life and rebirth, eggs are something we see at SPRING-TIME. Here is a lovely, simple way to decorate eggs that comes from Ukraine, Poland, Bulgaria, Russia, and other countries in this region. Painted eggs are also used in other cultures, such as to celebrate Nowruz, the Persian new year (solar calendar) at the time of the Spring Equinox, usually on the 20th or 21st of March.

Key Activity: *1 hour plus, depending on how many eggs you want to do!*

- Keep one egg fresh, as you will need its fresh egg-white.
- Hard boil six eggs, trying not to crack them and set aside to cool.
- Taking your paper napkin, carefully separate out the layers, so you have the thinnest layer (napkins often have four or so layers to make the whole).
- Cut out some small shapes from the napkin layer with patterns.
  - E.g., a rabbit, chick, flower, or another decoration that will fit on the egg.
- Delicately place the cut-out of the napkin on your egg.
- Using the paint or basting brush, dip into the egg-white.
- Use the wet brush to attach the napkin cut-out to the egg, trying to avoid any creases.
- It's a bit like attaching transfers or fake tattoos.
- Let it dry and when finished place into an egg box.

Sharing/Reflection: *5 minutes*

Have a look together at what you've created and how it looks like a real printed egg, using simple and natural ingredients and designs!

Key Vocabulary/ Questions:	Extension Activities:
Eggs, egg-white, basting brush	Give these away as presents: people will love them! Experiment with different napkin designs.

SUMMER

*'It was June, and the world smelled of roses.
The sunshine was like powdered gold over
the grassy hillside.'*

Maud Hart Lovelace (American writer)

June, July, August in

Northern Hemisphere

December, January, February in

Southern Hemisphere

SUMMER SEASON, FOLKLORE AND CREATIVE ACTIVITIES

- Introduction to SUMMER

- Opening Activity – SUMMER Slow Walk/Lie-Down and Word Collection

A retelling of *The Birth of the Sun* from Australia

- Performing an Aboriginal Folktale

- Creating Animal Stones using the Dot-style from Aboriginal Culture

- Making A Sun Catcher

- Creating a Singing Map of Nature Trails based on a Sacred Song-line

A retelling of the *Huldufólk – The 'Hidden Folk'* from Iceland

- Sculpting 3D magical creatures – our own *Huldufólk*

- Creating a Crossroads Story about the Elves at MIDSUMMER

- Sketching Tree Trolls/Flower Faeries/Elves from Local Nature

- Creating Miniature Homes for *Huldufólk*

A retelling of *The Mysterious Midnight Fern at MIDSUMMER* from Northern and Eastern Europe

- Creating a Theatre-sketch – Power to Talk to Animals

- Creating Magical Spells to Protect the Fern Blossom

- Painting a Fern – Observing its Beauty and Symmetry

- Creating Cave Art – Travelling back to the Jurassic Era with the Fern

A retelling of *The Ten Suns and the Archer* from China

- Re-enacting *The Ten Suns and the Archer* folktale

- Creating a *Ten Suns and the Archer* Mixed Media Wall Frieze

- Creating our own SUMMER 'Dragon' Folklore Stories

- Creating Cyanotype Print SUN Dragons

DOI: 10.4324/9781003178682-10

A retelling of *The Hummingbird* from Peru, Ecuador, South America

- Creating a News Segment – Interviewing the Cast of *The Hummingbird* Folktale

- Creating 'Collage' Poems on the Migration of Hummingbirds

- Making a Hummingbird Mobile

- Caring for Our World Action Plan

Closing exercise

- Personal/collective associations with SUMMER and Giant Group Mandala

Try this at home

- Eco Printing with Flowers and Leaves

Introduction to SUMMER

As SUMMER arrives, we experience nature in full abundance and bloom. With the sun at its closest and highest in the sky, SUMMER brings hotter weather and the longest daylight hours. Fruit ripens and crops grow tall. Trees are bushy with green leaves. The colour palette changes again, bringing a range of bright/bold or more saturated tones. In countries at higher and lower latitudes in the hemispheres, we can switch off our central heating, put away our jumpers and enjoy being outside. This is the season of SUMMER holidays. Many people try to head to the sea. It's a time for ice-creams!

In relation to agriculture and farming, SUMMER is a crucial season to grow crops for the upcoming harvest. Good weather – both rain and the sun's heat – is essential to create the abundance in nature that humans depend upon. Yet, SUMMER can also bring with it more extreme and unpredictable weather patterns. Some places see weather arrive in the form of thunderstorms, tornados, floods, and monsoons. Other countries suffer drought and forest fires. As ancient people lived the land so closely, we find that SUMMER folklore stories and rituals are often based in invoking good weather for farming. As seen in other seasons, many characters in folktales personify natural forces. Some of our religious festivals, symbols and holidays also tap into older traditions linked with nature's rhythms; some linking in with the SUMMER Solstice, the astronomical start of SUMMER. The SUMMER Solstice or MIDSUMMER, either June 21/22 in the Northern Hemisphere or December 21/22 in the Southern Hemisphere, is the longest day of the year, with the most daylight hours. In Reykjavik, Iceland, the sun stays visible for 21 hours. It's called 'the midnight sun.'

In the following story section, we've collected folklore stories for SUMMER in the Northern and Southern Hemispheres. Although we've rooted folktales in specific countries, versions of these stories often cross borders and live elsewhere in different forms. Some stories explore the SUMMER solstice. Others explore specific aspects of SUMMER life or how nature and cultural/religious rituals interconnect. In selecting our five folktales for SUMMER, we've tried to choose lesser-known stories. Equally, we recognise that there are many other stories out there. We hope ours are useful starting places that can encourage your own interest in collecting SUMMER folklore tales.

SUMMER offers children, families, and classrooms a range of creative possibilities to explore the unique essence of this season. A selection of activities is offered for each folklore tale across different arts media – storytelling, visual art making, drama, and movement. With the warmer weather that comes with SUMMER, there is a real opportunity to run creative sessions outside, to enable children and adults to enjoy the natural world.

OPENING ACTIVITY: SUMMER SLOW WALK/LIE-DOWN AND WORD COLLECTION		
Subject: Wellbeing **Curriculum Links:** English, PSHE	**Key Skills:** Sensation, mindfulness, observation	**Duration:** 1 hour

Resources & Creative Materials:	Location:
Our senses and sensations, nature Strips of paper in seasonal colours, pens/pencils, a box	Outdoors on a dry, warm day

Learning Objectives:

- To teach mindfulness techniques and support children in mind/body wellbeing
- To introduce concepts of growth, blooming, harvesting associated with SUMMER
- To create a box of SUMMER words, sensations, feelings, objects, and images

Introduction & Warm-Up: *15 minutes*
Explain mindfulness and walking meditation principles behind a SUMMER-Walk/Lie-In:

- A way of observing and moving through the world without judgement.
- Slowing down and allowing our bodies and minds to relax in the natural world.

Invite children first to stand in a circle outside to practice noticing through the senses:

- In silence, feel ground beneath your feet and notice what is happening around you.
- What do you see and hear, what temperature do you feel on your skin?

Key Activity: *20 minutes*
Activity 1: *SUMMER Slow Walk/Lie-In – 20 minutes*

- Explain how in SUMMER, animals, plants, humans... enjoy the warmth of the sun's rays.
- A time of ripening and growth – trees grow fruit and animals take care of their babies.
- Invite children to walk in silence in the outside space and observe their environment.
  - Give attention to their senses – colours, sounds, feelings.
  - What do they notice as they look around them? Weather, clouds, sky?
  - Any sounds – birdsong, insects?
  - What do they see around them – any growing fruit on the trees, any birds, insects?
  - Are there any natural objects that they find on their way – leaf, stone, feather etc

After some slow walking in silence, invite children to find a space to lie-down (if dry) and put an ear to the ground, and look up to the sky, and to let their bodies relax... to feel the earth support them, the sun on their faces (hopefully!). After a few moments, invite children back into a sitting circle.

Activity 2: *Gathering together of SUMMER words, images, sensations – 15 minutes*

- On a strip of paper, each child writes a few spring words or sensation.
- Place these and any objects in a SUMMER box or create a display.

Sharing/Reflection: *10 minutes*
Invite participants to share their responses to the SUMMER Walk/Lie-Down
Any feelings, sensations, surprises? Any objects that they picked up along the way?

Key Vocabulary/Questions:	Extension Activities:
Ripening, Fruit, Mindfulness, Senses, Creativity What kind of senses and words are unique to SUMMER	SUMMER words can be fanned out and displayed.

SUMMER Folktale 1 from Australia
A retelling of the folktale *The Birth of the Sun*

This story comes from the Aboriginal Australia. Story and nature continue to hold a significant importance in Aboriginal culture in Australia, with oral storytelling equally held as a sacred and valued tradition. 'Dreamtime' stories are important stories, passed down from the time of 'Dreaming', that tell us creation myths of how the world came to be. Aboriginal storytellers use a range of arts forms to tell Dreamtime stories... the story may be told in pantomime, drama, dance, and in the visual art forms. Facial expressions, hand gestures, and mime were, and still are, very important in the telling of a Dreaming story.

In sharing and retelling this story, we hope that children and group participants can learn from Aboriginal people about how we are all a part of nature, and the need to honour, respect, and nurture that connection. In this time of climate change, there is a lot we can learn from the Aboriginal perspective. Equally, we hope that participants can also respect the oral storytelling traditions of indigenous peoples.

When the world was very new, there was no sun. Humans and animals had to hunt using only the light of the moon.

One day, Emu and Brolga – an Australian crane – had an argument. Each bird said that they were the best creature. In anger, Brolga threw one of Emu's eggs into the sky. As the egg flew through the air, it broke and its yoke burst into flames, lighting up the ground below. A kind-hearted sky spirit was dazzled by Earth's beauty and thought it would be a great idea if the world was lit up like this every day.

And so, as soon as the sky spirit saw the morning star, he lit a fire in the sky. At first, the fire released only a little heat and light as it began to burn. Then it grew hotter and brighter. But as the day came to an end, the fire would burn out and the light would dim again.

But the sky spirit had a problem. If it was a cloudy day, the morning star could not be seen. So, he turned to the kookaburra for help, asking him to call out using his strong wondrous voice when the sun needed to be lit.

ACTIVITY: PERFORMING AN ABORIGINAL FOLKTALE		
Subject: Performing arts **Curriculum Links:** English	**Key Skills:** Drama, mime, story telling	**Duration:** Two 1-hour sessions

Resources & Creative Materials: *The Birth of the Sun* folktale	**Location:** Inside or outside

Learning Objectives:

- To learn from Aboriginal people's beliefs in the sacredness of nature
- To show how Aborigines value oral storytelling
- To retell a story using song, mime, and drama
- To work out the key moments in a story
- To create a 'part two' using the first story as inspiration

Introduction & Warm-Up: *15 minutes*

- Explain how Aboriginal Australians could be the oldest population of humans living outside of Africa, where one theory says they migrated from in boats 70,000 years ago. They used mime, drama, and song to retell tales, and kept their stories closely guarded within their own communities and still do. They believe strongly in the sacredness of nature, and hold huge respect for all creatures and life on this planet.
- Listen to the story *The Birth of the Sun*.
- Discuss the key points in the story.

Key Activity:

1st session: *30 minutes*

- In groups, work out how you wish to retell the story. Imagine you are in Australia 50,000 years ago trying to explain how the sun came to be. Try to include mime, song, dance, and drama in your play.

2nd session: *30 minutes*

- Can you create a part two to the story – using mine, song, dance, and drama? One day, the kookaburra loses his voice, so the sky spirit doesn't light the morning start and the world is plunged into darkness. How can we get the sun back? Could another creature help the sky spirit?

Sharing/Reflection: *15 minutes*

Invite the groups to perform their stories after each session. What are the similarities and differences in the first performance? How did the children get the sun back into the sky in the second performance?

Key Vocabulary/Questions: Aboriginal, Emu, Brolga, Kookaburra How did you come up with your ideas? What's it like working collaboratively? Learning to be aware of an audience in a performance	**Extension Activities:** Write up plays, either making them into a story or a comic using images to support the story.

ACTIVITY: CREATING ANIMAL STONES USING THE DOT-STYLE FROM ABORIGINAL CULTURE		
Subject: Visual arts **Curriculum Links:** Art, RE, Geography	**Key Skills:** Art, mindfulness	**Duration:** 1 hour 45 minutes

Resources & Creative Materials: Paper, acrylic paint, paintbrushes or 'Poska' pens, varnish (optional) Large pebbles or stones (ask participants to bring one in) Dot-style animal image examples from Aboriginal culture Pictures of Australian animals	**Location:** Outside

Learning Objectives:

- To learn about the practices of Aboriginal people in honouring nature
- To give an insight into some of the sacred art practices of Aboriginal people
- To learn that dots were not just a visual style but an important language
- To engage with the essence of animals in a mindful and respectful manner
- To learn what kind of animals live in Australia

Introduction & Warm-Up: *15 minutes*

The Aboriginal people of Australia can teach us a lot about how to respect animals in nature. Their art captures a sacred aspect of animals. The dot and x-ray style that many people associate with Aboriginal art is actually quite recent. In the 1970s, this was a way to disguise sacred meanings in their art to protect it from outsiders.

- As a group, let's imagine what it might mean to put nature first in our culture.
- Imagine what it must have been like for Aboriginal people for visitors to arrive with their cameras, wanting to capture photographs, just to take memories away.
- In the modern world, we can rush around and be so fast, but in other cultures they move at a pace that fits in with the natural world.
- Look together now at the dot images of animals and share feedback.
- What feelings do you have looking at how animals are represented?
- What kind of animals do you recognise?

Key Activity: A slow art exercise, giving time to each phase – *1 hour and 15 minutes*

Activity 1: Individually, getting to know your animal – *15 minutes*

- From a selection of pictures, choose an animal to represent.
- Spend time thinking about its unique nature/qualities – is it fast, slow, nocturnal, etc?
- What kind of habitat does it live in – dry, desert, sea, ground, sky?
- Imagine what it might feel to be this animal? What might the world feel like?

Activity 2: Sketching the dots and deciding on your colour schemes – *30 minutes*

- On a piece of paper first, practice bringing your creature to life through dots (don't make your practise-piece too big as your pebble will be small).
- Think about what kind of contrasting colours might suit your animal and its habitat.
- Take your time… allow yourself to be slow with the dot making.

Activity 3: Making SLOW-ART of dot animals – *30 minutes*

- Once you have practised your animal on paper you are ready to paint onto your pebble.
- You have the option of painting a pale flat colour (white/pastel) onto your pebble before painting on your dot animal OR you may decide to paint dots directly onto the pebble if it's a light colour.
- If you create a base colour first wait for it to dry before painting on your dot animal.
- Take your time (if it helps, lightly sketch the animal shape onto the pebble first with a pencil).
- Paint in the animal using the dot technique – use one colour at a time, wash the brush in between so the different dots are distinctive and the colours stay clean.
- Enjoy! It could be nice to listen to music whilst doing this activity.

Sharing/Reflection: *15 minutes*
Create an animal pebble trail. Invite participants to place their pebble next to someone else's to create an animal trail.
Spend time as a group walking around the animal pebble stones in silence.
Afterwards, invite each participant to stand by their animal pebble, sharing their creative process – how do the colours express some of the energy and essence of their animal?
Discuss together feedback and responses to both making and seeing other's stones.

Key Vocabulary/Questions:	**Extension Activities:**
Aboriginal, dot-style art, cultural appreciation (rather than cultural appropriation) What can we learn from this way of making art?	An outdoors exhibition or Pebble Trail.

ACTIVITY: MAKING A SUN CATCHER		
Subject: Creative arts **Curriculum Links:** Art, Biology, Geography, Physics	**Key Skills:** Making, Creativity	**Duration:** 1 hour

Resources & Creative Materials:	Location:
The *Birth of the Sun* story Coloured A4 card (any colour works) Coloured tissue paper Petals and leaves – not freshly picked preferably Clear sticky back plastic Hole punch and string	Inside and outside

Learning Objectives:

- To engage children with the power of the sun's rays
- To use nature – petals/leaves/feathers – in art and design patterns
- To look at light play

Introduction & Warm-Up: *5 minutes*

- A suncatcher filters colour through it by reflecting the rays of the sun.
- This activity focuses on creating a suncatcher in the shape of the Emu's egg thrown into the air to light up the sky. It's also a good way to use up petals from flowers that are on their way out and found leaves. (There's no need to pick new flowers – these can be left to bloom.)
- Think about how stained glass in churches and cathedrals capture so much colour.

Key Activity: *Making the suncatcher – 45 minutes*
Cut an egg-shaped hole out of the A4 card – make it as large as possible within the frame of the card. Emu eggs are big! Cut a hole in the top of the card with a hole punch so you can hang it later. These tasks could be done in advance of the session – save the egg shapes that you cut out from the middles of the A4 as you will need them.

1. Collect a selection of small petals/ leaves/grass/small feathers (so each child has a handful); these could be collected on a nature walk or brought from home.
2. Using the egg-shaped pieces of card as a base (that were cut from the middles of the A4 sheets) practise making designs with the petals and leaves – be gentle with the petals as they bruise easily. (If there are any blank areas in the designs you can add some bits of coloured tissue paper later to fill in the spaces.)
3. Once you have a final design you like (using leaves and petals) leave it on the card.
4. Peel the back off an A4 piece of sticky back plastic and place it sticky side up on the table (you may need to stick the edges to the table with tape).
5. Carefully place the A4 card (with the egg-shaped hole in it) on top of the sticky backed plastic so you have an egg-shaped sticky area.

Transfer the leaf/petal design from the card onto the sticky area, smoothing each item down carefully – if there are any sticky bits remaining tear up small bits of coloured tissue paper and carefully smooth them into the gaps so no sticky areas remain uncovered.

Sharing/Reflection: *10 minutes*
Tie a piece of string through the hole in the top of the A4 card so that you can tie the sun catcher in a window.
If it's a sunny day hang OR hold the sun catcher up to the light to see the way the light moves through the decorated area and what patterns/colours may emerge in the shadows. If you aren't lucky enough to have a sunny day you could use a torch to see how the light passes through the suncatcher.

Key Vocabulary/Questions:	Extension Activities:
Colour, pattern, design, shadow, sun catcher	Decorate the card frame of your sun catcher using collage or colored pens. You could even write words on your frame inspired by the voice of the Kookaburra. What words did he use in his strong wondrous voice when the sun needed to be lit?

ACTIVITY: CREATING A SINGING MAP OF NATURE TRAILS BASED ON A SACRED SONG-LINE		
Subject: Art, Geography, Music **Curriculum Links:** Geography, music, RE	**Key Skills:** Song, mindfulness, observational skills	**Duration:** 1 hour

Resources & Creative Materials: Our senses and our attention, a place for a nature-walk	Location: Outside

Learning Objectives:
- To give an insight into some of the sacred land practices of Aboriginal people
- To move through the land in a mindful and respectful manner
- To learn how to observe and map out the land through natural landmarks
- To listen to nature – the trees, birds, plants, animals, etc
- To show what the Aboriginal perspective and relationship to nature can teach us

Introduction & Warm-Up: *15 minutes*

The Aboriginal people of Australia can teach us a lot about how to respect our lands and all that live within it. As a nomadic people moving through the land, when Aboriginal people came to a new place, they created songs to share what they saw. These are living maps, known in English as song-lines. These are seen a sacred process, honouring nature. Not only are natural landmarks sung about, but also events that have happened.

- As a group, let's look at what natural landmarks we can see around us.
- In silence, look around – what can you see... from the very small to the very big?
- Is there a cluster of trees, a bend in the path, a tree root that sticks out, etc?
- Invite children to look around them and report back on their observations.
- Encourage using metaphor, e.g. old man tree, broken wing branch, hard nose rock.
- Share some of the observations together.

Key Activity: *30 minutes in a contained nature area*

Activity 1: *In small groups, have a mindful slow-walk and nature trail together – 15 minutes*

- Firstly, agree where participants are moving towards – where is the final destination?
- As groups move through the terrain, encourage a mindful, silent walk of concentration.
- Invite children to open their eyes, ears, senses, and 'listen' to all natural things.
- Be open to letting the land speak, and seeing landmarks in metaphor form.
- What do things look like? Can write notes to remember if needed.

Activity 2: *Create our own singing map, or song-line – 15 minutes*

- In the same small groups, share all the observations – what did you see, hear, etc?
- Create a singing map together to capture all the observations that lasts a few minutes.

Use prepositions: UNDER, BY, BEHIND, THROUGH.

- Choose someone in the group to write down the words.

Sharing/Reflection: *15 minutes*

Invite each group to share their singing map/song-line using either voice or song.
How did it feel to listen to the different singing maps – how easy was it to recognise places?
How does it feel to relate to the natural world in this way?

Key Vocabulary/Questions: Aboriginal, Nomadic tribes, song-lines, sacred land, reverence, metaphor, landmark What can we learn from moving through land this way?	Extension Activities: Be taken on a journey on other peoples' singing maps.

Summer Folktale 2 from Iceland
A retelling of the *Huldufólk* – the 'Hidden Folk'

In many northern and European countries, MIDSUMMER and the SUMMER Solstice, around June 21/22 in the Northern Hemispheres and December 21/22 in the Southern Hemispheres, was a time people believed that elves, fairies, and magic folk would allow themselves to be seen. Shakespeare's famous play A MIDSUMMER Night's Dream picks up on this ancient folklore.

One country full of faery lore about elves and trolls is Iceland. If you look at the unique landscape of Iceland, its twisted lava formations, it's easy to see why humans could have imagined magical, otherworldly creatures. There are even stories that modern building and construction works have had to be moved, so not to disturb the special elf places rooted in the landscape!

In Iceland, Huldufólk are the hidden people thought to live in enchanted rocks and cliffs and only let themselves be seen at MIDSUMMER, the longest day. Huldufólk is a polite way to describe elves! Folklore said that at MIDSUMMER, if you sat at a crossroads, the elves would attempt to trick you into eating their food and drink, and you must resist them at all costs. Given that there are 21 hours of daylight at MIDSUMMER, otherwise known as the Midnight Sun, the Huldufólk had lots of opportunities to trick you!

Throwing stones is frowned upon as you might hit an elf or one of their homes. All around Iceland you will see rocks with doors painted on them or tiny wooden houses, álfhól. These homes are all built for the hidden people to keep them safe. Food and drink offerings are left at these houses at MIDSUMMER and other important festivals of the year.

ACTIVITY: SCULPTING 3D MAGICAL CREATURES – OUR OWN *HULDUFÓLK*		
Subject: Creative arts **Curriculum Links:** Art, English	**Key Skills:** Art, sculpture, storytelling	**Duration:** 1 hour 15 minutes

Resources & Creative Materials:	Location:
Huldufólk folktale Clay, natural objects such as twigs and stones Paint, wool, eco-friendly glitter, recycled sequins, textiles	Outside if possible

Learning Objectives:

- To teach children about the *Huldufólk* and other mythological creatures
- To create our own magical creatures, little people – born from the landscape
- To locate and give our magical creatures a specific place to live

Introduction & Warm-Up: *15 minutes*

As we've seen, in Iceland, the *Huldufólk* – elves – were hidden people who lived in enchanted places in nature – rocks, sea-cliffs, waterfalls, trees. Iceland is also home to trolls and faeries. Ancient peoples in many countries believed in little, magical people living in nature. Often they had special powers. Invite participants to have a group discussion on:

- Special places we know in nature, that inspire our imagination.
- Have we ever imagined magical creatures that lived near us? What kinds?
- What places might home these creatures? What kind of landscape?
- What magic powers in nature might these *Huldufólk* have?
  E.g. creating fire, controlling the winds, water, healing trees, etc...

Key Activity: *45 minutes*

Create your own *Huldufólk*, in whatever shape or form, be it elf, faery, or troll!

- Encourage participants to follow their own ideas, and not copy anyone else's – that there is no right or wrong outcome – we are here to have fun with our imagination.
- Use clay to mould your magical creature's body – using twigs as frames or limbs.
- With twigs, create limbs and/or a body frame to mould clay around.
- Decorate and dress up your magical creature with any resources available.
  E.g., painted stones, recycled sequins, textile pieces.
- Experiment with making your *Huldufólk* look as magical or as grotesque as possible!
- How does its form tell you about its identity – is it earthy or flighty with wings?
- Give your *Huldufólk* a name and a place to live in nature to live, e.g., under a rock, a waterfall, a tree root...

Sharing/Reflection: *15 minutes*

Invite participants to sit in a circle outside and share their *Huldufólk* creature.
Introduce each *Huldufólk* by name, where they live, and their magical power in nature.

Key Vocabulary/Questions:	Extension Activities:
Huldufólk – elves, faeries, trolls, mythology Why do you think people believed in little people? What is it about nature that inspires magic and myth?	Write a story about your *Huldufólk* and where it comes from.

ACTIVITY: CREATING A CROSSROADS STORY ABOUT THE ELVES AT MIDSUMMER		
Subject: Creative writing and Performing arts **Curriculum Links:** English	**Key Skills:** Storytelling, oracy	**Duration:** 1 hour
Resources & Creative Materials: *Hulufólk* folktale	**Location:** Inside or outside	

Learning Objectives:

- To create your own story using the *Huldufólk* as inspiration
- To develop confidence in story telling
- To tell the story through oracy

Introduction & Warm-Up: 20 minutes

- Share how people from Iceland believed in *Huldufólk*, a term for elves/little people.
- Folklore said that at MIDSUMMER, if you sat at a crossroads, the elves would attempt to trick you into eating their food and drink, and you must resist at all costs.
- Ask the children to close their eyes and picture walking through the woods. Can they feel the breeze on their cheeks and see the sunlight trickling through the trees?
- Invite children to imagine they go along a pathway and reach a crossroads where some elves appear with a picnic. They try to trick you into consuming food and drink.
- Ask the children to open their eyes and then brainstorm some ideas on how the elves could make people eat food and drink. Perhaps they cast a spell so you forget you can't eat the food; they make your favourite food, and it looks so enticing...
- Brainstorm some ideas about what happens once you've consumed the food. Examples include shrinking or turning into a shrub or a rock.

Key Activity: *35 minutes*
Activity 1: *Creating the story – 25 minutes*

- In pairs, ask the children to create a story where the elves try tricking a human into consuming food and drink. Perhaps the elves succeed. What happens to the humans?
- Or perhaps the elves achieve in tricking some humans, but your main character is too smart.
- Invite the children to plan the story – they can make notes or write the story out if they wish.

Activity 2: *Telling the story – 10 minutes*

- Once they've created their stories, ask the pairs to tell their stories to each other. Each child needs to speak.
- This could be done outside. See if they can keep eye contact with the audience, rather than reading the story aloud.

Sharing/Reflection: *5 minutes*
What are benefits of oral story telling?
Which do you prefer – writing or telling a story?
Do you prefer being told a story or reading one?

Key Vocabulary/Questions: Storytelling, oracy *Huldufólk*	**Extension Activities:** Invite other year groups to listen to your *Huldufólk* stories.

ACTIVITY: SKETCHING TREE TROLLS/FLOWER FAERIES/ELVES FROM LOCAL NATURE		
Subject: Visual arts **Curriculum Links:** Art, Geography	**Key Skills:** Art, observation	**Duration:** 1 hour 30 minutes

Resources & Creative Materials: Our imagination, a nature walk *Flower Fairies* by Cicely Mary Barker, illustrations by Arthur Rackham and John Bauer Paper and pencil, clip frames	**Location:** Outside in a nature area Can be inside for sketching

Learning Objectives:

- To help participants understand why the natural world inspired so much mythology
- Invite participants to connect with nature using their imagination
- To spend time with trees and other natural objects to search for *Huldufólk*

Introduction & Warm-Up: 15 minutes

- If we look at the long history of faeries, trolls, elves, and witches their actual forms often come from nature. Why might this be?
- If we look closely at landscapes, we start to see why. Many artists have been inspired by nature to create their magical creatures. Introduce illustrations of artists such as Cicely Mary Barker, Arthur Rackham, and John Bauer.
- As a guide, choose some examples from your nature area – a tree, root, rock, etc. As a group, invite participants to imagine what they can see – what kind of magical creature?
- Now, it's going to be their turn to find their own imaginary creatures in nature.

Key Activity: *45 minutes*
Activity 1: *Nature walk – 15 minutes*

- Walk around the nature area in silence looking at trees, rocks, flowers, etc.
- Can they start to see faces, figures, or forms in natural objects? Trees, roots, rocks?
- Or imagine what kind of little magical creature made of flowers, grass, moss?

Activity 2: *Sketching your own elf, witch, tree troll, flower faerie, or other – 30 minutes*

- Decide on what you want as inspiration – a tree knot/root, a flower, a rock, etc.
- Sit or stand in front, spending time really looking at your source of inspiration.
- The closer you look, what do you notice and see?
- With your paper and pencil, start to sketch what you see.
- Let your imagination meet nature!

Sharing/Reflection: *30 minutes*
Treasure Hunt – in small groups, invite participants to sit in a circle to share sketches.
Invite other people in the group to try to find the source of the mythological creature!
In the big group, reflect on the creative process of making your creatures, and also what it was like to find the sources of inspiration, how easy/hard...

Key Vocabulary/Questions: *Huldufólk* – elves, faeries, trolls, mythology Why do you think people believed in little people? What is it about nature that inspires magic and myth?	**Extension Activities:** Create a more detailed image of your magical creature in colour. Create a magical creature face in clay on trees/rocks.

ACTIVITY: CREATING MINIATURE HOMES FOR *HULDUFÓLK*		
Subject: Creative art **Curriculum Links:** Art	**Key Skills:** Creativity, observation, imagination, creative play	**Duration:** 1 hour
Resources & Creative Materials: (per child) Natural materials Clay, feathers, sticks, grasses, small pieces of wood, pinecones, acorns, leaves, rocks, stones Art materials (paint and brushes)	**Location:** Outside preferably	

Learning Objectives:

- To learn to make things using natural forms
- To inspire imaginative and creative play
- To experience working outside

Introduction & Warm-Up: *10 minutes*

- As an outside exploration this activity would work best in a small group.
- The *Huldufólk* or hidden people are elves in Icelandic folklore who live outside in nature. They are hidden from us but can apparently make themselves visible at will. The little homes where the *Huldufólk* live are also hidden from us but might be right under our noses – where are they and what do they look like?
- Have you ever been anywhere that feels a bit different or magical, where you can imagine elves livings? Discuss together.

Key Activity: *Creating a home for the* Huldufólk *– 40 minutes*
Step 1: *Nature-walk as inspiration.*
Go on a nature walk outside and carefully explore the outside space, imagining where the *Huldufólk* might make their homes. Would it be in the base of a tree, in the branches, in a hole in the ground, in a hedgerow? What natural objects would they use in their homes? E.g. leaves to protect from sun or rain, mushrooms, or stones to sit on?

- OR if you have been outside recently you can spend some time imagining where and how the *Huldufólk* live.

Step 2: *Let your imagination lead the way...*

- Create a home for the *Huldufólk* using natural objects. If you can do this activity outside, you might just want to add a little wooden door to a tree and paint it a bright colour*, or you could create a little house out of twigs and leaves. You could also arrange twigs, leaves, and moss to make a garden for the house – there are no rules here, use your imaginations and see what natural forms inspire you!
- OR if you are working with natural materials indoors you could use them to create a room where the *Huldufólk* might live, once again letting the natural materials you have inspire you into imagining what they could become. Maybe you have found a little acorn shell that could become a cup or bowl? Maybe a feather could be a soft bed? Add as little or as much detail as you like. You could create your room within a cardboard box OR just on the table.

Step 3:

- In the process of making your *Huldufólk* home or room, you will have already imagined who the little people who live there are. Write down some information about them in connection to what you have already created.
- Think about the following questions when you write down the information:

1. Was it a family or group of friends or was it a single little person?
2. What did they look like?
3. How do they live in the space you created?
4. Do they have friends who live nearby? These could be other *Huldufólk* or even bird, animal, or fish friends (the *Huldufólk* house might be near the water's edge).
5. Do they have any special magical signals to warn them of any danger approaching from big human people?
6. Add anything else you may have imagined...

*Please don't paint growing trees or bushes and show respect for the plants and flowers in the area where you are making your home. Leave a small footprint...

Sharing/Reflection: *10 minutes*
Share the *Huldufólk* home OR room with your group along with the notes you have written down.
Invite other members of your group to suggest/make an observation/add an idea to your *Huldufólk* home to make it even better.
Make connections between all the homes in the group – do the folk that live there know each other? Do they visit each other? Are they related? Do they meet for special occasions?

Key Vocabulary/Questions:	**Extension Activities:** Using
Imagination/creativity	your home/room and notes as well as the ideas from sharing session, create a short story about the *Huldufólk* home you created.

Summer Folktale 3 from Northern and Eastern Europe
A retelling of *The Mysterious Midnight Fern at MIDSUMMER*

The fern, a spiralling, unfurling plant, has lived on our planet for 360 million years. Ferns witnessed the coming and going of the dinosaurs and the birth of human civilisation.

For so many years, the fern plant has confused people. Unlike other plants, there were no seeds. If there were no seeds, how did the fern reproduce itself?

Perhaps that's why across Northern and Eastern Europe the fern has inspired so many myths and legends. The hunt for the mysterious fern blossom is spoken about in countries such as Estonia, Poland, Belarus, Sweden, Finland, and Ukraine... There are many slight variations, and this one below is a bit of an amalgamation!

On MIDSUMMER's eve, legend says that you can find the mysterious fern blossom which has special magical properties. Only at midnight at this special time of year is when the flower will bloom and can be plucked.

To find it, you'll have to enter the forest, and get through the protection the fern receives from magic spirits.

Legends say that if you do find the fern flower that you will be given the power of speaking with animals. And perhaps earthly riches, and your greatest wishes may even come true!

It was only in the last century that scientists discovered the truth, that ferns reproduce by spores rather than by seeds! But we can see why the mysterious fern has inspired so many wonderful stories...

ACTIVITY: CREATING A THEATRE-SKETCH – POWER TO TALK TO ANIMALS		
Subject: Performance art, creative writing **Curriculum Links:** English, Drama	**Key Skills:** Mindfulness, creative writing, improvisation, drama, and theatre	**Duration:** 50 minutes

Resources & Creative Materials: *The Mysterious Midnight Fern* folktale Paper, pencils/pens	**Location:** Inside or outside

Learning Objectives:

- To learn how to step into the paws, hooves, claws of animals
- To use our imagination and connect with animals through dialogue
- To create a creative dialogue piece and theatre sketch, with a specific animal

Introduction & Warm-Up: *15 minutes*

In the *The Mysterious Midnight Fern at MIDSUMMER*, one of the magic powers that the fern flower could give you is the power to talk to animals. In many ancient cultures, shamans (a healer/medicine person) were believed to have this gift... they could converse with the natural world. Can we imagine what it would be like to have this gift?

- Sit outside with eyes shut – listen out for flies/bees buzzing, birds singing.
- Choose an animal, however big or small, and imagine what it might be saying.
- Don't worry about it being silly or non-sensical... just see what arises...
- What specific questions might you want to ask it?
- E.g., What do you like to do in your spare time, what are you afraid of? What's your favourite food, what do you think of humans? Etc...

With a partner, discuss what kind of animal speech came out from this creative activity.

Key Activity: *Individually – 20 minutes*

Activity 1: *Guided visualisation to connect and speak with an animal – 10 minutes*

- Sit or lie down with your eyes closed and feel the earth supporting you.
- Imagine that you now have the power to speak with animals.
- Picture an animal in your minds' eye that you'd love to have a conversation with.
- It might be an animal you know (a pet) or a wild animal in a forest, anything.
- Take some time to get 'to be' with your animal – getting to know it through speech.
- What does it have to say to you? And what do you have to say back? What kind of conversation do you have?

Activity 2: *Capturing the conversation – 10 minutes*

- With a pen and paper, write down the conversation as if a drama or theatre-sketch.
- Don't worry about spelling or grammar.
- Allow the conversation to flow and see where it takes you...

Sharing/Reflection: *15 minutes*

In a circle, ask for volunteers to act a part of their animal conversation/theatre
What was it like to try and imagine what an animal might say to you?
How easy or hard was it? Any surprises? What did you find out about your animal?
What's it like to hear other people's animal conversations through drama?

Key Vocabulary/Questions: Fern, Shaman, dialogue, theatre-sketch, improvisation	**Extension Activities:** Create a role play with a partner – an animal and human.

ACTIVITY: CREATING MAGICAL SPELLS TO PROTECT THE FERN BLOSSOM		
Subject: Creative writing **Curriculum Links:** English, Science	**Key Skills:** Creative writing, observation	**Duration:** 1 hour
Resources & Creative Materials: *The Mysterious Midnight Fern* folktale Paper and pencil/pen	**Location:** Inside or outside	

Learning Objectives:

- To swap position with a forest and the natural world
- To use our imagination to create challenges and spells to test humans
- To create a magical spell book for the forest

Introduction & Warm-Up: *15 minutes*
The *Mysterious Midnight Fern at MIDSUMMER* folktale
tells us that the forest creates all kinds of protective spells and charms with the help of the natural world. Part of the reason for this is to make sure that the person who finally finds the fern blossom is worthy. Let's brainstorm together a few ideas for what kind of magic spells a forest might come up with to test humans.

- Let your imaginations fly on this one – there are no silly or crazy ideas...
- Are there camouflage spells, or special flowers that if you step on them they put you to sleep? Or a riddle that you must find out? Or a forcefield...

Key Activity: *Small Group – 30 minutes*
Create a series of spells and challenges from the forest for humans.

- Together imagine that you are the Forest, and need to protect the fern blossom.
- What kind of person would you like to find the fern blossom?
- What spells, tests do you need to create to help find this kind of person?
- Write down each spell on one piece of A4 paper.
- Try to write in swirly, curly handwriting to make it look ancient and wise.
- What kind of little decorations might you put on the borders?

Sharing/Reflection: *15 minutes*
In a circle, ask for groups to share their spells out loud.
What impact do these spells and challenges have on you?
Share feedback and responses.
Would you rather be the forest casting spells or the human trying to get past them?

Key Vocabulary/Questions: Fern, botanist, zoologist Did you know that some medicines come from plants that do have specific healing powers/ properties?	**Extension Activities:** Use a teabag to create ancient looking paper to write spells. Come up with the counter-spells for the botanist or biologist trying to find the fern!

ACTIVITY: PAINTING A FERN – OBSERVING ITS BEAUTY AND SYMMETRY		
Subject: Visual arts **Curriculum Links:** Art, Science, Maths, Design	**Key Skills:** Creativity, Art, Observation, Mindfulness	**Duration:** 1 hour
Resources & Creative Materials: (per child) Fern leaves or a fern plant Watercolour paper or good quality cartridge paper A3/A4 Watercolour paint/acrylic with water/or watered-down poster paint – silvery greens/blues/limes (fern colours) Thin paint brushes Tissue/water pots	**Location:** Inside OR outside on a warm, sunny day	

Learning Objectives:

- To learn about the significance of the fern in Māori culture
- To practise mindful art making and explore the qualities of a fern
- To practise observational painting

Introduction & Warm-Up: *20 minutes*

The fern is very significant in Māori culture. The new curled shoot of the silver fern is called the *koru* and represents growth, hope and development.

- The literal word meaning of *koru* is 'loop', which signifies connection and beginning.
- The shape of the curled fern shoot is often used in design, especially in traditional greenstone carvings to symbolize growth. Each tribe (*iwi*) has their own stories.
- To *Pakeha* (New Zealanders of non-Māori descent), the silver fern is also a symbol of bravery, sacrifice, and allegiance; the fern symbolizes a sense of attachment to their homeland and appears on commercial logos and in sports and the military as a symbol.
- There are some stories about the silver fern being turned upside down and used to guide people through the dark, as moonlight would shine on the leaves.

Q&A with class: Exploring the fern

1. Examine a fern – what do you see?
   Ferns are fractals – infinite complex patterns that are created by repeating a simple pattern over and over. Each leaflet on a fern represents a miniature of the whole frond as they branch from the main stem in escalating size. The fronds illustrate a graceful curve and symmetry, they are very inspiring.
2. What other leaves, flowers, and animals are perfectly symmetrical?
   E.g., sunflowers, aloe plants, broccoli, citrus fruits, spiders' webs, snowflakes, peacock feathers, butterfly wings, ice crystals, beehives, natural whirlpools.
3. How does symmetry make you feel?
4. Natural symmetry in nature is meant to inspire calm, peace, and joy – do you feel that?

Key Activity: *30 minutes*
Fern Painting: Watercolour fern painting and drawing – slow and mindful – aim to do this activity silently to concentrate.
Key Tips: Just draw a single fern leaf on your page – fern paintings are beautiful in their simplicity.

Stage 1:

- Examine the fern – it's made up of very simple lines.
- On scrap paper – practise drawing the fern with a pencil.
- Start with painting in the stem.
- Paint in the leaflets alongside the stem – using minimum brush marks for each leaflet.
- Start small and slowly work your way down the stem getting bigger.
- If you are not happy with your first fern painting – try again.
- Try using different shades of green to create your paintings.

Stage 2:
Although they are called 'silver ferns', the undersides of the fronds are only silver in some populations and are more normally white. These white undersides reflect moonlight, making them useful aids to navigate bush paths at night!

- Make a night fern painting.
- Repeat the painting steps in Stage 1 using silver or white paint on black or dark blue paper.

Sharing/Reflection: *10 minutes*
Create a gallery display of finished fern paintings (night and day).
Examine the fern paintings with each other. Discuss how you felt whilst fern painting? Did it feel different from say painting something from your imagination?
Look at the difference between your day and night fern paintings – do you have a preference?

Key Vocabulary/Questions:	**Extension Activities:**
Colour, pattern, design, symmetry	Examine and explore more symmetrical shapes in nature and paint them.

ACTIVITY: CREATING CAVE ART – TRAVELLING BACK TO THE JURASSIC ERA WITH THE FERN		
Subject: Creative art **Curriculum Links:** English, History, Science	**Key Skills:** Art, Research	**Duration:** 1 hour

Resources & Creative Materials:
The Mysterious Midnight Fern at MIDSUMMER
folktale Internet or books – looking at the
Jurassic era
Pictures of cave art, chalks – red and black
Playground or brown paper

Location:
Inside or outside

Learning Objectives:

- Discover how long the fern has been on this planet
- Research which other creatures and plants are still around today from that time
- Research which creatures and plants are now extinct from that time
- To see the simplicity and effectiveness of cave art
- Create a piece cave art

Introduction & Warm-Up: *10 minutes*

- Show the extraordinary time scale of the fern – think about what sort of things the fern might have seen. How it survived the extinction of the dinosaurs, the birth of birds and mammals, the Romans, the Greeks, the World Wars etc...
- In groups, research which other creatures and plants have survived and which haven't.
- Take note of the size of plants and creatures in the Jurassic era.
- Look at pictures of cave art – how they were normally made from red or black pigment. The images are simple yet very effective and are a great way of recording what man has seen.

Key Activity: *40 minutes*

- Individually, imagine finding a fern in the woods. Suddenly it shimmers and before you know it, you find yourself being transported back in time – to the Jurassic period. What do you see? What creatures do you encounter? Remember, there is no technology.
- Create a piece of cave art showing an adventure you have back in time. Imagine you are with the dinosaurs and want to record your experience in the cave for people to find thousands of years later... (Dinosaurs and humans weren't on the planet at the same time, so people in the future will be very puzzled by your creation.)
- You can either create your cave art on pieces of paper or on the playground using chalk. Can you tell a story with pictures only and no words?

Sharing/Reflection: *10 minutes*
Invite the children to share their cave art. Can the audience work out what is happening without any words? Imagine what it would have been like where everything is so vast in size and there is no technology. Do you think the planet was healthier then or now?

Key Vocabulary/Questions: Jurassic, prehistoric, cave art Why do you think the fern survived?	**Extension Activities:** Create a cave art story showing an extinct creature coming back to present day with you and the feather. What chaos might they cause?

Summer Folktale 4 from China
A retelling of *The Ten Suns and the Archer*

This folktale comes from China and is thought by many to be thousands of years old. Although this story is often told within a longer tale related to the Mid-Autumn festival, we have placed it in our SUMMER section because of the theme of hot suns burning. Given the increasing concerns about climate change and global warming, this story feels like an important inclusion.

At the beginning of time, when the Earth was young, ten suns shone in the sky. At the centre of each sun, was a magical bird, a three-legged red raven. These ten Sunbirds were the grandchildren of the Jade Emperor who had told them that each must take turns shining in the sky. However, the Sunbirds did not listen.

With all ten suns shining at the same time, the lands and forests on Earth began to burn. Crops and animals perished. Homes were destroyed. This was ten times worse than any hot summer!

A Chinese archer named Hou Yi went to the emperor and told him that if the ten Sunbirds didn't stop shining at the same time, he would be forced to shoot them down. The Jade Emperor tried to make the Sunbirds listen. When they did not, he finally gave Hou Yi permission to shoot nine down. Hou Yi had special fire-arrows for his bow made from dragon tendons.

Hou Yi climbed to the top of the highest mountain and gave the ten Sunbirds one last warning. When again they did not listen, Hou Yi shot down them down, one by one. Burning red feathers were seen falling from the sky. In his enthusiasm, Hou Yi had to be reminded to leave one to shine for Earth!

Only this last Sunbird was afraid, and retreated into a cave, leaving the world cold and dark. Finally, a rooster cried out for the sun to appear. Unable to ignore this loud piercing cry, the last Sunbird rose again. To this day, the rooster will call out to the sun, just before it arrives.

ACTIVITY: RE-ENACTING *THE TEN SUNS AND THE ARCHER* FOLKTALE		
Subject: Performance art **Curriculum Links:** English, Geography, Dance/Movement	**Key Skills:** Storytelling, Movement, Drama	**Duration:** 1 hour 30 minutes

Resources & Creative Materials: *The Ten Suns and the Archer* folktale Textiles, scarves, pieces of material	**Location:** Outside and inside

Learning Objectives:

- To reflect on the vital power of the sun when it shines too much and when not!
- To bring to life a folktale through drama and movement
- To personify nature through drama
- To learn how excesses in nature, in whatever form, upset the balance of planet

Introduction & Warm-Up: *15 minutes*
Read the story to the group/class, and invite participants to give their responses.

- Reflect on the power of the ten sunbirds and what that would be like – ten suns!
- Discuss what it's like when anything is out of balance, too much or not enough.
- Examples from nature – droughts, floods, etc...
- Discuss the actions of Hou-Yi the archer and the danger of taking out the last sun.
- What would happen if we had no suns?

Key Activity: *30 minutes*

- In groups, you are going to bring to life the story of the *Ten Suns and the Archer*.
- Invite children to bring to life the story through drama, movement, and music.
- In mime, they say that the slower we move, the better we are at capturing the essence of something – experiment with slow, gentle movements.
- If there are fabric pieces/scarves, find ways to use them in the performance.
- Groups to decide themselves if they wish to narrate the piece or purely act it out.
- How do they want to bring to life the sunbirds' dying?
- How can they incorporate movement and sound?

Sharing/Reflection: *15 minutes*
Invite each group to perform their piece of *Ten Suns and the Archer*.
Share feedback and responses.
Discussion on the importance of balance in nature.
What about balance inside us? What might that look like?

Key Vocabulary/Questions: Mime, nature's balance, harmony, personification	**Extension Activities:** Write the story from the point of view of the remaining sun.

ACTIVITY: CREATING A *TEN SUNS AND THE ARCHER* MIXED MEDIA WALL FRIEZE		
Subject: Visual art **Curriculum Links:** English, Art	**Key Skills:** Art and storytelling	**Duration:** 1 hour 30 minutes

Resources & Creative Materials:
The Ten Suns and the Archer folktale
Large roll of white paper (or A2 sugar paper taped together) to make a wall frieze/hanging large enough to hold the 12 key elements (suns/mountain/archer)
Collage materials, art materials, feathers
Masking tape, wax crayons, hair dryer, iron
Plastic bags (recycled), pencils, crayons, brushes

Location:
Outside and inside

Learning Objectives:

- To bring to life the Ten Suns/Sunbirds and the archer story through a wall hanging
- To find creative ways to express the power of the Suns in the story
- To use the power of the sun to transform creative art materials

Introduction & Warm-Up: *20 minutes*
Re-read the story to the group/class and share how in the olden days pictures painted on walls and then wall hangings were ways to capture important stories across cultures.
Discuss what visual elements from this story would need to be shown in the wall hanging – imagine it as a large illustration for the story.

- Split the group/class into (13) groups that can work on separate key visual elements in the story; each of the 10 suns, the archer Hou Yi, the rooster, the background (including the mountain).
- Make the background for the tapestry – sticking together pieces of lining/craft paper with masking tape on its back.
- Work flat on the floor, with a view to hanging it up one wall of class/group-room.

Key Activity: *In small groups/pairs (or split into shorter sessions over a term) – 60 minutes*
Activity 1: Groups 1–10: The ten Sun groups.

- Cut out different circles of card for each sun – each sun can be a different size and have a different appearance. Each group will work on one circle.
- Each group to try a different technique to create their sun.
- Groups can explore techniques such as melting wax crayon shavings in the sun (or under a hair dryer) to create a melted wax surface as part of the artwork – the process replicating the power of the sun.
- Groups can also explore tearing up plastic bags (orange/yellow) into strips, laying them on the circle shape and ironing the plastic to melt it. **IMPORTANT: When ironing the plastic, place a sheet of baking parchment or greaseproof paper between the iron and the plastic. Adult to do the ironing.**
- Other sun groups could paint/collage or explore another technique to create their suns.
- You may want to add feathers or feather affects too.

Group 11: The background group.
The background group will need to paint the background of the scene. They could paint the sky and the land including the mountain range and the highest mountain.

Group 12: The archer.
The archer group will need to create the archer including his bow and dragon string arrows.
Use a collage approach to make the archer, you could even use real feathers to make the arrows.

Group 13: The rooster.
The rooster group could also paint or use a collage approach to make the rooster – this could feature torn paper to resemble the feathers or trace/draw/collage real feathers.
Once all the elements are created – stick them to the background piece.

NB: Adult supervision is needed with each of the groups who use the iron or the hairdryer.

Sharing/Reflection: *15 minutes*
Present the final piece – hang on a wall if possible.
Stand back and ask each child to say which image attracts them to the piece of work.
Ask for volunteers to re-read the story with the frieze in the background as a backdrop OR use as a backdrop for an enactment of the story. (See previous activity.)

Key Vocabulary/Questions:	**Extension Activities:**
Wall hanging, mural, art making, illustration	Wax crayon experiment – all children to create a picture using melted wax shavings (individually or in groups) – these could be left in a sunny spot to see if they melt!

ACTIVITY: CREATING OUR OWN SUMMER 'DRAGON' FOLKLORE STORIES		
Subject: Creative writing **Curriculum Links:** English	**Key Skills:** Storytelling, Writing	**Duration:** 1 hour

Resources & Creative Materials: *The Ten Suns and the Archer* folktale Examples of dragons in Chinese culture Dragon kings, and the red dragon of SUMMER	**Location:** Outside if possible

Learning Objectives:

- To learn about how dragons are seen as forces of nature in Chinese culture
- To engage with dragons as a metaphor for the seasons
- To create own stories about nature dragons

Introduction & Warm-Up: *15 minutes*

In the story, the archer Hou-Yi uses magical fire arrows made from dragon tendons. In China, dragons are seen differently to how they are shown in the West.

- In China, dragons are seen as a symbol of huge power, and mainly as positive and wise forces. It is said that the Dragon Kings were rulers of seas, water, and weather gods. Ancient people would seek their blessings of good weather for harvests, bringing offerings to try and stop droughts or floods. Dragons are believed to be older than time, and the ancestors of the Chinese people.
- Four Dragon Kings were seen to rule different seas, and the seasons across the year. The Dragon King which ruled the South Sea was Ao Qin 敖欽 and held the essence of SUMMER. This dragon was otherwise known as the Red Dragon, or Torch Dragon (赤龍 *Chìlóng* or 朱龍 *Zhūlóng*), and embodied the element of fire, a symbol of good luck.

Key Activity: *30 minutes*

In groups, come up with a story about how the Red Dragon might bring SUMMER- using the six-parts story structure – just a sentence or two for each section.

1. Introduce your dragon in its setting.
2. Where does it need to travel/what does it want to do?
3. What/who gets in the way of the dragon?
4. What/who helps the dragon?
5. Main action and turning point.
6. What happens afterwards?

Sharing/Reflection: *15 minutes*

Agree which section of story will be read by each person in group.
Read the folktale aloud to the other groups.
Share feedback and responses.

Key Vocabulary/Questions: Six-part story method, Dragon Kings, Red Dragon	**Extension Activities:** Draw the Red Dragon, researching Chinese dragon styles.

ACTIVITY: CREATING CYANOTYPE PRINT SUN DRAGONS		
Subject: Visual arts **Curriculum Links:** Art, Science, Photography	**Key Skills:** Process, Creativity, Patience	**Duration:** 1 hour 40 minutes

Resources (per child):	Location:
Resources (per child): Cyanotype paper (also known as sun paper and nature paper) Simple dragon images A4 glass clip frame – 1 per child Flat leaves/ferns/flower petals of different shapes and sizes Water trough (sink or washing up bowl)	**Location:** Inside or outside (This session would work in groups of 5/10 children at a time rather than a whole class activity)

Learning Objectives:

- Exploring how to use cyanotype printing
- Creatively using natural forms i.e., leaves to create a design

Introduction & Warm-Up: *15 minutes*

1. Practise looking at the shape of different dragons in the pictures you have found.
2. Practice making a simple dragon shape using different shaped leaves and grasses – for example use a larger leaf shape for a head and a few smaller ones to create parts of the body and the tail of the dragon.

Key Activity: *Making the cyanotype dragon print – 1 hour 15 minutes including drying time*

- To make the sun print place a piece of the cyanotype paper on top of the cardboard (use the cardboard base of the clip frame).
- Next, place flat objects from nature onto the paper (make sure they do not overlap). Use different leaf sizes and shapes plus grasses and flowers to make a simple dragon design (like the one you will have practised in the warm-up stage).
- Place the glass of the clip frame on top of the leaves etc to keep them in place – clip the glass into place over the leaf design.
- Place in direct sun for 10–20 minutes. (Sometimes a bit longer – the longer the better.)
- Unclip the glass from the frame, remove the natural objects, and rinse the cyanotype paper in cold water for one minute and then leave it to dry in the sun. As the paper dries it will darken and leave a beautiful imprint of the design on the paper. The dragon will appear!

Sharing/Reflection: *10 minutes*
Share the 'sun dragon' prints with each other as soon as they have dried – look at the variations in shades of blue and discuss how the heat of the sun has created the image on the paper. This really is quite a magical process which totally relies on the heat and the light of the sun to work effectively.

Key Vocabulary/Questions:	Extension Activities:
Key Vocabulary/Questions: Colour, pattern, design, photography, exposure	**Extension Activities**: Repeat the process using different shapes and textures including cut paper. Experiment with timings to create different effects.

Summer Folktale 5 from Peru and Ecuador, South America
A retelling of *The Hummingbird*

Hummingbirds are very much part of cultures in South America. Aztecs revered them. Despite the birds' size, they were thought of as warriors due to their speed, agility, sharp beak, and fiercely territorial nature. Often they were also seen as carrying messages from the gods. In this story, the hummingbird shows a warrior spirit. She will not give up regardless of the odds against her.

Once there was a great fire in a forest in Peru. Anteaters fled to a watering hole to escape the smoke and flames. Tamarins and tapirs were already there, trying to look after their terrified families. The smoke and flames grew, and different birds perched on a thick tall tree, near to the watering hole. Jaguars climbed high onto its branches. More animals raced to the lake, fearing the terrifying fire, including howler monkeys, cougars, and sloths.

"What can we do?" they cried in panic. "We are losing our homes."

But no one knew the answer. And no one noticed the little hummingbird flying towards the watering hole and scooping some droplets of water into her tiny beak. She darted over to the fire and dropped the water onto the massive flames. Back and forth she went over and over again. The other animals began to notice.

High up in the tree, a Jaguar called, "Little hummingbird, your beak is so small, and the flames are out of control, so what are you doing?"

The little hummingbird answered, "I'm doing what I can."

ACTIVITY: CREATING A NEWS SEGMENT – INTERVIEWING THE CAST OF *THE HUMMINGBIRD* FOLKTALE		
Subject: Performing arts **Curriculum Links:** English	**Key Skills:** Drama, investigative journalism, role play, prop making	**Duration:** 1 hour
Resources & Creative Materials: *The Hummingbird* folktale Props for your play such as desk, chairs, movie cameras, booms Drawings of background scenes	**Location:** Inside or outside	

Learning Objectives:

- To understand the important message in this folktale – how we can all make a difference and do what we can
- To retell a story in an unusual way
- To think about investigative reporting – what sorts of questions would you use? How would different characters respond to those questions?
- To understand how the news is a form of oral storytelling

Introduction & Warm-Up: *15 minutes*

- Read *The Hummingbird* folktale.
- Think about the cast of the story – why did they behave in certain ways? How would you describe their character and qualities?
- Have you ever seen anything on the news about droughts, floods, or natural disasters?

Key Activity: *30 minutes*

- Imagine you are creating a news programme on the fires in the jungle.
- The news is told orally and visually and is an interpretation of the facts.
- Possible scenes include:
  - a news reader in the studio interviewing members of the cast;
  - a reporter in the jungle, where the hummingbird is stopping the fire;
  - the hummingbird receiving an award after the event, but the creature is incredibly humble.
- To bring this news report to life, you can include/make props. Perhaps you want to have a camera operator or a picture in the background of the studio showing the hummingbird and the fire. You can have a branding for your news programme with its own logo and theme tune.

Sharing/Reflection: *15 minutes*

Invite the groups to show their news reports. If possible, film the segments.
Which characters do they relate to the most? How do they think they would have responded if they were in the jungle?

Key Vocabulary/Questions: What is the main message of this story?	**Extension Activities:** Write an article for a newspaper covering the fires and interviewing the cast.

ACTIVITY: CREATING 'COLLAGE' POEMS ON THE MIGRATION OF HUMMINGBIRDS		
Subject: Creative writing **Curriculum Links:** English, Biology	**Key Skills:** Creative writing, collaboration	**Duration:** 1 hour and fifteen minutes
Resources & Creative Materials: Hummingbird facts and photos Paper and pencil/pen, a timer	**Location:** Inside or outside	

Learning Objectives:

- To help participants connect with unique qualities of a hummingbird
- To teach the concept of 'free writes' – free-flowing writing without judgement
- To use poetry to bring to life the migration of a hummingbird
- To collaborate and build confidence in improvisation and poetry-making
- To share poems aloud in a group setting

Introduction & Warm-Up: *15 minutes*

The hummingbirds are incredible creatures. The 'hummingbird' name comes from the sound their beating wings make – a sort of humming. Here are some amazing facts about how these birds are built for making incredibly long journeys! Try to show photos too.

- They are the smallest migrating bird. Instead of migrating in flocks like other birds, they will fly solo. The ruby hummingbird can fly non-stop for 500 miles at a time!
- They are long travellers – the rufous hummingbird travels for 3000 miles from Canada/Alaska to Mexico!
- Their wings can beat between 50 and 200 flaps per second. Their hearts beat 1200 times a minute (for us humans, it's 60–100 beats).
- They are the only bird which can fly backwards!
- They have incredible, iridescent feathers in different colours – like jewels!

Key Activity: *Individually and in pairs – 40 minutes*

Create a 'free-write' piece and collage poem on hummingbird migration.
Activity 1: *A 'free write' piece – individually – 10 minutes*

- Imagine you are making the journey of a hummingbird.
- Write for ten minutes, anything you'd like to capture from the imagined journey.
- A free write is a stream of thought and consciousness – you can write slowly but try not to stop. Just keep going without crossing out words or worrying about spellings or whether your piece makes sense. Try to fill a page or two with your writings.
- You can choose any perspective – maybe you are the hummingbird, using 'I' or 'we', or perhaps you prefer 'she/he.'
- If you are finding it hard to write, you can try thinking about the senses of a bird, what it sees, hears, smells, and senses on its journey.
- Remember there is no right or wrong in this free-write.
- Your teacher or group facilitator will tell you when the first five minutes are over.

Activity 2: *Share free-writes and 'listener' tells 'reader' their five favourite parts –
20 minutes*

- In pairs, each person takes turns to read their 'free write' piece aloud.
- The 'listener' has a crucial role to play. After they've listened, they underline three favourite phrases or bits of sentences that stand out from the 'reader's' piece.
- These might be an interesting/different/curious way of describing something; phrases don't have to be long… they can be a mix of short and medium.
- The reader/listener swap roles – and the new 'listener' underlines three phrases.

Activity 3: *Create a 'collage' poem individually – 10 minutes*

- Each 'reader' now has three phrases on a piece of paper. Now it's the reader turn to re-read their piece to themselves, and underline three extra phrases – anything they like.
- The 'reader' copies out all six phrases in any order they like. They can add or omit words. Try not to worry about grammar too much.
- Now you will have six phrases, your very own collage poem of the Hummingbird!

Sharing/Reflection: *20 minutes*
In a circle, each person reads their hummingbird poem.
What was it like to create a poem like this, working with another person?
How did they find the creative process of a free-write?
Any surprises about how the poems turned out?
What have they learnt about their own creativity?

Key Vocabulary/Questions:	Extension Activities:
Hummingbird, migration, iridescence 'Free write' and 'collage poem' Collaboration	Write up poems, decorate them, and display in the classroom or group area. Record spoken poems.

ACTIVITY: MAKING A HUMMINGBIRD MOBILE		
Subject: Creative arts **Curriculum Links:** Art, Science, RE	**Key Skills:** Creativity, making, values	**Duration:** 1 hour 10 minutes

Resources & Creative Materials (per child):	Location:
Resources & Creative Materials (per child): *The Hummingbird* folktale Photos and images of hummingbirds Paper/card and pencils Colouring equipment Clear tape and glue String (cotton thread) Sparkly bits/small, coloured feathers (if possible)/metallic paint	**Location:** Inside Hang up outside on a good day

Learning objectives:

- To value the unique nature of hummingbird
- To learn about the different colours and displays hummingbirds come in
- To bring to life the energy and form of a hummingbird

Introduction & Warm-Up: *15 minutes*

- In myths and legends across the world, the hummingbird has been seen a special bird totem that can teach us to celebrate life and nature. If we look at their incredible iridescent jewel-like throat and wings, in so many bright colours, we can see why they may have inspired legends. But these aren't just pretty birds, they travel 2000 miles on their migration routes! They are determined flyers too. An ancient Mayan tale says that the Hummingbird carries human thought as a messenger, its wings beat so fast.
- Discuss together the different values the Hummingbird shows in the story with the fire – e.g. determination, bravery, hope, belief, faith, etc.

Key Activity: *Making the hummingbird mobile – 40 minutes*
Stage 1: Drawing Hummingbirds
Most species of hummingbird are 5cm–13cm in length (most are 7.5cm and longer but the bee hummingbird is 5cm).

1. Draw a line on a piece of paper between 5 and 13cm (children can choose) – this will give you the length of your hummingbird.
2. Look at images of hummingbirds and draw one no longer than the length of your line – practise a few times to get the shape right.
3. Once you have a hummingbird you are happy with, trace or draw it onto a thicker piece of card – then carefully colour it in with bright colours inspired by the hummingbird pictures. You could also use paint or glue on sequins or small coloured feathers to add more detail.
4. Once you have decorated your hummingbird, cut it out very carefully.
5. On the back write down in bold colourful letters one value that you appreciate about the hummingbird.

Stage 2: *Making the Hummingbird Mobile – 5 minutes*

- Attach a piece of string to the back of the bird (near the highest point) with clear tape and then tie to a hanging point.
- You could suspend the hummingbirds from a giant paper flower, or they could all be hung from a long stick suspended in a window.
- Children might like to individually hang them from a pencil/small stick to take home and remember the power of a little bird, or they could stick the bird to a gardening stick and pop them in a plant pot.

Sharing/Reflection: *10 minutes*
Share the different hummingbirds and make a note of all the different values children wrote on the back of them – which value was most popular?

Key Vocabulary/Questions:	Extension Activities:
Key Vocabulary/Questions: Colour, pattern, design, values What kind of values are important if we are going to protect nature?	**Extension Activities:** Create a story about your hummingbird's journey of migration.

ACTIVITY: CARING FOR OUR WORLD ACTION PLAN		
Subject: Visual arts, Creative writing **Curriculum Links:** English, Art, Geography, Biology, History	**Key Skills:** Creative writing, observation	**Duration:** 1 hour Plus 1 week for the challenge

Resources & Creative Materials: *The Hummingbird* folktale Paper and pencil/pen	Location: Inside or outside

Learning Objectives:

- To learn about how to engage with huge problems without feeling powerless
- To learn how little steps make a difference
- To create our own 'little steps' plan

Introduction & Warm-Up: *15 minutes*
Re-read the story to the group, and ask participants to give their responses.

- Why do you think the different animals responded in the way they did?
- What do you think of the Hummingbird's response to the challenge?
- What qualities did it show, and what can we learn from this story?
- What are some of the ways we can support ourselves when we feel overwhelmed?

Discuss how sometimes we can feel overwhelmed by big problems and feel powerless, when we don't see any change happening. Reflect together on how the hummingbird showed BIG courage and determination despite its SMALL steps.

Key Activity: *35 minutes*
Activity 1: *Whole class discussion on helping natural world in local community – 10 minutes*

- Discuss some of issues on the natural world in your local community.
- Is there anything that you see that really upsets you?
- If we learn from the Hummingbird, what little steps might you make?
- E.g., walking to school, picking up litter, recycling, switching off lights/computers.

Activity 2: *Individually create an Action plan – 25 minutes*

- Draw a large outline of a Hummingbird with plenty of room inside.
- Discuss with your partner/s what issues you care about in your community.
- List what little steps you can take to make a difference – starting with right now.
- Fill in the blank centre of the Hummingbird outline.

Sharing/Reflection: *10 minutes*
In a circle, share your action plan list What is the impact on the group hearing this list?
Weekly challenge: Can they adhere to their action plan?
Report back in one week.
How many days did they achieve? What supported them to continue?
What got in the way of completing their actions?
Discussion on some of the challenges of sticking to action plans.

Key Vocabulary/Questions: Hummingbird, conservation, activism What are some of the challenges to helping? How can we not give up hope when trying to help?	**Extension Activities:** Hold a school assembly showing how we can all make a difference.

CLOSING ACTIVITY: PERSONAL/COLLECTIVE ASSOCIATIONS WITH SUMMER AND GIANT GROUP MANDALA

Subject: Visual arts **Curriculum Links:** Art, Geography	**Key Skills:** Artmaking, collaboration	**Duration:** 1 hour
Resources & Creative Materials: Blank paper plate (one for each child) OR thick white paper/card cut into a circle – plate-size or larger Scissors, glue-sticks Lining paper/craft paper – masking tape Pens, paper, collage materials, fabrics, paints, chalks Any natural materials – leaves, twigs, etc		**Location:** Inside

Learning Objectives:

- To engage children in a giant creative activity to summarise the theme of SUMMER
- To teach collaboration in a shared art-making activity
- To engage children to capture their own *unique* relationship with SUMMER

Introduction & Warm-Up: *5 minutes*

Discuss how the Celts and other cultures saw the Sun as a wheel, turning for each season. In Hindu and Buddhist cultures, they use the Mandala, a circular template, to create images and patterns to represent the wholeness of the cosmos and of human beings. Today we are going to make our own SUMMER mandala to focus on our own personal relationship to SUMMER.

Invite children in silence to close their eyes and to think about the season of SUMMER.

- When you think of SUMMER, what comes up?
- E.g. images, words, sounds, sensations, places, drinks, foods, activities, plants, animals.
- Spend some time really allowing yourself to think about your memories.
- Any outdoor SUMMER scenes, festivals, or important community and/or cultural events?
- Invite children to think about their own personal connection to SUMMER.

Key Activity: *40 minutes*

Activity 1: *Individually create a SUMMER image – 30 minutes*

On the paper circle or plate, each participant creates their own SUMMER image.

- Invite children to draw/write their associations with the season of SUMMER.
- The challenge is for the children to fill in all the paper, leaving no gaps!
- If words, encourage children to decorate these in a SUMMER seasonal style/colours.
- Images can be abstract, showing warm colours, patterns or a scene. It can be a collage or 2D. The choice is theirs. Encourage children to play and experiment with images and ideas.

Activity 2: *Creating a group Giant SUMMER Mandala collage in a hall space OR outside – 10 minutes*

- Ask each of the children to lay their circular artworks on the floor.
- Starting in a central position (middle of the floor or playground) position the circles in a spiral starting in the middle and radiating outwards.
- You could also lay the circles out using a different formation or design or try a couple of ideas before deciding on the right one.

Sharing/Reflection: *15 minutes*

Stand around the final formation on the floor and invite participants to share their responses to the SUMMER Mandala.

Invite Feedback on the creative process – what is it like to contribute to the Giant Mandala?

How do they look as part of a collaborative design?

Teacher or adult helper to stand on a chair or higher point to photograph the collaborative artwork for posterity.

Key Vocabulary/Questions: Mandala, mindfulness, senses, creativity, collaboration What makes SUMMER so unique?	**Extension Activities:** If there is a wall space big enough the design could be stuck to a wall with white tack to be appreciated by a wider audience. At the end of term individual circles can be taken home by children to be hung up on the wall to mark the season of SUMMER.

As we close our SUMMER SEASON, here is one last exercise to try at home.

ACTIVITY: ECO PRINTING WITH FLOWERS AND LEAVES		
Subject: Visual arts **Curriculum Links:** Art, Nature	**Key Skills:** Creativity, Nature art	**Duration:** 35 minutes

Resources & Creative Materials: Cotton or linen fabric/sheet Hammer Leaves and flowers in yellows/red/pinks/bright colours Plastic sheet (same size as fabric piece) Cardboard (large piece to protect the floor or table)	**Location:** Inside or outside

Learning Objectives:

- To learn how to eco print
- To use plants and flowers in art making
- To learn how to create your own designs

Introduction & Warm-Up: *10 minutes*

- Collect leaves and flowers in bright colors! Make sure you have permission before picking flowers or leaves!

Key Activity: *25 minutes*

1. Place your cardboard on your work surface.
2. Place flowers and leaves on the cotton or linen fabric. Then cover half of the fabric. Fold the other half on top of the flowers and leaves.
3. Place plastic on top of the folded fabric.
4. Use a hammer (with adult supervision) to bash the plastic with a gentle pressure so that you don't totally destroy the flowers and leaves underneath. You can experiment with different pressure when using different fabrics to notice the difference. Have fun, this is one of the most enjoyable parts of the activity!
5. **The big reveal**. Remove the top plastic sheet and unfold the fabric. You should have an image reflecting all the leaves and flowers you laid down with a few unexpected shapes and beautiful colours.

Sharing/Reflection:
The print will fade over time as nothing in nature is permanent. This activity teaches the fleeting nature of seasons, each one bringing new texture and colour.
Allow the fabric to dry and steam press to fix the print (with adult supervision).

Key Vocabulary/Questions: Eco print	**Extension Activities:** Keep going. This activity always has a different result and it's fun to experiment!

CONCLUSION

As we come to an end of all the seasons, we hope that you've found our *Rewilding Children's Imaginations* a useful resource in helping to develop creative ideas inspired by nature. Yet, in life the seasons do not end, they continue their cycle and they begin and finish all over again. We hope that this principle applies to your own work and that you can develop your own ideas for creative sessions inspired by nature.

There are so many other ways to explore our connection to nature and creativity. We look forward to seeing other resources emerge in the world, from other countries, cultures, places, and habitats.

If you are interested in finding out more about folktales and rewilding children's play, we've included a list of useful organisations and websites (see page overleaf). There will be many more that we don't know, as new communities pop up all the time. Creative learning inspired by nature is an emerging field in so many new ways. Amidst the very real challenges of climate change, it is also important to recognise the work that is being done across the world to activate changes in attitude and behaviour. In the UK alone, there are multiple organisations working tirelessly to promote care and interest in our precious natural resources.

We believe that like the planting of new trees and protection of natural sites and habitats, children are also in need of care. Let's free up their imaginations so that they can have some space to dream up a different future and a new way of being with the natural world.

We're going to finish with the words of the Italian actress Eleanora Duse (1858–1924): 'If the sight of the blue skies fills you with joy, if a blade of grass springing up in the field has power to move you, if the simple things in nature have a message you understand, rejoice, for your soul is alive.'

Pia, Sarah, and Tamsin

DOI: 10.4324/9781003178682-11

LINKS TO ORGANISATIONS

We hope that *Rewilding Children's Imaginations* has inspired an enthusiasm to find out more about local nature, folktales, and art making. Here are links to a small selection of organisations in the UK. There are many more exciting grassroot organisations to be discovered, in the UK and across the world.

- Woodland Trust – www.woodlandtrust.org.uk who share a range of school resources
  - www.woodlandtrust.org.uk/support-us/act/your-school/resources
- Forestry Commission UK – www.forestryengland.uk/blog/forest-bathing
- The National Trust – www.nationaltrust.org.uk
- The Wild Network – www.thewildnetwork.com – wild time for children and families
- The Society for Storytelling – www.sfs.org.uk
- Institute for Outdoor Learning – www.outdoor-learning.org
- Forest Schools – www.forestschools.com
- Sensory Trust – www.sensorytrust.org.uk – creating engaging experiences with nature
  - www.sensorytrust.org.uk/resources/activities/sit-spot
- Folklore Scotland – www.folklorescotland.com
- Irish Mythology – www.bardmythologies.com
- Surrey Art School – www.surreyartschool.com – seasonal art school
- A New Direction – www.anewdirection.org.uk – supporting creativity in young people

Here are our own websites for further information on our work –

www.rewildingimagination.com

Pia Jones – www.silverowlartstherapy.com

Sarah Pimenta – www.social-fabric.co.uk

Tamsin Cooke – www.tamsincooke.co.uk

QUOTE SOURCES AND PERMISSIONS

Chapter One – Page 3

'I go to nature to be soothed, healed and have my senses put in order'

Webb, Liggy (2021). In Burrows, J. Environmental Wellbeing: How to connect well with nature, United Kingdom: Liggy Webb, 2021, p. 4. Accessed 13th December 2022. Available at: https://www.google.co.uk/books/edition/_ /7MKAEAAAQBAJ?hl=en&gbpv=1&pg=PA4&dq=John+Burrows+I+go+to+nature +to+be+soothed,+healed+and+have+my+senses+put+in+order

Chapter Two – Page 9

'The protagonist of folktale is always, and intensely, a young person moving through ordeals into adult life...'

Spoken by Jill Paton Walsh (author). Permission granted kindly by the Estate of Jill Paton Walsh.

Chapter Three – Page 15

'Guided by the place itself, you usher yourself into new territory, where you become creators, adventurers, takers of risk, generous givers and bestowers of beauty'

Permission kindly granted by Trebbe Johnson (author and founder of Radical Joy for Hard Times).

Chapter Three – Page 16

'Painting from nature is not copying the object; it is realising one's sensations.'

Attributed to Paul Cezanne. Accessed 13th December 2022. Available at: www.artandarchitecture.org.uk, from The Courtauld Institute of Art.

Chapter Four – Page 25

'Three apples fell from the heavens - one apple for the teller, one apple for the listener, and one apple for the person who takes the story to heart.'

An age-old Armenian proverb often used to sign off folktales, a little like our 'once upon a time' at the end of stories.

Avakian, A.M. (1987) 'Three Apples fell from heaven' Folklore, 98(1), Taylor & Francis.

Chapter Five
Autumn quote – Page 35

'AUTUMN glows upon us like a splendid evening; it is the very sunset of the year'

Mitford, M. R. (1876) Our Village. United Kingdom: G. Bell & Sons. Accessed 13th December 2022. Available at: https://books.googleusercontent.com/books/content ?req=AKW5QadKM28jVJaxNTqjinP8s2HD-2JRrl470VGzh5zi0R4DlwrAeNwDq4v6 jN6VMRCvvs0-ZG6w5YErlcMOnhylICR50ACYFsDY7yc1r84_ZyEtbvdpcvTOCSwukkx _vhPfXZdNCdVOJXDtmAF_IYmkrcsizPvdrYAiY-JGDcDo6yHspB1VJ-LQKhEbo8ujP R0qPH2bwln97RuN-tCm3Wg-cZsuE9jCuNcPVRkgjpptAP3SPHCtpoGlxamuANE alEW63mLbai2o

Winter quote – Page 75

'Don't think the garden loses its ecstasy in winter. It's quiet, but the roots are down there riotous.'

Rumi, J.M. Rumi Garden Quotes. Accessed 13th December 2022. Available at: https://www.rumi.org.uk/

Spring quote – Page 117

'It is SPRING again. The earth is like a child that knows poems off by heart.'

Rilke, M. R. (1976) 'Spring', Sämtliche Werke in 12 Bänden (Complete Works in 12 Volumes), published by Rilke Archive in association with Ruth Sieber-Rilke, edited by Ernst Zinn. Frankfurt am Main.

Summer quote – Page 161

'It was June, and the world smelled of roses. The sunshine was like powdered gold over the grassy hillside.'

Hart, L.M. (1941) 'Betsy-Tacy and Tib', p. 4. Accessed 13th December 2022. Available at: https://en.wikiquote.org/wiki/Maud_Hart_Lovelace

Conclusion

'If the sight of the blue skies fills you with joy, if a blade of grass springing up in the field has power to move you, if the simple things in nature have a message you understand, rejoice, for your soul is alive.'

Duse, E. Accessed December 13, 2022. Available at: https://www .brainyquote.com/quotes/eleonora_duse_307834

STORY SOURCES

As previously mentioned, sources are notoriously difficult to pinpoint in folktales. Many tales we hear in passing, and if they capture our imaginations, these stories stick. Working backwards to find their source is like trying to find the source of a river. You're not quite sure which way to follow, and whether it really comes from there. Folktales are often older than countries' modern borders and tend to travel. Some are translated by scholars who don't share the same cultural roots as the origin story. The authenticity of some sources is often contested between folklorists, historians, and keepers of culture.

We have done our best to find roots of stories and included sources where possible to thank and respect all the communities and storytellers who have shared their folktales and stories in the public sphere. In the end, we were guided by a wish to offer up great stories about nature and the seasons that children could enjoy.

Introducing oral storytelling

Anansi Brings Stories into the World

- Rattray, R.S. (1930) *Akan-Ashanti Folk-Tales*, collected and translated by author, unknown binding.
- Coleman Smith, P. (1899) *Annancy Stories* (illustrated), NY: Robert Howard Russell.

Autumn folktales

AUTUMN Colour from Oneida tribe, First Nation, Upstate New York, USA

- https://www.oneidaindiannation.com/autumn-color/

Magic Harp of Dagda – the Oak of two Blossoms from Ireland

- *Gods and Fighting Men: The Story of the Tuatha de Danaan and the Fianna of Ireland* (1919), arranged and translated into English by Lady Gregory, London, UK: John Murray.
- www.bardmythologies.com/the-dagdas-harp/

Two Brothers, a Swallow, and a Pumpkin from North/South Korea

- Allen, H.N. (1889) 'Hyung Bo and Nahl Bo, or the Swallow-king's Rewards', *Korean Tales*, New York & London: The Nickerbocker Press.

The Magic Herb and the Hedgehog from Baltic and Slavic regions

- Folklore collected by renowned Serbian folklorist, Vuk Karadžić (19th Century)
- https://en.wikipedia.org/wiki/Raskovnik

The Spirit-Wind Horse from the southwest of England, UK

- Tongue, R.L. (1970) 'Lazy Lawrence', *Forgotten Folk-tales of the English Counties*, Routledge.

WINTER folktales

The Cailleach, inspired by:

- Mackenzie, D.A. (1917) 'Beira, Queen of Winter', *Wonder Tales from Scottish Myth and Legend.* Dover Publications.
- www.mythopedia.com/topics/cailleach

Ameratsu, inspired by:

- *Kojiki* (2015, first published in 1969) Translated by Philippi, D. Princeton Legacy Library
- www.britannica.com/topic/Amaterasu

The Legend of the Spider, inspired by:

- Stories online posted by Ukraine cultural websites www.ukraine.com/blog/spiders-and-their-webs-are-not-showed-the-door-on-ukrainian-christmas
- A story of a museum visit to Canada bringing folklore from Ukraine www.ptashkablog.com/2015/12/15/christmas-spiders/

Rainbow Crow, inspired by:

- *The Rainbow Crow* is attributed by author, Van Laan (1989), to the Lenape tribe. She states that the story origin was told by Bill 'Whippoorwill' Thompson, principal chief of the Eastern Lenapé Nations, but this is disputed by the Lenape-Nanticoke Museum, and the story may well have come from a Tsalagi (Cherokee) story.

The Firefox, inspired by:

- Brekke, A. and Egeland, A. (1963) *The Northern Light from Mythology to Space*, Research Berlin, Heidelburg, Springer-Verlag

- 'tulikettu' – WordSense Online Dictionary. Available at: https://www.wordsense.eu/tulikettu/

SPRING folktales

Baba Marta, inspired by:

- The folklore around the Bulgarian 'Grandmother March', who ushers in the Spring, is still alive in the current celebrations of her festival that happens on 1 March.

- Website dedicated to Bulgarian life and traditions: www.openbulgaria.org/post/legends-of-baba-marta/

Eostre/Ostara, inspired by:

- First mentioned in The *Reckoning of Time*, Bede (1582), as part of the Saxon festivals. Although there are folklorists and historians unconvinced of her role, her name certainly stuck, and was followed up by Grimm.

- Grimm (1835) *Deutsche Mythologie/German mythology*, Dieterich'sche Buchhandlung: Göttingen.

The Red Bud Tree, inspired by:

- The Jakarta Tales (Birth Stories) are ancient tales relating to Buddhism. We were inspired by this version written especially for children:

- Babbitt, E.C. (Ed.) (1922) More Jataka Tales, New York, NY: D. Appleton-Century Company.

Beltane, inspired by:

- This ancient festival appears in medieval Old Gaelic texts, and is now spoken about on various blogs and websites.

- *Celtic Myth and Legend, Poetry & Romance* was abridged from an earlier first edition entitled *The Mythology of the British Islands*, by Charles Squire, published in 1905.

The Tylwyth Teg Doorway, inspired by:

- Davies, E. (1809) *Mythology and Rites of the British Druids*, unknown publisher.
- Jenkyn, T.W. (1908) *The Welsh Fairy book*. https://www.sacred-texts.com/neu/celt/wfb/index.htm

SUMMER folktales

The Birth of the Sun, inspired by:

- Langloh, P.K. (1896) *Australian Legendary Tales*, Melville: Mullen & Slade.

Huldufolk, inspired by:

- Faulkes, A. (1995) *Edda: Snorri Sturluson*. Everyman. (Prose Edda initially 13th century)
- Árnason J. and Magnús Grímsson J. (1852) *Íslenzk Æfintýri*, E. Þórðarson

Ten Suns and the Archer, inspired by:

- Mayers F.W. (1874) *The Chinese reader's Manual: a handbook of biographical, historical, mythological, and general literary reference*, American Presbyterian Mission Press.

Q'inti – the Hummingbird and the Fire, inspired by:

- This story is attributed to the Quechen people of Ecuador and Peru and has been retold by Wangari Maathi, environmentalist and Nobel Peace Prize winner.
- It has also been told by: Yahgulanaas, M.N. (2012) *Flight of the Hummingbird*, Greystone Books.

The Midsummer Fern, inspired by:

- Bane, T. (2020) *Encyclopaedia of mythological objects*. McFarland.
- en.wikipedia.org/wiki/Fern_flower
- www.oldeuropeanculture.blogspot.com/2021/04/?m=0

Note: All references were accessed between 5th July and 16 December 2022.

REFERENCES AND BIBLIOGRAPHY

Allen, R. (2021) *Grounded – How connection with nature can improve our mental and physical wellbeing*, London: Mortimer Books

Baker, N. (2009) 'Last of the pond-dippers', *Natural World*, September

Bettelheim, B. (1976) *The Uses of Enchantment*, London: Penguin

Bird-David, N. (1999) "Animism" revisited: Personhood, environment, and relational epistemology. *Current Anthropology* 40s: S67–S91

Campa, A. (1965) 'Folklore and History', *Western Folklore*, 24, January

Campbell, J. (1993) *The Hero with a Thousand Faces*, London: FontanaPress

Foreman, D. (1993) 'Around the campfire', *Wild Earth*, 2(3)

Forest Research (2022) *'Forest School: a marvellous opportunity to learn'*, Research Summary, Social and Economic Research Group, Forest Research. Available at: www.forestresearch.gov.uk

Fromm, E. (1964) *The Heart of Man: Its Genius for Good and Evil*. New York: Harper and Row.

Gay'wu Group of Women, Laklak Burarrwanga *et al.* (2019) *Songspirals: Sharing Women's Wisdom of Country through Songlines*, Allen & Unwin

Hanse, M.M., Jones, R. and Tocchini, K. (July 2017). 'Shinrin-Yoku (Forest Bathing) and Nature Therapy: A State-of-the-Art Review', *International Journal of Environmental Research and Public Health*, 14(8), p. 851

Hunter, J. (2020) 'Folklore, landscape and ecology: joining the dots', *Time and Mind*, 13(3), pp. 221–225

Johnson, T. (2017) *101 Ways to Make Guerilla Beauty*, US: Radjoy Press

Jones, P. (1996) *Drama as Therapy: Theatre as Living*, London: Jessica Kingsley Press

Jung, C.G. (1964) *Man and His Symbols*, London: Picador

Jung, C.G. (1984) *The Spirit in Man, Art & Literature*, London: Ark

Koscielniak, B. (2014) *About Time: A First Look at Time and the Clocks*, Boston: Clarion Books

Levine, S. (1992) *Poesis*, London: Jessica Kingsley

Li, Q. (2010) 'Effect of forest bathing trips on human immune function', *Environ Health Prev Med*, 15, pp. 9–17

Louv, R. (2005) *Last Child in the Woods: Saving Our Children from Nature-Deficit Disorder*, Chapel Hill: Algonquin Books

Maes, M.J.A., Pirani, M., Booth, E.R. *et al.* (2021) 'Benefit of woodland and other natural environments for adolescents' cognition and mental health', *Nat Sustain*, 4, pp. 851–858

Maslow, A. (1971) *The Farthest Reaches of Human Nature*, New York: Viking Press

Matthews, J. and Matthews, C. (1998) *The Winter Solstice: Sacred Traditions of Christmas*, Quest Books

Maudsley, M. (2007) 'Children's Play in Natural Environments', *Children's Play Information Service Factsheet no. 10*, National Children's Bureau

Moss, S. (2012) *Natural Childhoods*, National Trust report

Mills, J. and Crowley, R.J. (1986) *Therapeutic Metaphors for Children and the Child within*, New York: Brunner/Mazel

NHS digital report (2017) 'Mental Health of Children and Young People in England Surveys'. Available at: www.digital.nhs.uk/data-and-information/publications/statistical/mental-health-of-children-and-young-people-in-england/2017/2017

O' Brien, L. and Murray P. (2022) 'Such enthusiasm – a joy to see' *An evaluation of Forest School in England*, Forest Research. Available at www.researchgate.net/publication/228383499_Such_enthusiasm-a_joy_to_see

O'Brien, L. and Murray, R. (2007) 'Forest Schools and its impacts on young children', *Urban Forestry & Urban Greening*, 6, pp. 249–265

Oliver, M. (2016) *Upstream: Selected Essays*, New York: Penguin

Oxford University Dictionary (2012) Seventh Edition, Oxford University Press

Pyle, R. (2003) 'Nature Matrix: reconnecting people and nature', *Oryx*, 37(2), pp. 206–214

Sigman, A. (2004) 'Increasing Screen Time is Leading to Inactivity of 11–15s', Youth TGI Study, quoted in Sigman, A. (2007) *Agricultural Literacy: Giving concrete children food for thought*. Available at: https://slidex.tips/download/agricultural-literacy

Sigman, A. (2007) 'Visual voodoo: the biological impact of watching television', *Biologist*, 54(I), pp. 12–17. Research also quoted at https://www.ncbi.nlm.nih.gov/pmc/articles/PMC6586981/

Siddons Heginworth, I. (2008) *Environmental Arts Therapy and The Tree of Life*, London: Routledge

Siddons Heginworth, I. and Nash, G. (2019) *Environmental Arts Therapy: The Wild Frontiers of the Heart*, London: Routledge

Sheldrake, R., Amos, R., and Reiss, M. J. (2019) *Children and Nature: A research evaluation for The Wildlife Trusts*, University College London (UCL), Institute of Education

Shum, A., Skripkauskaite, S., Pearcey, S., Waite, P., and Creswell, C. (2021) 'Children and adolescents' mental health: One year in the pandemic (Report 10)', Co-SPACE study

Sobel, D. (1996) *Beyond Ecophobia: Reclaiming the Heart of Nature Education*, Great Barrington, MA: The Orion Society

Soule, M. and Noss, R. (1998) 'Rewilding and biodiversity: complementary goals for continental conservation', *Wild Earth*, 8, pp. 18–28

Stuart-Smith, S. (2020) *The Well Gardened Mind, Rediscovering Nature in the Modern world*, London: William Collins

Sabini, M. (Ed.) (2002). *The Earth has a Soul: The Nature Writings of C. Jung*, Berkeley, California: North Atlantic Books

Stonard, J.P. (2021) *Creation. Art Since the Beginning*, London: Bloomsbury

Trotter, R.M. (2014) *Sit Spot and Inner Tracking*. USA: Sagefire Institute for Natural Coaching

Wilson, R. (1993) *Fostering a sense of wonder during the early childhood years*, Columbus, OH: Greyden

Waite, S., Passy, R., Gilchrist, M., Hunt, A. and Blackwell, I. (2016) 'Natural Connections Demonstration Project, 2012–2016: Final Report', Natural England Commissioned Report NECR215, Natural England

Warner, M. (1994) *From Beast to the Blonde*, London: Vintage

Warner, M. (2014) *Once upon a time: A Short History of Fairy tale*, Oxford University Press

Wilson, E.O. (1984) *Biophilia: The Human Bond with Other Species*, Cambridge: Harvard University Press

Winkelman, M. (2002) 'Shamanism and Cognitive Evolution', *Cambridge Archeological Journal*, 12(1), pp. 71–101

Note: All references were accessed between 5th July and 16th December 2022.